Cosmopolitan Sexualities

Cosmopolitan Sexualities
Hope and the Humanist Imagination

Ken Plummer

polity

First published in 2015 by Polity Press

Polity Press
65 Bridge Street
Cambridge CB2 1UR, UK

Polity Press
350 Main Street
Malden, MA 02148, USA

ISBN-13: 978-0-7456-7099-7
ISBN-13: 978-0-7456-7100-0(pb)

A catalogue record for this book is available from the British Library.

Library of Congress Cataloging-in-Publication Data

Plummer, Ken.
   Cosmopolitan sexualities : hope and the humanist imagination / Ken Plummer.
      pages cm
   Includes bibliographical references and index.
   ISBN 978-0-7456-7099-7 (hardcover : alk. paper) -- ISBN 0-7456-7099-7
(hardcover : alk. paper) -- ISBN 978-0-7456-7100-0 (pbk. : alk. paper) -- ISBN
0-7456-7100-4 (pbk. : alk. paper) 1. Sex--Social aspects. I. Title.
   HQ21.P564 2015
   306.7--dc23

                                                                        2014041486

Typeset in 10.5 on 12 pt Sabon by
Servis Filmsetting Ltd, Stockport, Cheshire
Printed and bound in the UK by CPI Group (UK) Ltd, Croydon, CR0 4YY

For further information on Polity, visit our website:
politybooks.com

In fond memory of

Stan Cohen (1942–2013)
Mary McIntosh (1936–2013)
Michael Schofield (1919–2014)
Jock Young (1942–2013)

Four inspirations

Hate begets hate, violence engenders violence, hypocrisy is answered by hypocrisy, war generates war, and love creates love.

Pitrim A Sorokin, *The Ways and Power of Love* (1954, p. xi)

Few things have done more harm than the belief on the part of individuals or groups (or tribes or states or nations or churches) that he or she or they are in *sole* possession of the truth: especially about how to live, what to be & do – & that those who differ from them are not merely mistaken, but wicked or mad: & need restraining or suppressing. It is a terrible and dangerous arrogance to believe that you alone are right, have a magical eye which sees *the* truth, & that others cannot be right if they disagree.

Isaiah Berlin, 'Notes on prejudice' 1981;
in *New York Review of Books*, 18 October 2001

Contents

Boxes

Website

http://kenplummer.com/cosmosexualities/

You may also be interested to visit this website connected to the book which provides links to a broad range of further resources relevant to *Cosmopolitan Sexualities*.

Abbreviations

ACHPR	African Charter on Human and People's Rights
AI	Amnesty International
AIDS	acquired immune deficiency syndrome
APF	Asia Pacific Forum
ARSRC	Africa Regional Sexuality Resource Centre
ART	antiretroviral therapy
ART	assisted reproductive technology
ARV	antiretroviral
ASEAN	Association of Southeast Asian Nations
AU	African Union
AVEN	Asexual Visibility and Education Network
BDSM	bondage, discipline, sadism, masochism
CATW	Coalition Against Trafficking in Women
CBRC	cross-border reproductive care
CEDAW	Convention on the Elimination of all forms of Discrimination Against Women
CHS	*Culture, Health and Sexuality* (journal)
CLAM	Latin America Centre on Sexuality and Human Rights
CMA	critical medical anthropology
CRC	Commission on the Rights of the Child

CRPD	Convention on the Rights of Persons with Disabilities
CSA	child sexual abuse
CSO	civil society organization
CSS	critical sexualities studies
ECHR	European Convention of Human Rights
EU	European Union
FGM	female genital mutilation
GAATW	Global Alliance Against Traffic in Women
GCVP	Global Campaign for Violence Prevention
GDI	Gender-Related Development Index
GJM	Global Justice Movement
GIFT	Global Initiative to Fight Human Trafficking (UN)
GII	Gender Inequality Index
HDI	Human Development Index
HIV	human immunodeficiency virus
HRW	Human Rights Watch
HSI	Human Security Index
IASSCS	International Association for the Study of Sexuality, Culture and Society
ICCPR	International Covenant on Civil and Political Rights
ICERD	International Convention on the Elimination of All Forms of Racial Discrimination
ICESCR	International Covenant on Economic, Social and Cultural Rights
ICTY	International Criminal Tribunal for the Former Yugoslavia
ICJ	International Court of Justice
IHDI	Inequality-Adjusted Human Development Index
IHEU	International Humanist and Ethical Union
ILGA	International Lesbian and Gay Association
IMF	International Monetary Fund
INGO	international nongovernmental organization
IRRAG	International Reproductive Rights Research Group
IWHC	International Women's Health Coalition
LGBT	lesbian, gay, bisexual, transgender (other letters can

	be added as appropriate, e.g., Q for queer; I for intersex)
MDG	Millennium Development Goals
MDMA	ecstasy: empathogenic, phenethylamine and amphetamine drug
MSM	men who have sex with men
MENA	Middle East and North African
NATO	North Atlantic Treaty Alliance
NAMBLA	North American Man Boy Love Association
NGO	nongovernmental organization
OAS	Organization of American States
OHCHR	Office of the High Commissioner of Human Rights
OIC	Organization of Islamic Cooperation
PAL	Paedophile Action for Liberation
PIE	Paedophile Information Exchange
SPW	Sexual Policy Watch
SRHR	sexual and reproductive health and rights
SRI	Sexual Rights Initiative
UN	United Nations
UPR	Universal Periodic Review (United Nations)
UDHR	Universal Declaration of Human Rights
UNAIDS	United Nations Programme on HIV/AIDS
UNCHR	United Nations Commission on Human Rights
UNFPA	United Nations Population Fund
UNICEF	United Nations Children's Fund
UNIFEM	United Nations Fund for Women
WCF	World Congress of Families
WHO	World Health Organization
WSF	World Social Forum
WSW	women who have sex with women

Introduction

> O wonder!
> How many goodly creatures are there here!
> How beauteous mankind is! O brave new world,
> That has such people in it!
>
> Shakespeare: *The Tempest*, 1610

> Endless forms most beautiful and wonderful
>
> Charles Darwin, *On the Origins of the Species*, 1859

Planet Earth currently houses well over seven billion human beings in some two hundred nations with thousands of ethnic tribes often in conflict, and more than seven thousand languages, each with histories stretching back across the millennia. Imagine, if you dare, the sheer multiplicity of various gendered, sexual and intimate relationships and practices that these little animals, us, have experienced as they have walked the earth through time and space; and the different religions, states and economies that have been brought into existence that have helped shape them. Here is a truly vast labyrinth of desire, gender and reproduction. Think perhaps of the sheer complexities, or not, of your own life; and those of your parents, grandparents and their communities too. Think of all the films you may have seen, the novels you might have read, the television you might have watched, the music you have heard about human relationships and sex. Spend a few minutes searching some of the millions of sex sites on the web. Then massively multiply all this into *the global gendered world of human sexual complexity: the human sexual labyrinth.*

Now this is indeed a challenge – and it is what this small study is about. I want you to stand with me in amazement at this oh so 'incorrigibly plural' world (to quote Louis MacNeice's poem 'Snow'), this 'pluriverse of differences', and these 'endless forms most beautiful'. I want you to wonder, along with Shakespeare, how many goodly creatures there are here and, maybe, how beauteous mankind is. Or, just maybe, to ask how many of these creatures are really not so beautiful at all. And with this, to ponder just how it is we can live together with all this difference. In this book, I puzzle about these varieties of embodied, emotional human sexual and gendered experiences, and ask how we humans live, or fail to live, with them. I will not be aiming here to chart a topography of these 'world varieties of sexual experience', to document 'the global history of sex', to review the multiple forms of the 'world gender order', to detail any kind of global scientific truth about diverse and gendered sexualities, or even to provide a manual of titillating sex acts: all this has now been tried in very many places. In this book, my focus lies with the challenge of grasping human vulnerabilities and asking how we can live with the diversities of our genders and sexualities and their tangled, emotional, biographical bodies; how we can build some common cosmopolitan values that will enable us to connect such diversity; how we can appreciate just where boundaries and borders do indeed have to be drawn; and how we can start to build up cosmopolitan institutions that make all these tasks possible.

To help me in this, I draw on the long history of cosmopolitanism, which suggests a form of everyday practical *consciousness* that recognizes human differences and then struggles to build social *structures and cultures* that help make diversity a workable feature of the humane, good social life. It is a goal to strive for, it harbours utopian visions and there are a few signs to indicate that we may be a little on our way towards its development. At the same time, the path to its realization is cluttered with major problems and difficulties that need facing head on. My version of cosmopolitanism is a humanist theory; and my stance in this book will be broadly that of critical humanism. This takes seriously the centrality of a contingent human vulnerability, agency and meaning emerging alongside global human values: empathy and dialogue, care and kindness, dignity and rights, actualization and human flourishing, and fairness and justice. Despite a continual attack from many directions on humanism, it provides an imagination of great value.

A troubled world

And yet, everyday, as I have been writing this book, I have been torn with a dark hope. As the daily world news arrives, I am given a repeatedly clear vision of *the devaluing of human lives* across the world: the damaged and destroyed lives in the wars, violence and terrorist acts in Syria, the Ukraine, Iraq, Palestine, the Congo and elsewhere. We live in *a very cruel, nasty world of dehumanization* that is destroying lives for generations to come. Money, religion, nation and power (usually linked to gender and masculinity) seem to be the prime motivating forces for much of this misery and conflict. Yet, at the same time, I can also see *the flourishing of human lives* – in music and art, in education and care, in sport and science, in hundreds of little miracles of everyday human kindness. It is *a joyous world of human creativity and caring*. And this contrast will be a recurrent theme of this book. The bad news is humanity's inhumanity to humanity. Often with the help of the state and religion, unbelievable violence and cruelty are heaped on large numbers of people. Systems of ranking, honour and status are used to brutally destroy 'the other'. Powerful elites get away with murder, and tragic human suffering among the masses is ubiquitous. But the good news is humanity's evolving compassion, hope and creative activism. People in the world fight back: they do not like the horrors of the world, they create new movements to resist them and they bring dreams of a better world. Cosmopolitan sexualities, and this book, form part of that dream.

Just as embodied human vulnerabilities are displayed every-where, so too is human resilience. As I write, I hear of Meriam Ibrahim in the Sudan being sentenced to death for marrying a Christian man and committing apostasy from Islam. Following a worldwide response, her sentence was repealed and she was allowed to leave the country. A young student is gang-raped on a bus in Delhi in December 2012 and dies two weeks later; it leads to a public outcry about male violence towards women in India, where a woman is raped every 20 minutes. New social movements are born.[1] In Russia, gay men become objects of new regressive discriminatory legislation. A major campaign is organized on the Internet against this move. In the UK, the failure to deal with female genital mutilation (involving thousands of women each year) and child sexual abuse become national scandals, and public concern forces the government to act. And in Chibok, Nigeria, Boko Haram (meaning 'non-Muslim teaching is forbidden' and responsible for at least 10,000 deaths) kidnapped more than 250 female students as part of a widespread Islamic insurgency in northern Nigeria, professing their opposition to the education of girls and the Westernization of Nigeria. Many of the girls become so-called 'sex slaves'. Despite both a world response and a local one (the 'Bring Our Girls Back' movement), as I write, this remains a very bleak story.

Only a few incidents like these get reported. They take place against the backdrop of worldwide silenced human sexual suf-fering, where women are regulated in multiple ways, children are abused routinely, same-sex relations are outlawed, and much more. For example, in more than 70 countries, there are laws that criminalize homosexual relations. In Iran, Afghanistan, Saudi Arabia and Chechnya, gay sex can lead to the death penalty. From Europe to Africa to the Americas to Asia, case after case of torture, ill-treatment, violence and discrimination against lesbians and gay men is documented. There are also very many cases of transgender rights activists – the ultimate gender outlaws – being abused across the world. And so it goes on.

A tale to tell

In this book I puzzle over some of these problems and suggest a few pathways ahead, giving my account in two major connected parts. The first part examines the transformations of our sexualities in the early decades of the twenty-first century, suggests growing variety, and then charts some of the ways we are developing to try to live with this difference. The second part examines some of the problems encountered in doing this, taking the strong stand that if we are ever to advance we have to be clear about the universal values we all need to strive for and incorporate into our everyday lives now. The 'we' here is a global one, not a narrow Western one, which seeks progressive change for all and not for just a few.

Chapter 1 sets the scene by locating cosmopolitanism in a humanist tradition, describing it and suggesting the many problems it brings in its wake. My critical humanism is far from being a mainstream stance taken by others who research such matters. Indeed, for some it might seem dangerously old-fashioned. So I have to spend a little time saying what it is and why I use it. Above all, I highlight human actions and positive values. Chapter 2 then suggests that in the modern world the range of global possibilities for human sexual diversity is rapidly accelerating. It outlines some of the key conditions that are bringing about these sexual trans-formations and claims that as most of these changes are unlikely to go away this century, we had better learn to work with them. The next chapter then proceeds to demonstrate that the notion of *cosmopolitan sexualities* (or cosmosexualities) is already emerging as a set of developing structures and practical everyday responses to help us handle these problems of modern diversities. But it also claims this brings many problems; so I spend some time building a framework of critical issues that we need to bear in mind all the time when thinking about cosmosexualities. If we let these critical issues fall from view, we will be in trouble.

With these problems firmly in mind, Part Two can then examine some of the grounded utopian processes that might nudge us a little closer towards developing a theory of cosmopolitan sexu-alities, ultimately cultivating *inclusive sexualities*. Inclusive sexualities are those that can embrace sexual and gender complexity and variety. Chapter 4 shows the vital need to grasp the complexity of sexual and gender cultures and the importance of bridging cultural wholes with microscopic human actions. Chapter 5 highlights the importance of regulating sexuality, the importance of norms, and the ubiquity and inevitability of conflict. Human sexualities are everywhere embroiled in contested norms, and there are subterranean traditions at work that resist dominant orders (hegemonies) in many ways. Chapter 6 thus turns to the importance of fostering a cosmopolitan imagination through narratives, dialogues, empathy and common norms. It leads to a discussion of the kinds of societies in which all this can be fostered, and I look around the world to see where such ideas are being enabled. Finally, I suggest the importance of examining what I will call grounded everyday utopias, where we can find important human values already in practice in the world now, and suggest how these provide clues for pathways to better worlds and lives for all, not just the elite few. Although it is fraught with inevitable tensions and problems, I claim we have to champion a localism that will, in the future, blend with cosmopolitanism if there is to be any hope for a better world for all people, where human sexual differences will not cause so much pain.

As far back as we can trace, the human world has been a world of sexual difference. This has been well documented, and here I bring some of the key features of this complexity together. I see human beings as irrevocably plural, vulnerable and fragile; human social worlds as intransigently ambivalent, aleatory and agonistic; and human life as obdurately dwelling in perpetual contradiction, contingency and conflict. Six central but well-known ideas shape my thinking; there is nothing particularly fancy or complicated about them.[2] They are the ideas of social structure, human action, relations, culture, story and contingencies. I see structures, like gender, nations and inequalities, as the deep forces that underpin human life: they work like tectonic plates and move only slowly. I see human actions, like empathy and care, as the meaningful practices through which we actively make our human worlds and make sense of them. I see relations with others – loving, hating – as the key constituents of making human order. I see cultures, like media and religions, as symbolic meanings and skills we develop to make sense of our everyday problems: they work like tool-boxes of human action. Stories of all kinds and shapes are the key to these cultures: we make stories, live our lives through stories, make sense of our lives through them, even as they then exercise 'hegemonic' power over us.[3] Stories animate human life. We live lives, including sexual lives, through stories. And ultimately, I see contingencies as the chance and drift moments of these social lives as we actively move along continuously and creatively, making life chancy, precarious and risky, but, hopefully, also always worth living.

The book invites reflections on a wide range of complicated and important issues. In it, I seek to review, revise and ultimately challenge both the reader and myself to see the ubiquity of difference, the intransigence of conflict, the inevitability of disappointment and the importance and necessity of hope. It is a small work of synthesis; it stands a little on the shoulders of giants and could not have been written without the cumulative labours and insights of many brilliant scholars, past and present. While I acknowledge many of them in a very long bibliography and endnotes, this is not meant as a work of detailed exegesis or discussion of others' writings. My task is more formal, abstract and general, even though this does go a little against the grain. I do, however, give a little more background on the website that accompanies this book (see http://kenplummer.com/cosmosexualities). To present a full account of human sexual variety would require an encyclopedic multi-volume project, and my challenge is the opposite. I am attempting a succinct and readable overview of key themes and issues. In some ways, the book is a small companion piece to my earlier studies, *Telling Sexual Stories* and *Intimate Citizenship*.

No writing is a simple view from nowhere. Approaching the age of 70, I come with a lot of baggage and many people to thank (they know who they are: I do not list them here). I am a white male gay partnered UK citizen – and this has shaped much of my life. I illuminate this in an afterword epilogue where I show how embedded a personal life is in research findings. I would like to give the view from everywhere, but this would after all be nowhere. So, try as I may to be global, I come back to my home and my roots. In truth, it cannot easily be otherwise for any writer.

An infinity of lists

Finally, a brief comment on one unusual feature of this study: the lists. A little before I started writing this book, I stumbled across Umberto Eco's magnificent *The Infinity of Lists* (2009), which was inspired by an exhibition he arranged to suggest an imagery and art in awe at the complexity and infinity of all life, especially human life. Here are lists and visions of armies and martyrs, of the garden of earthly delights, of paradise, of fruits, fish and meats, of ships, of angels and demons, of the war dead, of perfumes and things, of places and cities – and on, and on, and on. Here is the ineffability of lists, their inexhaustibility, their infinity. As I delighted in the imagery of this book, I was prompted to add to his listings *the infinities of sexualities*. I have long sensed a difference between *closed sexualities*, which bundle our sexualities into a tightly restricted code, and *open sexualities*, which keep alive a vision of human possibilities. Lists can indicate this openness – a multitude of sexualities both experienced and awaiting experience: past, present and future. To capture a little of this, I turn in this book to the list. The list affords me the chance to briefly demonstrate a very wide range of examples, suggesting too that such examples are merely indicative. Much more could be said. Each item on a list could become its own book; each ending on a list brings its own etc. etc. etc. . . . The list could be extended with yet more examples, but it has to end somewhere. For a book about multiplicities, it is a good and, I think, effective little tool.

There are now a great many encyclopaedias, dictionaries and handbooks written on the wonders of the human sexual spectrum – whole libraries of millions of books in fact. The modern world brought with it a taxonomic zeal searching for order, and it was not long before this classificatory urge was applied to human sexualities in the controversial pioneering work of the early sexologists such as Krafft-Ebing, Hirschfield, Ellis and Freud at the fin de siècle. The great and persecuted Magnus Hirschfield calculated that there were 43,046,721 possible sexual types, and suggested running a 'Department Store of Love', 'where everyone can purchase their favourite fetish objects and achieve complete satisfaction of their desires'.[4] (This was, of course, before his library was closed down, his books burnt and his life destroyed.) Today, though, we can indeed click on any sex website and find that his wildest dreams have (almost) come true.

This book does not aim to get bogged down in all this detail. My challenge is to be crisp and clear, take stock of this diversity, ponder how we can live with it across the world, and look ahead. I will use the pleasure of the list as a tool to help with this and I will succeed in my task if I can demonstrate the ubiquity and global challenge of living with human sexual variety and can lay out a few pathways to move through what is surely a very troublesome sexual labyrinth. We are a long way from a better world for all, but this book hopefully makes one more small contribution to that end.

Part One

Humanism and the Making of Cosmopolitan Sexualities

It takes all kinds of people to make up a world,
All kinds of people and things.
They crawl on the earth, they swim in the sea,
And they fly through the sky on wings.
And brother, I'll tell you my hunch:
Whether you like them
Or whether you don't,
You're stuck with the whole damn bunch!

Rodgers and Hammerstein, *Pipe Dream*
(Used by permission of Williamson Music, A Division of Rodgers
and Hammerskin: An Imagem Company, © Imagem CV)

Cosmopolitan sexualities are those sexualities that live convivially and reciprocally with a variety of the diverse genders and sexualities of others, both within and across cultures. This usually entails an awareness of:

1 An ontology of a real global humanistic universalism of sexual and gender differences.
2 A recognition of human sexual differences as being part of what counts as being human.

3 An imagination of 'openness' and 'tolerance' towards sexual differences; often accompanied by a playful sense of irony, paradox, and contradiction.

4 An agon of perpetual conflicts about these sexual differences, the source of much human suffering.

5 A politics of sexual differences connecting local political struggles with global ones through dialogue and a search for common grounds.

6 A social structure of social solidarity of reciprocal inter and intra cultural awareness of sexual differences, becoming enshrined in rights, institutions and everyday practices.

7 A social psychology of tangled emotional and biographical differentiated gendered and sexualized bodies, suggesting the need for self-awareness, empathy and dialogue stretching through a 'circle of others' spreading across the globe.

8 An ethics which fosters a global sense of empathy, care, justice, dignity and a flourishing of different lives living together well.

9 A legal framework of international laws that provide frameworks for organizing the diverse sexualities in the modern world.

10 A pragmatic, grounded everyday 'utopian' process of people living together and learning from each other's sexual and gender differences, enabling the making of a better world for all.

1

Plural Sexualities:
Making Valued Human Lives

A pluralistic universe . . .
> William James, *A Pluralistic Universe* (1909)

Plurality is the condition of human action because we are all the same, that is human, in such a way that nobody is ever the same as anyone else who ever lived, lives, or will live.
> Hannah Arendt, *The Human Condition* (1958)[1]

The world in which we live is a 'pluralistic universe'. And human sexualities, like human life, are born of these pluralities. Even as we live under the dominance of singular coercive states trying to create singular hegemonic orders, we still live plural lives in plural cultures with plural values, religions, politics, identities and affiliations, as well as plural genders and plural sexualities. By plural, I highlight multiplicities, differences and variety. Human beings cannot help this plurality: it is surely one of the things that make us human. Even under totalitarianism, versions of variety survive. Indeed, it could be that a key to the human condition is this very difference between every human being. But plurality in this sense also forms the basis of many of our troubles as well as of politics. The dynamic and 'ethos' of pluralization are crucial to understanding social life.[2]

In this book I pick up this idea and apply it to the varieties of human gender and sexualities. I ask how we can best live with these differences in times ahead. These are political and ethical (normative) questions, for which I make no apology. In line with her statement quoted above, I take Hannah Arendt's maxim that 'politics rests on the fact of human plurality' very seriously and I look to the plural politics and cultures of the future by confronting the problems, politics and practices of what I will call 'cosmopolitan sexualities' head on. Drawing from a range of contemporary political and ethical theories, I give them my own pragmatic-humanist twist. This is not a fashionable view: so be it. My task is to draw a map of how this can be approached, but it is not meant as an encyclopedia of world details and answers. As if it could be.

Plural lives

My claim is that there exists a real world of global and essential human differences – we are all born and remain uniquely different – and that living with these differences is simultaneously the source of both the greatest joys and the miseries in human life. Exploring the multiplicities of human life can bring great pleasure; but the downside of this is that we have to live with the potential for perpetual conflicts and violence over these differences. The atrocities such conflicts can generate are often the source of horrendous human suffering and, sadly, they are not likely to go away. But these human differences also bring human interest, joy and delight. The challenge is to reduce the conflicts as much as we can (I doubt if we could ever reduce them completely), while encouraging the delights. Human beings with their differences and conflicts have to be treated as a key subject for human studies. And here my concern is with varieties of sexual experience.

Our selves, our tribes

The trouble is that everywhere this variety appears, it is foiled by the problem of our simultaneously limited and narrow views. Even as we have multiple commitments and affiliations bridged by variable and plural identities, we have a tendency towards *ethnocentrism*. W.G. Sumner's famous term – 'in which one's own group is the center of everything, and all others are scaled and rated with reference to it' – has quietly become one of the most influential of modern times.[3] It grasps an idea so vital in appreciating one of humanity's key predicaments: that we bond in narrow worlds, forge restricted identities and reduce life to our own limited worlds of self and tribe. We seem to prefer to have one story, with one voice, telling one truth. We prefer our own small monologic world to a global dialogic one. Obscured by the limits of our own small worlds, we find it so very hard to grasp the plural worlds of others; and to recognize that although they are not quite the same as ours, we are surely all bound by a common humanity. We are blinded by the restrictions of our little-minded parochialisms, provincialisms, patriotisms and patriarchalisms. Usually we do not even see this, let alone try to move beyond. And this is one sure pathway to the miseries of human social life: to its perpetual conflicts and, worse, to its human atrocities. We stigmatize, silence and ultimately slaughter those others who, in their millions, are not like us, those others who render vulnerable the safety of our world, those who become our enemies.

We can find this problem everywhere; and critical humanism, the view I take in this book, suggests three key strategies to help understand and maybe partially overcome it. Personally, it means cultivating multiple *empathies*; interpersonally, it means cultivating plural *dialogues*; and across cultures and societies, it means cultivating *cosmopolitanism*. Empathy demands an understanding of the other, especially our enemies. Dialogue demands the recognition of multiple voices not singular ones. And cosmopolitanism demands a search for *common grounds* that enable us to bring our multiplicities together. Taken together, I will argue that cosmopolitanism requires *a cosmopolitan imagination* to champion a certain openness of mind, bringing with it an imaginative sensitivity to others and a lightness of perpetual doubt. As cosmopolitanism bridges social institutions, social forms and structures, so societies come to organize the recognition of these differences of others as being crucial to what counts as being human.

Given the problems it raises, cosmopolitanism is something of a utopian idea. I will discuss these problems throughout, and highlight them in particular in Chapter 3. Cosmopolitanism has long had many enemies, moving under many names. Their critical voices can often be heard in religions, politics and even the universities – everywhere, in fact, where there is only one singular voice speaking only one singular truth. For that is the enemy of cosmopolitanism: the closed mind, the monologist, the absolutist. Wherever we fall pray to the unitary doctrine of sameness, the monologic programmes of the 'one and only way', cosmopolitanism is in trouble. And worryingly, such positions are everywhere.

Of course, living with too much plurality can push lives into chaos, and guides through this labyrinth are needed. But the recognition of pluralities, along with recognition of their limits, has long seemed to me to be a requirement for living. Human social life (then) is intrinsically about difference, diversity, plurality. We are the relational, dialogic animal who dwells in difference and we should never forget it. At the heart of this book lies the question: *how can we come together to live meaningfully, critically, empathically and peacefully with our often radically divergent differences, while setting reasonable boundaries?* I choose human sexualities as my example; but what I argue here may, I hope, be applied across the widest reaches of human life.

Contingency and the varieties of sexual experience

The human sexual world is part of this vast landscape of differences, a sexual labyrinth if you like; and this book can be seen as a case study in helping to map out pathways for living with sexual variety.[4] The varieties of human sexual experience have by now been very well documented, and it is not my aim to rehearse all this here.[5] I simply claim that human sexualities are contingent upon time and place; and that whenever we look closely, we will find *differences of desire* – of what sexually excites or fails to excite, from same sex to other sex, from self to objects, from passivity to activity. We will find *differences of gender* – of how we play out the modalities and challenges of varying masculinities and femininities. We will find *differences of relationships* – of how we connect to each other, coercively or voluntarily, monogamously or polyamorously, lovingly or full of malice. We will find *differences of reproduction* – of how we give birth to others and the conflicts over abortion and the new reproductive technologies. We will find *differences of representation* – of how we speak about and present out sexualities to ourselves and across groups. We will find *differences of disease* – of global pandemics like AIDS and old horrors like syphilis and the ways we can handle them. We will find *differences in danger* – of violence, coercion, rape, abuse and sexual murder, as well as the many kinds of threats and dehumanizations we experience around our sexualities. And we will find *differences in politics* – in the ways we practice controls over sexual lives. And so it goes on: *differences in actions and practices, differences in sexual and gender identities, differences in vulnerabilities, differences in sexual divisions, differences in motivation* – and on and on, so forth and so forth, etc., etc.

Some types of sexual variety may be unacceptable. Quite what these should be is a contested zone, and I will discuss this more in Chapter 5. At this stage, you may like to consider the kinds of sexual variety you find unacceptable. Here is my own listing. I think of these as *dehumanized sexualities*. The list includes sexual genocide and femicide, sexual murder, honour killings, hate crimes, sexual slavery, and rape in its many forms (from rape in war through prison rape to marital rape); also sexual assaults, genital mutilation, queer and trans battering, coerced marriage, pressured sex, sexual harassment, child sexual abuse and domestic abuse. The list could go on to include a great deal of prostitution and human trafficking where the selling of sex is out of the seller's own personal control (where there may be pimps and traffickers or women working out of sheer desperation in horrible conditions); and it could include the literatures of sexual violence and degradation, as found in parts of the pornography culture (many feminists would include these); and it could even extend ultimately

---

1.1   *Why do we do sex?*
Sampling a multiplicity of motivations

A good illustration of pluralities can be found in the multiple motives for having sex. Here are some of the reasons people give for having sex: maybe add more of your own:

> Anger, addiction, affection, aggression, attraction, babies, bonding, boredom, 'bug chasing',[6] closeness, commitment, curiosity, depression, duty, exercise, experience seeking, femininity, fidelity, frustration, fun, gratitude, habit, health, jealousy, laziness, love, marital duty, masculinity, mood changing, money, novelty, nurturance, passion, peak experience, play, power, pressure, procreation, rage, relief, reputation, revenge, self-esteem, self-expression, spiritual, status, stress reduction, thrill, 'to get the day going', ' to send to sleep', spiritual transcendence, transgression, violence, war . . . and on

A study by Meston and Buss (2007) reviews sex motivation studies, suggesting some 237 reasons for doing sex and clustering them into physical, goal-based, emotional and insecurity reasons. Perhaps people today offer many more reasons for engaging in sexual activity than in earlier times.

---

to the widest of cultural ideologies which promote sexual hatred through misogyny, homophobia, heterosexism, patriarchy: to all propagandists against sexuality and sexual vigilantes who will not tolerate the sexualities of others. As we move through this growing list of negativities, it becomes clear that more and more of these areas are as widely practised as they are contested. In many cultures throughout the world, rape in war is normal; so is forced marriage. Likewise, the pornographic abuse of women and the debate over this issue have raged for over a century in the Western world. These contested sexualities – so deeply linked to 'patriarchal sexualities' and 'hegemonic masculinities'[7] – will be my focus in Chapter 5.

Dehumanized sexualities cover a multiplicity of sins: and they render human sexuality dangerous, defiling and damaging. They are usually compelled by coercion, motivated by hatred and hostility, infused with abuse, dynamited by violence, structured by inequalities and lack any sense of care and fairness. They frequently protect the wounds and self of perpetrators. *Dehumanizing and desensitizing, they are profoundly without empathy or compassion for the other.* Found globally and across history, they may be seen as the dark side of human sexualities. Primarily, this is men on women; but it can also be women on men, men on men, and women on women. It is also heterosexual on homosexual, conventional on transgender – and the rest. It is a powerful force throughout history. And it is the enemy of humanism.

So I am fully aware of the need for boundaries, as we will see in Chapter 5. We need norms, or, as is often said these days, 'normativities'. But which norms and whose norms? Since this is a normative study, I will have to take the huge risk of suggesting what these norms might be. I will be aiming not just to look negatively at norms but also to start to suggest the need to look at them positively.

To help with this task, I turn to the ancient idea of cosmopolitanism, sensing its relevance to the modern problem of being able to live with most of our global sexual differences. The notion of cosmopolitan, sexualities suggests a humanistic imagination where minds are open to appreciate human sexual variety; a human social form that fosters cultures that can handle its conflicting sexual groups; and a human politics that champions living with our sexual differences. It acknowledges the ubiquity of human conflict and the need for limits, and it fosters empathy, dialogue and common grounds, while recognizing the need for fluid, mobile and porous boundaries and borders. It is part of a wider programme of intimate citizenship.

And it is humanism writ large. It is to this I now turn.

Critical humanism

In the preface to his classic study of orientalism, Edward Said (1978) writes that 'humanism is the only – I would go so far as saying the final – resistance we have against the inhuman practices and injustices that disfigure human history'.[8] As will become clear, my arguments in this book are based on a humanist position that places the well-being of the historical, embodied human struggling for a better world at the heart of its analysis: it puts our species to the forefront of critical thinking.[9] It sees that the world we live in is a human world: it is created through human beings, organized and disorganized by human beings, and ultimately transformed by human beings. It is people doing things together that make states, economies, institutions happen. It is people together who change the world and make it a better or lesser place. It is people that matter. They are most certainly not all that matter; and it may be that we also at times have to remind ourselves of our huge insignificance in the much grander scheme of things. We are indeed only a little animal and a little species with a short time on this planet in a colossal pluriverse. But as a distinctively little animal (born immature, big brained and bipedal), we try to make sense of ourselves. It is indeed partially what makes us human to do so. And humanistic research starts with the people around the world living their daily lives of difference. At the core of our concerns lie the talk, feelings, actions, bodies, vulnerabilities, creativities, moralities, sufferings, joys and passions of people as they share communities and social worlds, create human bonds, and confront the everyday constraints of history and a material world of inequalities and exclusions.

All this brings ideas of the 'human', 'humane', 'humanities', 'humanitarian' and 'humanity' to the fore. It can indeed even be claimed that although humanism has a long genealogy, the very idea of *humanity* itself, despite deep tangled roots, is an idea that was constructed and fitted for the twentieth century. Growing out of an awareness of 'crimes against humanity' (first in the genocide in Turkey of some million Armenians; later in the slaughters of the Second World War), the very idea of humanity has increasingly seeped into world consciousness during the twentieth century.[10]

And humanism is also always interested in its opposite form: dehumanization – the multiple and major social processes that degrade and rob humans of their humanities: the anti-human.[11]

Humanism simply suggests a multiplicity of ways of being human. It comes in an endless array of varieties. Almost every belief system can be linked with humanism, from Catholicism to communism, from Buddhism to pragmatism, from *Ubuntu* in Africa to *Ren* in Confucianism. Critical humanism embraces this multiplicity, but also puts it under scrutiny. Challenging any simple unitary view, it is critical of all claims that human beings can be understood 'transcendentally' and taken out of the contexts of time (history) and space (geography) of which they are always a part. For critical humanists, our 'human being' is most emphatically not a free-floating universal individual: rather, 'it' is always stuffed full of the culture and the historical moment, always in process and changing. Human beings 'nest' themselves in webs of contexts, relationships. To talk otherwise is to engage in the 'myth of the universal man'.

And of course this is also true of our sexualities. Recent critical sexualities studies have made it very clear that there is really no such thing as a universal fixed sexual or gendered being.[12] Sex for human beings is about many things: it is drenched in language, symbols and metaphor, and never mere biology. It can never, *should never*, be simply reduced to one thing only (as so much contemporary thinking likes to do). Box 1.2 suggests some of the multiple meanings of our sexualities.

Critical humanism has a very strong, pragmatic pedigree, espousing an epistemology of radical empiricism that takes seriously the idea that knowing is always limited and partial and should be grounded in the persistent plurality of obdurate experience. It makes no claims for grand abstractions or 'final solutions'. It assumes an inherent ambivalence and ambiguity in human life while simultaneously sensing the significance of politics, morality and value in all activities. It looks for practicalities that may help make the world a better place *for all*.

1.2   *How do we talk of sex?*
Sampling a multiplicity of sexual metaphors

The use of language is a distinctively human and social thing and its linkage to sexualities makes our sexualities distinctive too. In the human world, we have to give sexuality meaning and we often come to frame our sexual lives through metaphors. Here are a few.

Sex can be seen as a biological drive, an evolutionary force, a tool of repression, a liberatory act; as joyful lust, romantic longings, violence and hate, natural or unnatural, the machine that pumps, the disease that plagues us, the inner beast or the outer spiritual force. Sex can come to mean a body, a chase, a commodity, a disease, a form of filth, an expression of love, a feeling, a game, a gender, a hormone, an identity, a hobby, a hunt, a medical problem, a microdot, a passion, a pathology, a play, a performance, a perversion, a possession, a script, a scarred experience, a therapy, a trauma, a mode of transgression, a form, of violence, a form of work, a kind of war . . . and on.

Humanist troubles

Despite my admiration for humanist thinking, there is much critique and rejection of it. It is true that there is a deep seam of humanist thought that can never simply go away; but the intellectual project of 'humanism' has for a good while now been in a lot of trouble. It has been decried and dismissed from many directions, but especially by some very serious and high-minded intellectuals. A major influence here has been the tragic work (and nihilism) of Nietzsche, along with the dark critics of the Enlightenment – such as Horkheimer and Adorno in their *Dialectic of Enlightenment* (1944). More recently, it has been the object of attack from many poststructuralist, postmodernist and posthumanist writers, including Michel Foucault, who sees much humanism as itself constituting a repressive political regime disciplining human life. Contemporary social thought about sexualities has generally followed this path. I cannot examine these arguments closely here; but since I walk a different path, and they have dominated one wing of contemporary academia, I have to respond briefly here to some of the major objections.

First, critics link humanism solely with Renaissance and Enlightenment thinking. This is a truly serious error. There have been so many humanists throughout history and across all cultures and religions that it is simply wrong to identify it solely with the Enlightenment. I am baffled at how so many can make this erroneous claim. It is true that much harm was done in the name of humanism during the Enlightenment period. But to equate humanism solely with the Enlightenment is a dangerously restricting view. Indeed, much of our thinking about what it means to be human might be seen to start with the arrival of what Karl Jaspers (1951/2003: 100) has dubbed the Axial Age, a time where:

> Man everywhere became aware of being as a whole, of himself and his limits. He experienced the horror of the world and his own helplessness. He raised radical questions, approached the abyss in his drive for liberation and redemption. And in consciously apprehending his limits he set himself the highest aims. He experienced the absolute in the depth of selfhood and in the clarity of transcendence.[13]

This is the time, between 800 and 200 BC, that we find Confucius in China, the Buddha in India, Zarathustra in Iran, Isaiah in Palestine, and Homer, Plato and Archimedes in Greece. All can be seen as foundational 'humanists', the start, perhaps, of the 'great thoughts and great thinkers' about the human condition.

But this aside, even the detailed studies of the complexities of Enlightenment thought (like that found in the work of Jonathan Israel on the Radical Enlightenment[14]) make it fairly clear that the European Enlightenment was itself in a colossal radical crisis over the nature of what a human being was. Its great thinkers were in persistent disagreement over the nature of humanity and never settled upon one 'essence'. There was no *one* agreed-upon universal view on humanity, as is so widely and falsely claimed by critics.

Second, and closely linked to the above, humanists are often charged, mistakenly, of claiming that there is just one true universal and transparent essence of humanity (an 'unencumbered self', a 'universal man'). Certainly, there are (complex) boundaries with other species; but the humanism I understand fosters a view of the human being as 'open-ended': as a biological, historical, social and transformative being stuffed full of potentials, rather than a solitary being who strides through history as unified essence, essentially the same. The nature of the human being, and humanity, is a perpetual movement of possibilities. True, we can find versions of humanism that suggest one universal self; but we can also find a multitude of humanisms and selves.[15]

Third, a modern variant of this has tried to link humanism to the ideology of neoliberal capitalism by suggesting that this autonomous rational agent is the key actor in rational markets. But neoliberalism is about markets, money and profit; whereas humanism is about people not markets. It is about care, compassion and kindness; a better world will not simply arrive through rationality and markets, but needs emotional bonding and empathy. Even Adam Smith, in his important *The Theory of Moral Sentiments*, makes very clear the significance of the passions.[16]

Fourth, humanists are often seen as necessarily being atheists. Sadly, many groups, like the British International Humanist and Ethical Union (IHEU), the magazine *The Humanist* and some academic writers (for example, A.C. Grayling and Richard Dawkins), actually do work very hard to foster this misleading view. They want to make the word 'humanist' synonymous with 'secular' and 'atheist'. But this is neither fair nor correct: history shows that there have been many humanists who are spiritual and many spiritual leaders who just might be considered humanist too. There have been many great 'humanist' religious leaders, from Gautama the Buddha to Zoroaster, Jesus to Gandhi. Humanists surely have to recognize this world variety of religious experience as a part of humanity and, with this, the significance of a wide range of religious and spiritual meaning in the lives of human beings across cultures and history. In some accounts, religion becomes a functional necessity for humans. And we are moving into a world where an awareness of religious pluralisms generates the need for both multi-faith organizations and cosmopolitan religion.[17]

But that said, there are also very serious problems indeed with religion. For while one wing, I call them *open religions*, inspires us expansively to a range of significant human values, another dominant strand, *closed religions*, hurls us to the most vicious misogyny and vile hatreds for humanity's differences, often committing the most extraordinary violence and atrocities in its name (think: Inquisition, witchcraft purges, moral crusades, terrorism).[18] Humanists have to be very critical of religions when they become institutionalized and presume a level of absolutism, 'fundamentalism', fanaticism and monologic terrorism that is unbecoming to our humanities. Religions have a well-deserved bad reputation for their historically (patriarchal) appalling neglect and treatment of women. They also have a great deal to say about sexualities, much of it negative. Although there may be perpetual divisions both between and within religions, much of these can lead to a negative and nasty view of sex. So even though some varieties of religion are open and can be compatible with humanism, others, those that are closed, most certainly are not. Some religious variants are the enemies of cosmopolitanism; others are not.

Another critical claim is that humanists are often seen as cheery, simple-minded people who want everyone to 'feel good', believe in the goodness of people, search for common happiness and fight the good fight for progress in the name of humanity. Well, there are some humanists like this; but much humanist writing these days takes a very different track. Here we find humanists who often struggle to hold their heads up in the face of the clear and stark knowledge of the truly dreadful nature of humanity throughout its history: its bloody wars and genocides, its colonizations and slavery, its violence, exploitations and hatreds of all kind. It is the dark story of 'humanities inhumanity to humanity'. Indeed, it is precisely this suffering and tragic story that drives many of them to ask the very question of how we can live with this. What kind of human is it that does so many terrible things? The testimonies of concentration camp survivors (Primo Levi, Bruno Bettelheim and the rest) speak to this.[19] At the heart of this humanist vision is a little creature of great vulnerability and fragility that is capable of dreadful things – tragically, in the name of humanity. I will have a lot more to say about all of this.

A final, more recent, critique comes from the new posthumanist scholars who claim we are currently rupturing the confines of the merely human to become posthuman. By means of radical technological transformations, we are moving beyond the traditional human being, the human species, and even human death. New, exciting life that we can hardly imagine is in the making.[20] I have more sympathy with this critique than any of the others, because transformations are surely under way that are likely to change the way we live (see Chapter 2 for a partial documentation). Of course, much of the world remains untouched by these transformations; but change is certainly on the agenda. What is not clear is why this should be anything more than the long historical evolution of humanity: is it not just humanity reworking itself yet again for a new time and place?

I am working, then, against a background of many critics. So be it. But it should be noted that the humanism I appreciate and value is an altogether more critical vision than the one created by many of its opponents.

Vulnerability and the dignity of the self

In his biography, Desmond Tutu (1999: 31) remarks:

> My humanity is caught up with, is inextricably bound up with yours. We belong in a bundle of life. I am a human because I belong. A person with *Ubuntu* ... belongs in greater whole and is diminished when others are humiliated or diminished, when others are tortured or oppressed, or treated as less than who they are.

Our humanity is necessarily bound up with others. Box 1.3 suggests some common versions of humanity that we need to bear in mind. I do not see them as being particularly contentious. Some features are shared with other animal life (we share much genetically); but many are not to be found commonly, or so complexly, among other life forms. The evolution of the human brain surely plays a key role in much of this, and while our humanity may, or may not, be born with us, we are certainly born with an 'open-

1:3 *Ecce homo:* Sampling a multiplicity of human beings	
Homo Duplex	the double animal of body and culture
Homo Sapiens	the brainy, thinking animal
Homo Rationabile	the rational animal
Homo Socius	the social animal
Homo Politicus	the political animal
Homo Loquens	the talking, linguistic animal
Homo Symbolicum	the symbol-manipulating animal
Homo Narrans	the story-telling animal
Homo Poetica	the meaning-making animal
Homo Dialogus	the communicating animal
Home Faber	the tool-making animal
Homo Practicus	the practical animal
Homo Vulnerot	the vulnerable animal
Homo Ethicus	the moral animal
Homo Caras	the caring animal
Homo Dignita	the animal with dignity
Homo Reciprocans	the reciprocal animal
Homo Adorans	the religious, spiritual animal
Homo Amans	the loving, benevolent animal
Homo Creativius	the creative animal
Homo Investigus	the curious animal
Homo Economicus	the economic animal
Homo Ludens	the playing man
Homo Necans	the killing animal
Homo Sentimentalis	the empathic, feeling animal
And on . . .	

ended' potential, and with capacities or capabilities to become human. There is a long history of attempts to discover just what this humanity means, and prominent in many accounts is a sense of our vulnerability and dignity.[21]

There are many features of the human condition then; but one that is central to my arguments in this book concerns the facts that we are 'needy' social animals who live in aleatory, agonistic, ambivalent human worlds: little creatures of great vulnerability and fragility. Vulnerability is derived from the Latin *vulnus* – wound – which makes us the wounded animal; and these wounds come from four main sources – our bodies, our relationships, our cultures and our environments. We have bodies that bleed and die; we have relationships that fail us; we have cultures that prescribe unliveable lives; and we have environments prone to scarcity, tsunamis and earthquakes. Vulnerability, and the potential for suffering that comes with it, seems to be our lot.[22] The prolific nomadic world sociologist Bryan S. Turner put this bluntly: 'Suffering is inevitable and misery is universal . . . We suffer because we are vulnerable and we need, above all else, institutions that will give us some degree of security.'[23] Ironically, it is often these very institutions of security that can so often traumatize us and leave us feeling intolerant of human differences.

Vulnerability is closely linked to ideas of human dignity, a key concept that underpins much philosophical thinking on humanity (even though it has its critics: Schopenhauer once called it 'the shibboleth of all the perplexed and empty-headed moralists'[24]). It can be found in the writings of Cicero, is developed in much religious writing and gets its humanist associations from the 24-year-old Pico Della Mirandola in his *Oration on the Dignity of Man* (1486). In addition, it is central to Kant's belief in human agency, and has been embedded in most of the fundamental human rights documents since the 1940s: 'All human beings are born free and equal in dignity and rights.' Versions of it are also found across cultures, originating as a term for people with elevated status from China to Persia, who required respectful treatment, and trickling down from this bourgeois use to the masses. Its roots also connect it to ideas of 'honour', about which much more will have to be said later.

'Dignity' is undoubtedly a word used in many ways. Sociologists have had difficulties with the idea, but recently there have been significant signs of a rediscovery of interest in it.[25] 'Dignity' seems to be central to much thinking about justice, rights and human flourishing. It is bound up with the value of the human self. At its most general, it means that the human race as a whole is given a distinctive stature and that each individual in it has the right to be valued and treated well. People are vulnerable and they need security from others: they need to be valued. But so often societies fail them: they build systems of rank, privilege and status that devalue whole swathes of people; and life becomes a struggle for honour and esteem. Sadly, dignity can also be found in those who terrible things.

Plural values, valued lives

There is a long and voluminous history of writing on ethics and morals, of imagining lives that are good or bad for a person to live (ethics), and suggesting principles about how a person should treat other people (morals).[26] And these concerns lie at the heart of humanism: of *'aiming at the good life with and for others in just institutions'*.[27] Centrally, human ethics and moralities have been historically assembled from practical activities around diverse situations, global religions and philosophies, which themselves have been in persistent dispute over the core values. These have genealogies. As the pragmatist Philip Kitcher says in his historical study *The Ethical Project*: *'Ethics is something people work out together, and in the end, the only authority is that of their conversation.'*[28]

Religion and philosophy especially are renowned for suggesting key ideas on what a good life might look like: between them they provide a multiplicity of rival normative systems. Positively, and valuably, religions have long made claims about social justice, human rights, love and care, dialogue and the good life of virtue. The Golden Rule, *'to treat others as one would like others to treat oneself'*, can be found throughout history in many cultures.[29] But more negatively, and destructively, past systems of ethics have regularly not practised what they preached: the history of religions in particular show an astonishing human wreckage of war, conflicts, persecutions, inquisitions, torture, terrorism and other hatreds conducted in the name of virtue.[30] As I look around the conflicts and horrors of the modern world today, I can see religion as being rarely far away. So often, and sadly, the search is on for the one and only Holy Grail – the key value around which the good life can be organized. And terrible things have developed from this.

Although the 'golden rule' strikes me as a good practical

general rule, it can never be the only one. The search for one unified ethical system is very dangerous and not the view taken by humanist pragmatists. They would, rather, follow William James in claiming that '[t]he elementary forces in ethics are probably as plural as those of physics are. The various ideals have no common character apart from the fact they are ideals'; or Isaiah Berlin, who comments: 'Human goals are many, not all of them commensurable, and in perpetual rivalry with one another.'[31] There is really no reason to believe in just the one unified system of ethics: values are multiple yet interconnected. There may also well be an *incommensurability of ethical systems* when differences are agonistic and in tension.[32] Pragmatically, we have to live with this.

Search for common humanities

Over the past few decades, there have been serious attempts to sort out these multiplicities and to help find practical ways of bridging *common grounds of difference* for a global humanity.[33] Increasingly, this is on the agenda of many groups. For example, the Global Interfaith Movement, arising from the 1893 Parliament of World Religions (with more than 4,000 people of different faiths crowded into a hall in Chicago) was long ago established to speak across religious differences – and remains one of the major organizations today (the International Association for Religious Freedom was born from it in 1900; and it flourishes to this day[34]). Much later, the celebrated theologians Küng and Kuschel (1993) drew on the key principles of the world's major religions to build 'a global ethic'. It was signed at the Parliament of the World's Religions gathering in 1993 by more than 200 leaders from 40 or more different faith traditions and spiritual communities, and many thousands more have signed since then. It claimed four essential affirmations as shared principles essential to a global ethic. These were:

- a commitment to a culture of nonviolence and respect for life;
- a commitment to a culture of solidarity and a just economic order;

- a commitment to a culture of tolerance and a life of truthfulness;
- a commitment to a culture of equal rights and partnership between men and women.

This was only one of the earliest of such listings. Nowadays, we can find a major mission for a discourse across civilizations and religions and the development of interfaith dialogue.[35]

But the major modern example comes from the United Nations in the aftermath of the horrors of the first and second world wars. Both the UN Charter (1945) and Declaration of Human Rights (1948) created a global vision of a collective ethics with practical implications. It does well to remind ourselves of these. Amongst many concerns, it was determined that the people of the United Nations would:

- save succeeding generations from the scourge of war, which twice in our lifetime has brought untold sorrow to mankind; and
- reaffirm faith in fundamental human rights, in the dignity and worth of the human person, in the equal rights of men and women and of nations large and small; and
- establish conditions under which justice and respect for the obligations arising from treaties and other sources of international law can be maintained; and
- promote social progress and better standards of life in larger freedom; and
- practise tolerance and live together in peace with one another as good neighbours; and
- unite our strength to maintain international peace and security; and
- ensure, by the acceptance of principles and the institution of methods, that armed force shall not be used, save in the common interest; and
- employ international machinery for the promotion of the economic and social advancement of all peoples.

Although it is often decried as US-dominated, the creation of this charter was complex and involved the work of many people around the globe. It is a good example of world peoples struggling to agree on multiple common shared values. The history of this has now been well documented.[36]

Gradually, all this has turned into what is now sometimes called a 'global ethics project', arriving with its own professors, courses, associations, journals and textbooks.[37] These days, even nongovernmental organizations (NGOs) and big corporations employ 'global ethicists'. In these worlds, a key divide is between the abstractionists and the situationists, between those who provide general guidance lists of values and those who struggle over the daily process. Both, of course, are needed. We need 'the list' to give the vision to enable the struggle. But while there may be no universally agreed straightforward listing of universal human values, we do need attempts at such listings as starting points for struggling and debate.[38] Such listings are usually values that are historically based and found in many cultures, but once listed they seem trite: many people will find them to be a cliché. A full historical genealogy of these morals of our times must await us.[39] I will have more to say about these as we proceed.

A world ethics for critical humanism?

Ultimately, global values must be concerned with the practical incorporation of the best of many value systems, from Buddhism to Islam. The challenge is to dig deep into these systems, themselves full of contradictions and tensions, and find commonalities. Here I want to make a start and indicate a few of these potential global principles that guide me in my own humanist arguments. They are neither exhaustive nor fixed, but simply suggestive, open to change and debate, in need of continuous development.[40] They are transformative and can be reshaped through arguments. This is no dogma. It is simply a working tool for the present and provides a number of major domains of values to work with.

What is critical for humanists is the sense that there are multiple values, not just one, and they are grounded deeply in our humanities. They flow out of human relationships and inform personal lives; subsequently, they also help shape social institutions and practices. I believe they are quite widely held. They certainly have long lineages of serious intellectual and religious thought behind them and are not simply Western, but extend across many cultures.[41] Above all I think many people live by them.

The humanist search for these universal values is down to earth and practical. Grounded in the everyday bodies of human beings, it has to start with the importance of *care*, for, as the political philosopher Daniel Engster succinctly put it: 'Caring is at the heart of human existence.'[42] Wherever we find the birth of a new baby, it comes with the requirement of good care: all babies need looking after. But more: as we ourselves are cared for by others, so we learn to care for others. There is a gentle reciprocity in the task of care: just as we will sometimes need care, so too will we sometimes be required to care for others. And we do this across the life cycle to the final stages of dying. All this can direct us to a much wider sense of care, including care of the environment and, ultimately, the idea that a good state has a prime function of making sure of the care and 'security' of its peoples. Humanism directs us to an ethics of care, a practice of care, the development of a compassionate temperament and the importance of love and kindness in human lives. But it also means grasping its opposites: humanism wants to reduce violence and foster communities of kindness beyond self-interest, markets or nation-states. All over the human world people are forced to live with perpetual cruelty, violence, war and hatred that will be reproduced across traumatized generations. Such negative values are inimical to care and bring the potential for the nihilation of the human species. The value of care opens the door to looking after each other: and to 'love'. A goal of humanism, then, is harm and violence reduction, while creating a caring, nonviolent – even loving – society.

Locked within this philosophy of care comes a second key embodied humanist value: *empathy*. Again, right from our earliest infant days, we really have to acquire the ability to see the world from the viewpoint of others – initially, parents, siblings and peers; later, many significant others. Many scholars have written about role-taking and empathy. At the heart of this is the value of developing dialogues with others, asking about the nature of communication, of voice, of hidden and silenced voices, and of the importance of the recognition of others. The value of empathy opens the door to dialogue, and ultimately to sympathy and compassion. Humanist values lead us to want to foster an ability to live with the wonder of human differences, to dialogue well and to help shape an empathic, dialogic society.[43]

A third value moves one step further on: care and empathy lead to treating others with *dignity and rights*. I find it quite shocking that throughout history, as today, it has been possible to dismiss huge swathes of people as being worth nothing – in caste systems, in slavery, as refugees, in class and race ghettos, in wars – condemning them to lead excluded, wasted and sometimes genocidal lives. Should all humans be accorded dignity, or just a very select privileged few? The humanist stance is, of course, that all people have the right to dignity. And this introduces the key idea that people also have the rights to human life, raising the value and problems of the universality of rights, the variety of rights (individual and collective – i.e., group), their differentiations (civil, religious, intimate), and the international movements that crusade for them. The value of dignity opens the door to a multiplicity of human rights, and humanism wants us to foster them as part of a world global culture helping to shape a truly 'human' society – with human rights and dignity for all people.[44]

Ultimately, the search for grounded values for all people would be incomplete without also recognizing the importance of *human capabilities, well-being, actualization and flourishing lives for all*.[45] The humanist stance is that every human life on this planet should have the opportunity to flourish. How is it that our world structures have, throughout history, restricted the opportunities of so many people to lives that are wretched, damaged, dispossessed and lacking in any kind of quality? Why has the idea that people everywhere should be helped to lead flourishing lives not been seen as a human priority throughout the centuries? What are the good traits of humanity, which need to be cherished and valued, and what social conditions will bring this about? Here we find a very long tradition of philosophical thought that highlights telos and human goals, and which asks what is meant by human well-being (sometimes linked to happiness). What is meant by the good life and the wasted life? What are human capabilities and potentials? And what indeed might be a 'virtuous' life? The value of human flourishing opens the door to a multiplicity of human capabilities that need developing. Humanism wants to take seriously what it would mean for all to lead a good life and help shape a flourishing society.[46]

Finally, this in turn leads to a fifth major but interconnected value, perhaps the most widely known and discussed, but also the most contested: that of *justice*. Care, empathy, dignity and human well-being seem to me to be basic requirements for treating people humanely. But justice opens wider debates: if we aim to treat people fairly, we need to understand the importance of equalities and inequalities in the shaping of human lives. It could be that the greatest obscenity of human earth is its vast inequalities, which are perpetuated, even exacerbated, across generations. The human world is riddled with raging poverty, competition and stark inequalities across economic, gendered and racialized groups: and these lead to mass damaged and wasted lives. There is nothing new about this, although it could just be becoming worse.[47] So the challenge for humanists is to ask how human freedoms are restricted by intersecting social divisions across class, gender, ethnicity, health, age, sexualities and nationhood;[48] and how we can bring about a society with more social justice, redistribution, equalities and freedom. And this would be for all, not just the elite few. The value of fairness opens the door to justice, equality, freedom and democratization in relationships. Humanism seeks formal equality (likes must be treated alike) and substantive equality (given, for example, equalities of opportunity). It wants us to foster economic redistribution and interpersonal equality and respect to help shape a just society. And as we search for a world of cosmopolitan sexualities, it needs always to be alongside this search for a just world.[49]

This short listing could never be complete. Very quickly, I could add the value of global hope and amelioration: the desire to make the world a better place for all. Humanism, not succumbing to negativism and despair, wants to help shape a progressive society, rationally advancing forward to a better world for all. And likewise, modern humanism is born of a pragmatism that suggests that the world does not work well with grand rulers and despots, or authoritarian systems of any kind that trample on the human. And the abstract writings theories of political theorists often do not serve people well. They simply do not work for the majority of those who live ordinary everyday practical lives doing ordinary everyday practical actions. These little actions should be cherished. Humanism identifies practical grounded and practical worlds, working with small-scale, local, contingent and endlessly pluralistic actions as the locus of human life. I could go on.

I have introduced some opening possible global values, which I will return to throughout the book.[50] An astute observer may note that many of them are at odds with the contemporary economic values that tend to dominate government policies. Again, I must be very clear: I have not just conjured up these values from my magic bag at a whim. There are deep-rooted, evolving intellectual global traditions behind all these simple statements, frequently to be found in religious and philosophical arguments, and I have simply briefly identified some of them, even as I have also struggled personally with them for decades. More than this, they are indeed deeply rooted in the very processes of becoming human. If, for example, we are not cared for in our earliest years, it becomes harder for us to care for others in later life. If we do not develop empathy, we can hardly interact with others. If we are not accorded dignity, why should we give dignity to others? Our values and our beings are deeply connected. And they are at the heart of our search for positive norms.

Valued sexual lives

We can briefly conclude this opening chapter with a sense of the values that can also be seen to provide guides to a good sexual life, to *humanist sexualities*. Here are the values of caring and loving sexualities, empathic and compassionate sexualities, a respectful and dignified sexualities based on rights, a flourishing sexualities with sexual well-being, as well as sexual and gender justice: a fair and just sexualities. Making these clear also creates a sense of oppositional malevolences – *a troubled sexualities* – to be challenged

and resisted: cruel and violent sexualities, non-empathic monologue sexualities, dehumanized sexualities, damaged sexualities and
unfair sexualities. Box 1.4 lays these out. Cosmopolitan sexualities
depends on the sense of a practical common ground and it is well
to be clear at the outset what I suggest these to be. There is much
to discuss here and I return to it all throughout the book.

1.4   *Ethical sexualities*:
Sampling a multiplicity of better and lesser 'human' sexualities

Humanist values suggest we should:

- understand others
- be kind
- foster human rights and dignity
- encourage lives to flourish
- seek justice

Applied to sexualities this means:
Positively: The better side of sexual life seeks out:

- Empathic and dialogic sexualities – understand others: appreciate and dialogue with your sexual partners and their worlds.
- Caring and loving sexualities – be kind and look after others:
  care for the sexual other as well as your self.
- Respectful and dignified sexualities – cultivate sexual and
  gender rights and dignity: respect others, their dignity and
  their rights, being aware of their fragility and vulnerability.
- Sexual well-being – encourage lives to flourish: enabling sex
  and relationships to work well.
- Sexual and gender justice (just sexualities) – create free, fair
  and equal sexual relations.

Negatively: The dark, damaged side of sexual life is revealed in:

- Intolerant sexualities: the lack of appreciation of sexual differences and the closure of dialogues about sexualities.

- Unkind sexualities, sexual violence and cruel sexualities: sexualities become embroiled in being unkind to the others; often cruelty, violence and hatred.
- Dehumanized sexualities: treating sexual others with no dignity or respect and lacking any rights to their own sexualities.
- Wasted sexualities: unfulfilled sexualities lacking in any kind of 'quality'.
- Unfair and unequal sexualities: sexual lives damaged through poverty, competition, greed and the stark inequalities of intersecting class, gender, race, age and nation.

2

Transformational Sexualities: Making Twenty-First-Century Sexual Lives

All fixed, fast-frozen relations, with their train of ancient and venerable prejudices and opinions, are swept away, all new-formed ones become antiquated before they can ossify. All that is solid melts into air, all that is holy is profaned, and man is at last compelled to face with sober senses, his real conditions of life, and his relations with his kind.

Marx, *Communist Manifesto* (1848)

Another world is not only possible, she is on her way. On a quiet day, I can hear her breathing.

Arundhati Roy, *The God of Small Things* (1998)
(Reprinted by permission of HarperCollins Ltd, David Godwin Associates and Penguin Random House, © Arundhati Roy (1998))

The early twenty-first-century world of sexualities is a world like no previous one. We are drifting, and not with a whimper, into new sexual forms. Here are folk from all kinds of backgrounds transforming their emotional, embodied sexualities with the aid of dazzling technology (think: reproductive technologies), spiralling new media (think: digital sexualities), greedy capitalism (think: sexual commodification, consumption, sex markets and sex trafficking), widening inequalities (think: gender violence and pauperized sexualities), reforming religions (think: secular sexualities and fundamentalist sexualities), shifting subjectivities (think: individualism and informalism), pandemic disease (think: HIV and AIDS), family diversification (think: gay marriage, child marriage, forced marriage), democratic politics (think: sexual rights, movements and queer politics) and global mobilities (think: local and global sexual lives increasingly interconnecting through travel, migration, media and business). It is a world marked by the intensification of nations, even as there are moves from collective community-based lives to individualist ones: from absolute religions through secularism to post-secular and complex ones; from honour societies to post-honour societies. Here is modernity and its continuing move from unified, collective worlds to pluralizing, individualizing, differentiating ones. Such change suggests that new forms and diversities of sexualities are in the making across the globe. And, with these, the vulnerabilities of human life may be increasing. Many breathe this new sexual air everyday; but, equally, many do not. It tells both a positive story and a negative one. In this chapter I examine some of these broadest of sweeping transformations to suggest some of the contemporary challenges of human sexual variety that we must confront.

Transformational sexualities

'Transformational sexualities' are those sexualities that are emerging under conditions of twenty-first-century modernity. Just what this modernity is has been widely documented and explained. It is not my task to rehash all this here.[1] Some see this 'modernity' (the word itself is always a problem) as starting way back in the fourteenth century, others at the moment of the Renaissance and Enlightenment; still others in the early twentieth century, with the avant-garde and the first world war. Some claim it is Western; others that it is universal. It has been variously linked to the advance of capitalism, the decline in religion, the exploitive march of colonization, the rise of nation-states, the growth of technologies and new media, and the rise of a new mentality or consciousness of individualism. Sometimes it is celebrated, frequently it is portrayed darkly (as with Max Weber's disenchantment of the world); regularly it is put into contest with tradition. Usually, it brings an enormous sense of the rapidity of change, of transience and speed, of 'All that is solid melts into air'. It brings us to the brink of the post: postmodern, postreligion, postcolonialism, posthuman. It suggests new worlds of emotion and bodies in the making. It means multiple things, then.

Whatever account is preferred, it always flags a complex history that is now culminating at a time when the diversities of the modern, the late modern and the postmodern have brought a variety of 'newish' sexualities wrestling with the past and bringing transformative implications for social life. Historians have long documented the diversities of sexuality throughout history,[2] and in recent times they have highlighted the move from classical orders to modernist ones, showing the changing historical nature of gender, heterosexuality, homosexuality and orgasms – along with the arrival of a so-called 'sexual revolution'.[3] The older orders of seemingly more traditional, tribal and religious sexualities are very far from gone, especially in agrarian and theocratic societies; but newer ones are most certainly appearing alongside them. To use a rather overdrawn and slightly old-fashioned phraseology, we could claim that the world we live in now simultaneously brings traditional, modern and postmodern sexual worlds (though at different paces and to differing degrees). And one key problem for transformative human sexualities is the very tension that exists between these worlds.

With so many terminologies and shifting arguments, I find the language of the sociologist Shmuel Eisenstadt (1923–2010), amongst others, to be useful. He suggests that we dwell in *multiple modernities*.[4] Here we can trace every contemporary society back through different routes into the past, while sensing both parallel and different pathways into possible futures. My concern is with the diversities of *multiple modernist sexualities*. Just as there are 'multiple modernities' across the world, following different trajectories and differing outcomes, so there are multiple modernist sexualities with deeply varying routes moving on different trajectories across different countries in the world and displaying their own local rituals. These various modernities have been achieved in different ways: through colonization, through conquest, through innovation, through evolution, through diffusion.

And this means that the pathways into contemporary global and plural sexual worlds are varied. As many countries like Nigeria, Pakistan and Syria move towards their own and very different versions of modernity, so they also struggle with the contradictions posed by their vast inequalities and past traditions, conflicts, religions and tribalisms. So we have a fragmented contemporary Africa, whose sexualities have been shaped by poverty, corruption, Christianization, civil war and colonialism; a China struggling with sexualities where Daoist, Confucian and Communist pasts meet each other at a capitalist turn; Muslim cultures with sexualities torn by variant antagonistic interpretations of Islam facing enormous conflict with the West; and, indeed, a Christian West caught in a tension between its former patriarchal puritanism and an emerging secularizing gender-equal and highly sexualized culture. All flow from different past complex and multiple sexualities and all lead to possibilities for differing future plural sexualities. Clearly, the contemporary sexualities of Shanghai have not been shaped in the same historical ways as the routes through the Ottoman Empire to modern Istanbul, and these are definitely not the same as the paths of sexual development of Nigerian, Indonesian or Iraqi sexualities. It could hardly be otherwise as different histories unfold, but it is crucial to bear this in mind when we consider cosmopolitanism later.

And yet: despite all these differences, there are surely also potential common problems facing human sexualities across the globe. For there are unmistakable new global trends: of technology and commerce, of travel and migration, of media and digitalization, of fundamentalisms and secularization, not to mention the rise of international governance. And these have all worked to make the world increasingly connected, while raising new sexual possibilities and problems even as they also highlight conflicts. So just as there have then been many different pathways into multiple sexual modernities, so many convergences are also taking place. Even so, this terminology can smack of the hegemony of the West over the East, the North over the South. And indeed, the very idea of modernity symbolizes for some countries a major threat and something to be resisted. I will look at this later (see Chapters 3 and 4).

So we have to be careful. In what now follows, I provide an over-simple sketch of a few sightings of these multiple modern

---

2.1 *Modern sexual worlds*: Sampling a multiplicity of social worlds

Long ago, the sociologist Tamotusu Shibutani remarked that 'modern societies are made up of a bewildering variety of social worlds'.[5] In fact, today we can find an equally 'bewildering' variety of sexual social worlds displaying every kind of human sexualities. At the quickest glance, we can find the following social worlds all over the modern world. Believe it or not, all have been researched and I provide just a partial listing here – a good few are mentioned again in this book. For ease, I put them in alphabetical order:

abortion worlds; AIDS/HIV worlds; androgyny worlds; asexual worlds; barebacking worlds; BDSM (bondage, domination, submission, masochism) worlds; 'bear' worlds'; bisexual worlds; celibacy worlds; chastity worlds; circuit party worlds; drag worlds; drug sex worlds; 'faerie' worlds; 'feederist' worlds; female genital mutilation worlds; fetish worlds (including foot fetish, undie fetish, urine fetish and many more); feminist worlds; fraternity and sorority worlds; gang rape worlds; homosexual, gay, lesbian, queer worlds; honour-shame worlds; 'leathermen' worlds; macho/machismo worlds; macho slut worlds; modelling worlds; nudist worlds; paedophile worlds; 'polyamory' worlds; pornographic worlds; prostitute worlds; rape worlds; rape survivor worlds; religious, moral and purity crusade worlds; safer sex worlds; sex abuse survivor worlds; sex addiction worlds; sex education worlds; sex offender worlds; sex therapy worlds; sex tourist worlds; sex trafficking worlds; sex work worlds; singles bars worlds; sexual diseases worlds; 'swingers' worlds; teenage sex worlds; transgender worlds; transsexual worlds; transvestite worlds.

The list goes on and we could add many more routine examples, such as: mundane heterosexual worlds; courting worlds; wedding worlds; divorce worlds; and the like. And on, and on.[6]

---

sexualities, their transformations and the vulnerabilities they bring with them. They form the critical background to the development of cosmopolitan sexualities.

Reproductive sexualities, techno sexualities

A first striking feature of the modern world has to be the new technologies it has created. If, in a first wave, the industrial revolution brought science and machines, a second wave has surely brought the new electronic, pharmaceutical and genetic revolutions. Unsurprisingly these many deep developments radically transform the sexual, creating a plethora of new sexualities along the way. We now have new *assisted reproductive sexualities* (ART), resulting in pregnancy by artificial means and developing new forms of reproduction, globally leading to cross-border reproductive care (CBRC); *digital sexualities*, with the ubiquitous presence of connectivity (computers, mobile phones and the rest) in sexual life; *prosthetic sexualities*, with sex gadgets from vibrators and penile toys to G spot manipulators, erotic furniture, erotic electro stimulation and life-size sex dolls; *pharmaceutical sexualities*, where drugs – Viagra, Ecstasy (MDMA), nitrite inhalants ('poppers') and other forms of 'sexuopharmacy' – bring new possibilities of sexual practice and pleasure. There is even now the possibility of *posthuman sexualities*, whereby an array of technologies transcend the physical sex, gender and reproduction we have known in the past into a new cybersex. To some, these may sound like eccentricities and fringe diversions; but in fact they are changing our sexualities at their very core. Each raises major controversies.

What is most striking about many of these new technological sexualities is that they bring a very clear potential to disconnect human sexuality and gender from their very long presumed biological essence and their coupling with reproduction. Viagra can now prolong sex way beyond the reproductive years; contraceptive pills, morning after pills (and condoms for men *and* women) can facilitate sex without reproduction; new reproductive technologies can make pregnancy and childbirth possible without sex. Put these

together and we have a heady mix: the idea historically that reproduction is the universal and most widespread bases of sexualities is
now challenged, and the linking of sex, gender and procreation so
widely held to have been a fundamental truth throughout history
has been broken.

Above all, this has transformed the lives of women. Throughout
history, women have spent much of their lives in child bearing,
birthing and child rearing. Now, the modern world makes reproductive sex less central and allows a move to sexualities that are
more relational, even recreational. Many women now have time
to live lives beyond, and outside, child bearing and child rearing:
they have the conditions for a 'life of their own'. Some countries
like China regulate reproduction; and a booming global surrogacy
market also now exists across the world. All this raises many challenges for religions, as they watch old 'truths' and authorities being
eroded. And, indeed, for the transformations of traditional gender,
these changes become the basis for much new conflict.[7]

Mediated sexualities

Throughout history, cultures have come to represent human sexualities in various ways through texts and objects that then fold back
into our lives (*textual sexualities*). The Greeks represented sex on
vases and in art; the Hindu captured sexuality through dance and
music; the Egyptians constructed giant phalluses for Gods. (Only
the Islamic faith challenges representation in such ways.) All give
(varying) meanings to those who see them. But the decisive factor
in the development of modern sexualities has to have been the
gradual evolution of modern media from Gutenberg to Facebook.
It is not that the media directly shapes sexual life, but that it indirectly helps us to imagine the sexual lives of others. As the media
has grown, so we have learnt more and more about the possibilities
and the plausibility of the imagined and actual worlds of sexualities
that others inhabit.

In many ways, we can even trace the history of modern sex
through the history of modern media: the making of the printing

press (and with it the making of both sex scandal news media, the 'sexualized' novel, and the language of perversion); the invention of the camera (and with it the 'dirty pictures', pornographic photos and a hyper-visualized 'voyeuristic' sex culture); the creation of the telephone (and the possibility of 'telephone sex', 'dirty/silent calls', 'call girls' and auditory/'dirty sex talk'); the rise of first the film/movie industry (and abounding in sex controversies ever since) and eventually the television, the 'video nasty' and, ultimately, as we will see, the Internet. And although there have been attempts at regulation and censorship in all countries, it is an unmistakably global trend.

Each culture has generated its own literature – from *The Perfumed Garden* in Islam to *The Kama Sutra* in India. In the Western world, the novel became significant from the eighteenth century onwards in helping to appreciate, imagine, create and extend our visions of private and subjective feeling worlds. Here are 'torrents of emotions'; of wider empathies, worlds of complex desires different from or maybe similar to yours. Many, now classic, novels opened fresh windows: Rousseau's *Julie* (1761), as well as his *Confessions* (1782–9), Samuel Richardson's *Pamela* (1740) and *Clarissa* (1747–8), Henry Fielding's *Tom Jones* (1749). These are hardly 'sex novels' by today's standards, but they do open our eyes to sense other worlds of intimacy and desire. The great 'love novels' like *Anna Karenina, Madame Bovary* and *Effi Briest* spoke so much of the desires of their time: love, passion – and adultery. And alongside these came the more explicitly sexual and titillating: John Cleland's *Fanny Hill* and *Woman of Pleasure* (1748–9) 'the most licentious and inflaming book', as Boswell called it.

From the mid-nineteenth century, we find an explosion of writings around what has been called 'sexual perversion' or 'aberrations' – the naming of homosexuality, sadism, voyeurism and the like. For this was not only the time of the emerging sexologists (Iwan Bloch, Sigmund Freud, Richard von Krafft-Ebing, Havelock Ellis, Magnus Hirschfeld, William Reich) but also the new modernist literary imagination of desire (Marcel Proust, Oscar Wilde, D.H. Lawrence, Thomas Mann, Paul Valéry, Frank Wedekind, James Joyce and a host of others).[8] From this inventive writing there has been a steady drip of literature and text turning now into a monsoon of 'sex writings' across the world. It is a story that leads us from the work of de Sade in the eighteenth century, through Joyce's *Ulysses* (1922) and to others like Bataille's *The Story of the Eye* (1928) in the twentieth century, with various strands of sexual anarchism, sexual libertarianism, queer radicalism and transgressive sex.

Over my own life time, I have witnessed one *cause célèbre* after another, including: *Lady Chatterley's Lover* (1928, but not allowed to be published in the UK until 1960), *Fear of Flying* (1973), *Emmanuelle* (1974), '*Belle de Jour*' (2003) and, even as I write in 2013, E.L. James's *Fifty Shades of Grey*, which is simply the latest erotic bestseller to outsell all others – and in this case to reintroduce us all, yet again, to the world of bondage, discipline, dominance, submission and sadomasochism, those most popular and widely discussed of all our secret passions. By early 2014, the book had sold 100 million copies worldwide, been translated into 53 languages and turned into a 'hot' film. Thus, different sexual lives become available in print for all to eventually read and reimagine the sexual life. Since the 1990s, the *Guardian* newspaper in the UK has even been providing an annual 'Bad sex award' for the worst sex writing in a novel.[9]

Electronic sexualities

This transformation of texts has gradually moved into an electronic age. Once hidden in private spaces, diverse sexualities now proclaim their stories loudly from both old mass media – a *screen sexualities* found in film, video and television – and new social media – a *digital sexualities* found through mobile phones, websites and social networking. And this has most surely had a worldwide impact on creating and shifting sexual variety. A new public telling of sex invades what was once seen as the private: once experienced as a very personal and hidden sphere, it is now made increasingly accessible to all.

Screen Sexualities

The cinema became the twentieth-century art form that gradually permeated the lives of billions around the world, bringing new and different messages about the intimate life, about love, passion and sex. Implicitly, it fostered a new kind of voyeuristic sexualities. The very earliest of films brought newly styled erotic bodies (for example, the 45-second-long first outrageous screen kiss shown in William Heise's *The Kiss*, 1896, which was denounced by the Catholic Church), through grisly tales of sexual murder (Fritz Lang's *M*, Hitchcock's *The Lodger*) and in titillating dance sequences (the controversial body shots of Busby Berkeley's crotch shots), and bosom exposures (Jane Russell – and so on). The history of cinema is one of enhanced sexualization: from *The Kiss* (1896) through *From Here to Eternity* (1953) with Burt Lancaster and Deborah Kerr rolling over as the waves crashed orgasmically over their bodies; and on to the now widespread acceptance of extreme sexual violence in films like Lars von Trier's *Nymphomaniac* (2013). And the film industry, including film festivals, is of course a global one: for example, in India, Bollywood films; in Sweden, 'sensation films'; in Japan, 'pink films'. Today, sex on the screen is a staple diet of most non-Muslim countries, even though major restrictions do exist.[10] Across the world, film has opened up realms of sexual possibilities.

Digital sexualities

It could be, though, that it is with the digital screen that the most widespread and revolutionizing of transformations is taking place. For with the convergence of computers, phones, cameras, videos, scanners, televisions, webcams and screens comes a new array of digital sexual services: *camsex* (with video), *cybersex* (with computers), *phone sex* (with phones), *gamesex* (with computer games), *'sexting'* (with mobile phones), *teledildonics* (with robots and remote controls) and *sexual networking* (with social networks). Taken together, they signpost multiple new intimate relationships and sex practices that simply did not exist before the late twentieth century. And they potentially bring complex new global languages: *cybersex, cyberdating, cyberqueer, cyberporn, cyberstalking, cyberbullying, cybergrooming, cyberrape, cybervictim, cybercottage, cybercarnality*. The lists go on.[11]

These digital sexualities transform our sexualities in at least five ways. First, they change how we gain *information* and knowledge about sexualities in all their diversities and forms across the world, from guidance pages on infertility (there are more than a million sites on sperm banks) to sites engaged in mail-order brides. Second, they use *social network sites* to create new possibilities for making new local and global sexual and intimate contacts (Grindr, a gay line, was set up in 2009 and claims some five million active users in 192 countries worldwide). Third, they make available a vast flow of sexual *representations* (the 'people's pornography'[12]) hitherto unavailable: every sexual fetish or curiosity can now develop its own complex imagery, and we can make it ourselves too – the new DIY/Gonzo porn: 'The Internet is for Porn', as the song in the musical *Avenue Q* goes. Fourth, they generate new *erotic embodiments*, making possible new eroticisms and providing actual direct physical sex contact through the technology itself, often through masturbation. Finally, digital sexualities can also make sex *political*, creating new global activisms around sexual politics, both conservative and radical. Much of this is achieved through the click of a Google search – a *google sexualities*.

These are all startling new issues for the twenty-first century to confront. Space gets reorganized: sex and sex partners now become locatable across the globe. Time gets transformed: sex now becomes accessible instantly with the possibility for many of 'perpetual sexual contact' through a mobile phone. Representations mutate: as sex becomes 'mainstreamed' and sexual images that were once rare or impossible become ubiquitous. The private reconfigures: sex, once private, now becomes more and more publicly visible as old splits of private/public change. Inequalities sharpen: as new hierarchies of accessibilities and cyberclasses appear; of those who have access to all this across the world, and those who do not. And new global issues are raised concerning both regulation (how states control these new communications) and surveillance (how states monitor what is going on).[13]

Familial sexualities

Despite what some critics say, families are central and universal in all societies. But they develop in multiple varieties across the world and are open to change. Centrally, they help organize reproduction (fertility, birth control and the politics of reproduction become key issues), gender (raising issues of patriarchy, patrilineage and patrimonialism), child rearing (raising issues of child abuse, child marriage, etc.), and relationships (where the main concerns are polygyny, arranged marriage, polyarmory, spouse abuse and 'honour crimes', and, more recently, same-sex marriage). But they also become the foundation of what the sociologist Carol Smart has called 'personal life': our relationships, connectedness, emotions and memories. How might these be changing under multiple modernities?[14]

Although families are surely found everywhere across the world, they are clearly not the same. More than 100 years ago Edward Westermarck's classic, if anecdotal, study, *The History of Human Marriage* (1891), demonstrated this. And a century later the leading world sociologist Göran Therborn, in *Between Sex and Power* (2004), delineated five very basic differences between contemporary global types, linked to sub-Saharan African (Animist), European/North American (Christian), South Asian (Hindu), East Asian (Confucian) and West Asia/North Africa (Islamic). He also identified further subforms such as the Southeast Asian and the Creole American (and even this, I suspect, is far from complete). Each of these family types provides contrasting cradles in which human sexualities nest. And, of course, these family structures also change over time within any one country. John D'Emilio and Estelle Freedman's classic account of the history of sex in the United States over the last three and a half centuries cogently, if rapidly, suggested that family there had moved 'from a *family-centered*, reproductive sexual system in the colonial era; to a *romantic, intimate, yet conflicted sexuality* in nineteenth-century marriage; to a *commercialized sexuality* in the modern period, when sexual relations are expected to provide personal identity and individual happiness apart from reproduction.'[15] Changes indeed.

In the twenty-first century, families are changing everywhere, even as such changes are resisted by what might be called the global family protection movement.[16] According to Therborn, the 'Western family' (European/North American) reveals the most radical transformations, changing through what he calls, rather clumsily, the 'de-patriarchalization of families', whereby the hitherto central role of the man becomes weakened, and patriarchy is 'forced to retreat'.[17] In any event, a greater emphasis comes to be placed on equality within the family, and this has prompted many other changes. In many much discussed books – for example, Beck and Gernsheim's *The Normal Chaos of Love* (1995) and *Reinventing the Family* (2002b), and Anthony Giddens's *The Transformation of Intimacy* (1992) – these transformations have been welcomed. Many new trends have been suggested: from single parents and divorce to polyarmory and transnational and global families. The family has increasingly become the home to complex emotional personal lives.[18] And alongside all this has come the claim for gay marriage too. Detested and resisted in many African and Arab states as further evidence of Western decadence and imperialism, by 2015, some 20 countries across the world had nevertheless legislated for it.[19]

Many other changes are afoot globally. China, for example, faces a serious gender imbalance as a consequence of its 1979 One Child Policy, where, to control population size, a strict policy was enforced. As a consequence, female foetuses were often aborted because of the importance given to the male child. As a result, we now see in China the 'bare branches' of millions of unmarried men (and a rising crime rate), the prediction that there will be a shortage of brides of 24 million by 2020 and the arrival of 'the Little Emperor Syndrome', where single children become very spoiled.[20] Challenges are also being made to age-old practices like child marriage and polygamy. Despite near universal commitments to end child marriage, one out of nine girls across the world are married before their 15th birthday, and, in 2010, some 67 million 20–24-year-old women had been married as girls (most are poor). Likewise, polygamy is widely practised across the world – and usually to the serious disadvantage of women.[21]

Gendered sexualities

One key to assist in understanding the transformations of modern sexualities comes through a focus on gender, and especially in grasping the partial changes in women's status, lives and sexualities. *Patriarchal sexualities*, whereby gender inequality organizes sexualities, have been the norm throughout history. Women's sexuality has been silenced, rendered passive or sanctified. While gender inequalities surely remain deeply entrenched in all societies, there have been changes. Through major transformations in reproductive possibilities, many women no longer have to spend all their lives in child bearing and child rearing, with large families and high infant mortality. Likewise, secularization in parts of the Western world has reduced some of the restricting claims of religions on women's lives. And along with major developments in health, work, education and political activity, the historically subordinated position of women has started to change in many countries around the world. Women's sexuality has come to be recognized, becoming both more visible, more active and more under the active control of women themselves. For some there has even been a 'feminization of sex', as the stories of Mae West, Madonna and Lady Gaga reveal on the public stage.[22] This is a big story for cosmopolitanism and we will look at it in more detail as we proceed.

The story, however, is very uneven. Despite much talk of a global gender revolution and an equalizing between men and women in terms of work and educational opportunities, most women and girls remain very poor. The Global Gender Index published every year ranks countries on four dimensions: economy, health, politics and education. While there are a lot of interpretive problems here, it does suggest some countries are doing well: Norway, Sweden, Iceland, Finland, Denmark, New Zealand and Ireland are usually at the top (and there are surprises like the Philippines and Nicaragua). But other cultures fare much less well: with Yemen, Chad, Saudi Arabia, Pakistan and Syria (all Muslim) having the very worst results. One survey suggested that Afghanistan, the Democratic Republic of Congo, Pakistan, India and Somalia were the 'most dangerous places for women to live'.[23]

And it may well be that, as women's sexualities change and become more visible in some parts of the modern world, there exists more and more of a challenge for men and their masculinities, resulting in an intensification of violence against women. Hegemonic masculinity may well be under threat, as new masculinities are in the making.[24]

Violent sexualities

Patriarchal sexualities reveal a long history of sexual violence. The entanglement of sexuality with violence is multiple: from femicide and so-called 'honour killings' to rape and sexual murder. We cannot be sure if these have increased under modernity – they have a long history[25] – but certainly the global awareness of the unacceptability of such sexual violence seems to have grown along with its visibility. And this is increasingly recognized in legal change. The naming, recognition and attempts at prevention of this hidden and secret horror started significantly in the West in the 1970s with the Rape Crisis Movement, and gradually it has became more and more of an issue in many countries across the world.[26] For example, as I write, a major movement against sexual violence is developing in India. Sexual violence is now on a world agenda for action.

Part of this shift in awareness has been a change in the documentation of the 'global brutalization of women', country by country.[27] Measurement problems apart, we now know that something like one in every three women in the world has been beaten, coerced into sex or abused – usually by someone she knows; that as many as 5,000 women and girls are killed annually in so-called 'honour' killings (many of them for the dishonour of being raped!); that worldwide some 140 million girls and young women have undergone female genital mutilation (FGM); that an estimated 4 million women and girls are bought and sold worldwide each year, into either marriage, prostitution or slavery; that some 700 million women alive today were married as children (under 18), and some 64 million women and girls today become child brides;

and that each year women undergo an estimated 50 million abortions, 20 million of which are unsafe, and some 78,000 women die and millions suffer. The specific figures are open to critique, the terms may be contested, but the visible debate about the horrors of widespread sexual violence globally is a key feature of the modern world.

This growing awareness of sexual violence over the past half century has meant that we have also identified and named many 'new' problems, from child sexual abuse (CSA) and FGM, to child marriage and date rape. In some countries, these are still not recognized as violence. One major recent 'discovery' has been that of the sexual horrors of wars. In *Sexual Violence and Armed Conflict* (2011), Janie Leatherman argues that 'no part of the world has been unaffected by wartime sexual violence'. Both the numbers she produces (500,000 raped in the Rwandan genocide, 60,000 in Bosnia, and 32,000 in one small province of the Eastern Congo – the worst in the world) and the harrowing accounts she gives of violence 'so brutal it staggers the imagination' can leave one in no doubt how much rape in times or war and its linkage to hypermasculinity are part of the modern world.[28] While wartime rape may have existed throughout history, it has now been identified, named and acted upon. This new awareness has brought about a significant change: what has being going on throughout history has now become a new public issue for modernity. And at the same time it seems to say something about how traditional masculinities are coming under greater threat in many countries.

Post-honour sexualities

'Honour' has played a major role in the regulation of sexuality throughout much of history. It works to maintain a sense of 'honourable men and women'. Under modernity, this starts to wane as the values of what it means to be a man or woman change and patriarchal gender finds itself under threat and in crisis. Something of its traditional importance can be revealed from the well-known folk saying in Pakistan: 'When wealth is lost, nothing is lost; when health is lost, something is lost; when honour is lost, everything is lost.'[29] Honour codes are built into the emotional and the normative hearts of many cultures, bringing both an inner and an outer dimension.

An outer world of *public* expectations, a recognized code of worth, confronts an inner *personal* world of respect or shame. The public violation of honour can lead to irrevocable damage: honour killings, duels, and revenge, etc. are the honourable response and should be public: there is no shame attached to such public acts.

Honour can take many forms. It has been documented throughout history in wars, in sport, in academia, in patriotism and across different groups such as gangs, prisoners and ethnic cultures.[30] In England, it can be found in the workings of the early medieval system and becomes part of the military and education systems. In Mediterranean countries, honour has been seen as being at the centre of the family, the purity of bloodlines and the chastity of women. Today it remains central in many Arab cultures. More than 40 million live in Pakistan and Afghanistan under the Islamic Honour Code and the Pashtun traditions of honour. In the modern world, it can be used to defend the abuse, rape and murder of women and girls. The case of Mukhtār Mā'īm in 2002, who became the victim of a gang rape as a form of honour revenge, helped raise the issue of honour crimes on a worldwide scale (see Chapter 6).

Another transformation is under way here too. For the shift away from honour codes in the modern world marks a move from local values to universal ones; from group esteem and public shame to guilt cultures and self-esteem. The sociologist Pierre Bourdieu puts his finger on it when he says: 'The ethos of honour is fundamentally opposed to a universal and formal morality which affirms the equality of dignity in all men and consequently the equality of their rights and duties.'[31]

Honour may indeed be a key driving force in humanity's inhumanity against humanity, not only by generating shame and violence but also in the transformations of a 'moral revolution'.

The philosopher Kwame Anthony Appiah has argued that modern worlds have slowly moved away from such culturally sanctioned but morally dubious activities as slavery, the customs of

Hindu Sutee, European duels, Chinese foot binding, the vengeance of Samurai Bushido and others – all customs linked to honour.[32] He claims that change comes about through a shifting sensitivity to honour and a weakening of its traditional claims. Indeed, the prominent Middle East emissary Akbar S. Ahmed (2004) suggests that much of the contemporary fundamentalist response from Muslims to the West (as exemplified in the Twin Towers bombing) stems from this crisis of honour: it is to be found in the very language of Osama Bin Laden and many 'terrorists'. Today, the practices of female (and male) genital mutilation, dowry and child marriage, wife beating, rape in general and rape in war, and homophobia can all in some ways be linked to problems of honour, especially male honour. And they are all being challenged. As new forms of masculinity emerge under forms of modernity, so traditional honour is under threat. One of the problems of transformative sexualities may well be bound up with changing perceptions of masculinity, honour and dignity. Increasingly, this can all (once again) be linked to a growing crisis in masculinity.[33]

Secular, sacred and fundamentalist sexualities

The world now shivers with its multiplicities of fragmented religions: everywhere they play their positive and negative roles in shaping human sexualities. Judaism, Hinduism and Islam, for example, have not historically been 'against sex', but they do give very detailed and restrictive instructions on its performance. Buddhism is very ambivalent; and Christianity has highlighted negativity. Women play subordinated roles in all of them; and religions have little positive to say about many of the diversities, especially same-sex relations.

But modernity has brought about changes. Traditional, patriarchal sexualities have continued to grow and remain dominant in world religions, but in some 'modernist' (mainly North European) parts of the world, they have gone into decline as secularism and atheism have grown. This growth has been accompanied with significant transformations in gender, family and sexuality.

The post-9/11 world, though, brought an abrupt end to any straightforward secularization view, putting Islam and the full orbit of world religions with their multiple schisms back into sharp focus. This 'Return of the Gods', a 'post-secular' age, has started to make very apparent the transforming rifts and conflicts of modern sexualities around both gender and sexual orientation, as debates on Muslim women, Islamic masculinities and the gay international start to appear. Alongside a limited, partial secularization, we now see a resurgence of interest in the mainstream traditional world faiths as they explode into a wider variety of Pentecostal and Fundamentalist forms, attracting a very wide group of followers who seek a return to traditional gender and sexual norms. Secularism is now under attack, new violent Islamic and Hindu religious organizations are on the increase, and both the Muslim faith and Christianity are globally becoming stronger and more radically conservative. In Africa alone, the number of Christians grew from 10 million in 1900 to 360 million by 2000.[34] And what is really striking about this change is the way these expanding Christian countries are much more fundamentalist – traditional, morally conservative and evangelical. By 2050, it is estimated that 72 per cent of Christians will live in Africa, Asia and Latin America. They are often Pentecostal. Many are inclined to deal with faith-healing, exorcism and mysticism. Frequently, they raise huge funds from the relatively poor. This new 'Christendom' arriving in the poorer world is often the proselytized product of the West, as religious crusades, failing in the West, have turned their attentions elsewhere.

What all this means is that many of the new 'transformative sexualities' outlined here are significantly under attack, as many growing religious movements seek a return to a more absolutist past. Making serious, even violent, demands to reinstate traditional gender roles and traditional sexualities (patriarchal sexualities), they set the ground for increasingly contested sexualities under multiple modernities.[35]

Commodified sexualities

Capitalism, even with its many varieties, has become the default economic system of most countries in the modern world. This is ironic because it is a system that manifestly fails everywhere: fostering inefficiency, inequality, selfishness and widespread global suffering for the majority.[36] The critique of capitalism is truly extensive, but the system survives in the hands of the small groups it benefits.[37] It cannot be surprising therefore that modern capitalism also creates extensive global sexual marketplaces where human bodies can be consumed and commodified and sexualities given a cash value.

Some of these markets involve the explicit and direct selling of sex, while others are more covert and indirect. Mainstream sites now become sexualized: holidays are linked to sex tourism, media is saturated with imageries of sellable sexual commodities, and underground black market organizations are challenged by 'ordinary' multinational corporations that vie for their share of sex markets. Dispersed everywhere, the old distinctions of private and public crumble: selling sex is no longer confined to the old red light districts, but is carried out everywhere. This has resulted in the normalization and mainstreaming of sex[38] and the new technologies become endemic in much of its organization. Such commodification takes many forms, as can be seen in Box 2.2, which suggests that sex commodification has become more diversified than ever before, offering a wider and wider range of services. Some sociologists, like Elizabeth Bernstein, argue that new 'relationship meanings' are evolving, where there is no longer a simple cash nexus and market relation, but, increasingly, the provision of erotic acts premised upon the promise of an 'authentic' interpersonal connection – a 'bounded authenticity', as Bernstein (2007) calls it. The public/private boundaries between intimacy and commerce are, then, being reworked in new and challenging ways.

There are many contrasting accounts of this new commodification. Richard Poulin (2011) suggests that routine sexual marketing is a direct outcome of growing exploitation under capitalism.

2.2   *Selling sex*:
Sampling a multiplicity of sexual commodification

We can see modernity transforming sexualities into interlocking circuits of producing, selling and buying global sex, involving millions of people across the globe as never before in history. We can find global markets engaged in

- *Selling relationships* – e.g. mail-order brides and 'cyberbrides', dating agencies, the global wedding industry and a 'Pink Economy' to market gay life; and all this on both a national and international scale.[39]
- *Selling emotions* – from expensive sex therapy to standardized self-help books selling 'the 12 steps needed for a perfect relationship'.[40]
- *Selling 'stuff'* – like drugs (Viagra, birth pills, nitrate inhalants – 'Poppers'), chemically and electronically developed sex aids ('electrosex') and 'sex toys', clothes (BDSM costumes, and whips/harnesses to dildos, vibrators, inflated blow-up dolls). In China alone, there are estimated to be some 200,000 sex shops, 2,000 of them in Beijing.[41]
- *Selling representations* – this includes the major global industry of pornography. Its global economic value is almost impossible to estimate (much of the market is underground; no statistics are kept) but in 2007 it was estimated to be worth $97 billion globally – more than Microsoft, Google and Amazon combined. The widespread nature of this has been called the 'pornographication' of culture.[42]
- *Selling marketing* – the massive worlds of advertising, entertainment and sport selling items through their sexual iconography and giving many objects a sellable erotic connection: perfumes, clothes, holidays, music, dance are all linked to sex.
- *Selling bodies* – real 'live sex acts'[43] of all kinds are up for sale through sex work: stripping, table dancing/lap dancing, escort and call girls, brothels, street prostitution, massage parlours, beauty shops, peep shows, sex tourism, telephone sex. Again, much of this is global, and involves rich/first world

men as purchasers, with excluded poorer women selling from low-income countries. Examples include Taiwan's betel-nut beauties, Amsterdam's red light window women, China's *xiaojie* and money boys, the Caribbean's beach boys and widespread sex tourism, the Dominican Republic's *bugarrones* and *sanky pankies*.[44]

- *Selling people* – and the sex trafficking trade. An estimated 21 million men, women and children are trafficked for forced labour around the world today. Sex trafficking is a small part of this – between 500,000 and 1.8 million; but its measurement (and regulation) is notoriously difficult.[45]
- *Selling life itself* – the global commercialization of new reproductive technologies (online, on Google) with one-stop shopping for surrogates to hire and the making of 'the industrial womb' (Twine, 2011). Gamete donation, surrogacy and adoption have become multibillion markets that pose new ethical and legal challenges. There is also a costly and growing transgender, intersex and cosmetic surgery industry.[46]
- And on, and on.

Although it is impossible to even estimate its market value (it has so many 'outlets'), it is undoubtedly a major world industry amounting to multibillions of dollars. Poulin claims:

> The sex industry, previously considered marginal, has come to occupy a strategic and central position in the development of international capitalism. For this reason it is increasingly taking on the guise of an ordinary sector of the economy. This particular aspect of globalization involves an entire range of issues crucial to understanding the world we live in. These include such processes as *economic exploitation, sexual oppression, capital accumulation, international migration,* and *unequal development* and such related conditions as *racism* and *poverty*.[47]

Others link this capitalist exploitation to the development of neo-patriarchy, reminding us that it is *women's* bodies that are being sold. Thus, the radical feminist critic Sheila Jeffreys sees sexual exploitation as linked to the creation of a vast 'Industrial Vagina', where an often violent and extensive world of regulating women's lives becomes more and more entrenched.[48] (It should be noted, though, that the world of male sex has also become much more prominent.) Still others point to the ways in which sex workers have become increasingly active in very poor parts of the world, enabling them to save and support their families even though they may not always like such work.[49] This has also led to the creation of a worldwide sex worker movement in an attempt to get better conditions for sex workers. Others, by contrast, see this explosion of sex work as human sex trafficking, and there has been a major international response to it.

In these contrasting accounts of sex work versus prostitution, we see continuing tensions between those who see sex as pleasure and those who see it as brutal exploitation; between those who see commoditized sex as necessary work and those who see it as abusive prostitution; between those who delight in erotics and those who attack pornography. New global institutions emerge to regulate prostitution and trafficking, even as the development of a worldwide movement appears to fight for the rights of sex workers. It is one of the many irreconcilable dynamics of transformative conflicts of sexual life today, which we will return to in Chapter 5.

Urban sexualities and their assemblages

Cosmopolitanism is widely linked historically to the great cities of the world, from Istanbul to Shanghai, where travel and different cultures meet. Recently, the scale and numbers of these cities has grown. A hundred years ago, two out of ten people lived in urban areas; by 2010 over half the population did – and figures are estimated to be seven out of ten people by 2050. As more and more people have moved from rural to urban locations in search of better economic opportunities, the size of cities has grown from half a million in preindustrial societies to the current megacities of 17–20 million or more. And with this, sexual life changes.

Most visibly, cities become 'zoned' and recognizable sexual

lifestyle enclaves emerge. Changes in housing can create new spaces for singles. And here too can be found the massage parlours, 'porn' stores, street hustling, strip joints, gay bars, sports clubs, sex clubs, gay networks and communities, all creating a new 'moral geography of sex'. Any interested tourist can find such neighbourhoods ('no-go' or 'red light' districts). And they have long histories, even as their fortunes come and go: Kabukicho in Tokyo, Mia-ri in Seoul, Patong in Bankok, the Tenderloin and the Castro in San Francisco, London's King's Cross and Soho, Koinange Street in Nairobi, the Reeperbahn in Hamburg, Zeedijk in Amsterdam, Dashilan in Beijing, Kamathipura in Mumbai. They are popular spots for researchers who have investigated, for example, sex trafficking in Tokyo, Bombay's dance bars, life in Delhi's red light district, the sex industry in Singapore, and much more.[50]

Less tangibly, there has been a shift in mood. The city, as the great historian of the city Louis Mumford said, brings a 'constant titillation of the senses by sex'.[51] It fosters a blasé attitude whereby modernity becomes what poet and wanderer Charles Baudelaire (1821–67) called 'the transient, the fleeting, the contingent'. The city brings segmentation, anonymity and 'massness', cultivating a new feel or tone, an 'urban sexuality', widely depicted in early modern art, for example by George Grosz (1893–1959) and Otto Dix (1891–1969) with their mutilated urban sexual subjects in Berlin, full of *lustmord* – sexual murder. The *film noir* of *Double Indemnity* (1944), *Scarlet Street* (1945), and *City That Never Sleeps* (1952) beautifully captures this attitude, as does the later *Midnight Cowboy* (1969). Nowadays, it takes a new turn in the hugely successful television series (and film) *Sex in the City*. Even musicals like Kander and Ebb's *Cabaret* and *Chicago* have captured it. There may even be an affinity between these features of the city and the homosexual form: indeed, the male homosexual may be emblematic of the modern urban condition.[52]

Despite this major global urbanization, half the world population do still live outside the city. And in these cases, transformations to 'modern sexualities' have been much slower. In parts of Asia and Africa, especially, urban modernity is altogether another land. Sexual modernity arrives in these areas much later, if at all.

AIDS and sexualities

The global AIDS crisis became, in many ways, a symbol of transformative sexualities and a key harbinger of cosmopolitan sexualities. Identified in 1981, by 2014 about 39 million people had died of AIDS (and some 75 million people had been infected with the HIV virus). This major modern tragic pandemic of human suffering has changed our understanding of sexualities. It has transformed sexual behaviour patterns, while generating modern international arenas of sexual debate and awareness, bringing new languages, movements, politics, schisms and agendas. In many ways, AIDS has brought a modern globalized sexual awareness, at the same time showing us that local contexts bring different cultures and meanings of sex (I develop this in Chapter 4).[53]

In its earliest days, AIDS became a freeze-dried copy of a society's prejudices and stereotypes. Hookers, heroin, homosexuals, Haitians and haemophiliacs (The 'five H club', as it was called) were its stigmatized emblems, marking out global fears over sex, drugs, race, disabilities and deviance. The inability to handle the problems was largely due to religious, governmental and racial hostilities that generated ignorance and blocked progress. Very gradually, debates on stereotypes, ignorance and prejudices made the working hatreds and structures of homophobia, sexism and racism more and more globally transparent.

And from this has grown an international world of sexual politics activism (which I will investigate a bit further in Chapter 3). An astonishing world circuit of organizations – an AIDS industry – in a hierarchy of levels from the UN and WHO, through NGOs, and on to grass-roots activism, has shaped a new global awareness of sexualities and suggested new patterns of sexual conduct. Most notably, we saw the global development of 'safer sex campaigns', a range of sexual practices that avoided the exchange of body fluids and explored, even celebrated, 'non-penetrative eroticism'.

In recent years, the global awareness of AIDS has also started to highlight the extreme inequalities between nations and the shapes of the HIV problem alongside the linkage to big business. The availability of antiretroviral therapies (ARV/ART) is not evenly distributed: whereas wealthy countries can enable people with HIV to live productive lives, for many poor countries this is out of their reach. They are trapped in cycles of poverty. Divided sexualities become more and more apparent.

Divided sexualities, pauperized sexualities

For most people in the world, life is hard.[54] All sexual lives face the divisions of social location: people and their sexualities are stratified and divided by economic groupings (such as caste, class, slavery, the rich and the poor), by gender orders (of men, women and the linked 'third' or intermediate worlds of gender muddle), by age and generation, by health, by ethnic and racial divides, by religions, as well as by nations and cultures. They face the 'pathologies of power' whereby many come to be marginalized, colonized and subordinated. In the simplest terms, wealthy white rich men have usually ruled the world; poor indigenous women have usually been pushed into the margins of the wretched. Their sexual worlds have differed accordingly.

The most extreme division across the globe is between the rich and the poor. The total global *income* by fifths of the global population shows that the richest 20 per cent receives some 74 per cent of all income. At the other end of the social scale, the poorest 20 per cent of the world's people struggle to survive, living damaged lives as refugees, the global poor, the dispossessed. Their lives fall into the cracks or are pushed beyond society, beyond care, beyond rights.[55] This clearly has major consequences for sexual lives. Who has the time to debate the polemics of gay marriage in such societies? We might instead start to ask just what happens to sexual lives:

- When more than 2.2 billion people (about a third of humankind) are vulnerable to (extreme) multidimensional poverty; when some 1.2 billion people (22 per cent) live on less than $1.25 per day; and when you have no money for anything. Are the best things in life really free? *Pauperized sexualities*.
- When some 2.4 billion people lack basic sanitation. You have

no toilet, you cannot wash with ease – how to have sex with the great unwashed? *Unhygienic sexualities*.

- When over 20 per cent of the people (about 1.3 billion) lack the nutrition they need to work regularly – how to have sex when you are hungry, emaciated, looking for food? *Emaciated sexualities*.
- When some 50,000 people die each day from poverty-related causes – a third of all human deaths – how to have sex when you are very ill? *Sickness sexualities*.
- When some 10 million people worldwide are homeless: you have no house or home – where do you have sex when you have no home? *Homeless sexualities*.
- When some 10.4 million people are refugees: you have to flee from your country or enemy – where do you have sex in a refugee camp? *Exiled sexualities*.
- You have no private space, no way of being alone – who do you have to have sex in front of? *Public sexualities*.

It goes on and on and on: what is sex like when you sleep in beds with many others? When you smell, are dirty and have body lice? When a family that is ill and dying surrounds you? The transformative sexualities being discussed here have little impact on this experience. This is a world of varieties of modern human sexualities hardly explored. They are too often overlooked.[56]

Individualized, reflective sexualities

All societies harbour individual people living personal lives. Even the slave and the discarded poor live their own distinct lives. But it is only under conditions of capitalist modernity that this 'sovereign individual', with its 'reflexive self', comes into being; and that 'individualism' becomes an organizing principle. In the Western capitalist world, especially but not exclusively, there has been a long march of possessive individualism, which strides against the very strong collectivist spirit that is embedded in many other world cultures.[57] Just in my own lifetime, I have read hundreds of books and articles that have claimed, each in their own unique way, that the modern world has brought with it a new form of consciousness or subjectivity. The prevalence of modern selves and identity in the Western world has become a commonplace cliché for over a century (even as the latest books still manage to express some surprise at it). Some of these books delighted in this change; others were more critical.[58]

The overarching thesis claims that in the modern world, traditional modes of group thinking and subjectivities are weakened and become prone to emergent forms of reflective, individualized beings. It is this making of a 'sacral person' that shapes both modern 'humanity', and even a 'human rights culture'.[59] As modern worlds bring individualized subjectivities, so they also bring modern *individualized sexualities*. Choices now extend to how we will live our personal lives, who we will live with, the kinds of sex and love we pursue and, ultimately, what we will do with our lives.

Positively, this means enhanced empathy, choice, civility; negatively, it means selfishness, disconnection, commodification, struggles for survival. In reality, it probably means both.

Closely connected to individualism is the idea of informalized sexualities. From the late 1940s onwards in the Western world we begin to see a process of 'controlled decontrolling'.[60] There is a growing relaxation of public manners, symbolized by the 1968 student conflicts. All round the world, the old rules of order start to become manifestly challenged: we become more informal in forms of address, in body styles, in dance, in day-to-day interactions. Dress codes often signify the sexualization of the very young, and body modification (tattoos, rings, etc.) brings a new body code. More informal relations increasingly supplant the formality of sexual emotions, manners, language, groups and hierarchies found in many societies of the past. Sexual life is 'deregulated'. Tight codes and formal rules have given way to more fluid rules, a seeming 'endless hunger for instant change', 'self reinvention' and 'short-term living'. This is the liquid society – the liquid sexualities – that Bauman (2006) writes about.

Migrating, diasporic and hybrid sexualities

Migration is increasing: in 2013 there were more than 232 million international migrants (over 3 per cent of the world's population) with a range of patterns (colonial, 'guest' worker, legal and illegal, refugee). Furthermore, 51.2 million people were forcibly displaced (the largest since 1994), as were 16.7 million refugees and more than a million asylum-seekers. Most of these live in the less developed regions of the world (Asia and Africa), and the flow is roughly equal for men and women (though this does differ across regions). And as people move, so do their sexualities: a transforming world of sexualities moves with them. They carry with them the sexual contradictions of one complex culture into the sexual contradictions of another; along, possibly, with the burdens of nomadism, rootlessness and homelessness. As they become transnational sexual migrants, they confront border controls, regulation and even refugee camps. All of this provides very unstable grounds for sexualities; and new forms emerge from this situation that we are only just beginning to understand.

The challenge is the time-worn one of confronting a new sexual culture. Migrants cannot and do not simply assimilate their sexual lives to their new cultures: they bring their own experiences, confront conflicts and build new sexual lives that often have to be very different from what came before. New lives and new varieties of hybrid sexualities emerge in this process of human action. Research has shown quite a lot about this process of transformative sexualities arising from the struggles of Mexican immigrant men and women crossing borders into the United States; Filipino gay men arriving in New York City to become gay divas; Chinese men moving across London, Hong Kong and Shanghai and refashioning their identities; Cubans fleeing Castro's regime for Miami; and Peruvian migrant men in New York City negotiating modernity through their experiences and representations of masculinity. These, and others, all highlight the creativity and mix of people building new lives and new cultures: never simply absorbing the culture they arrive in, but struggling to create new forms and, with this, new forms of sexualities. Multiple modernities lead to a time of diasporic and hybrid sexualities.[61]

Global sexualities/mobile sexualities

Many of the themes of transformational sexualities are linked to globalization.[62] Human sexualities have always moved across the globe (through travel, migrations, armed conflicts), but this now accelerates under modernity. Globalization suggests the interconnectedness of much of the world through economies, cultures, religions, media and governance; and it implies changes in local cultures as they confront rapid world changes. Although this might suggest a world that is becoming more and more similar (the so-called homogenization thesis), a more likely outcome is that of making the local more hybridic and different ('glocalization' is the ugly term coined to capture this process). Thus, local situations adjust and modify in the light of global processes and, in turn, shape them a little.[63] Human sexualities become more internationally liquid and mobile, reshaping time and space, and making the world smaller. We can see it in all the features I have described. Thus, *global technologies* bring the new cross-border reproductive care.[64] *Global communications* bring globally mediated sexualities and digital sexualities with an international circulation of new forms of erotica and pornography alongside new forms of regulation. *Global relationships* bring migrating sexualities, tourist sexualities, transnational friendships, long-distance relationships – 'distant love', global marriage, gay global parties (the celebrated 'white parties') and 'cross-border marriage'. *Global capitalism* brings global sex commodification markets, with sex selling round the world: international sex work, sex trafficking, mail-order brides, international markets of pornography and the like. *Global cities* bring impersonal sexualities, 'metrosexual sexualities', red light zoning. *Global HIV* has brought a multibillion AIDS industry shaping new sexual practices, languages, laws, treatments and education. *Global professionalism*, linked to this, sees an army *of* new specialists in sex (sex researchers, sex medics, sex educators, sex therapists, and sex lawyers), each bringing their own languages, 'sex discourses' (and money-making activities), as they travel the world of international conferences. *Global individualism* has brought issues of choice. *Global migration* has increased hybridity and pauperization. And, ultimately, a new world of *global sex politics* has emerged. Sexualities are also migrating, transforming and moving across the world, creating a wider sexual diaspora with dialogues across the North and the South, the East and the West. Human sexualities, then, are now becoming more and more subject to global flows, fluidities and networks, perpetually in motion as they are reworked, redrawn and reshaped.[65]

Conclusion: making sexual politics

This chapter suggests that significant changes are now in the making, transforming sexualities. I have only scratched the surface; but some things are clear. Breaking the link with biological reproduction opens the door for a wider range of sexual practices. New electronic media enhances the visibility and plausibility of a wider range of sexual feelings and behaviour. Digitalization reorganizes both the time and spaces of sexualities, making sex perpetually available everywhere in the here and now. Capitalism puts more and more exploitative sex on the market. Urbanization creates ecological niches and social worlds of different sexualities. Plural religions lead to wider choices (along with the growth of fundamentalist responses). HIV and AIDS have carved out a global sexual health agenda. And individualization and informalization have led to greater reflexivity and choice. Ultimately, global changes have meant that sexualities have become increasingly mélanged, diasporic and hybridic.[66]

Out of all this has grown a new global awareness of the politics of gender, sexuality and social change, along with the possibilities for new cosmopolitan and inclusive sexualities. Overarching this have been the twin canopies of 'democracy' and 'rights', which have provided a home for struggles over the future of human sexualities in the modern world. New movements and debates around sexuality have developed not only in the West, but across the world: in India and Indonesia, in Argentina and Africa, in Malaysia and Malawi. It is this 'new world' of politics of sexuality and gender that I now start to examine.

3

Cosmopolitan Sexualities: Living With Different Lives

If our world is to be a decent world in the future, we must acknowledge right now that we are citizens of one interdependent world, held together by mutual fellowship as well as the pursuit of mutual advantage, by compassion as well as self interest, by a love of human dignity, in all people, even when there is nothing to gain from cooperating with them. Or rather even when we have to gain the biggest thing of all: participation in a just and morally decent world.

Martha Nussbaum, *Frontiers of Justice* (2006)

In this chapter, I start to examine one key response to human sexual variety: cosmopolitanism. This idea of 'living easily with diversity' has a long history, a complex pedigree and it signposts benign, even utopian, futures. Martha Nussbaum has been one of the leading contemporary thinkers on debates concerning both the good life and cosmopolitanism and the quote above provides a dream of a world to come. It is my dream too. But it is also an idea that is always under attack and one that is riddled, even ridiculed, with problems. It often gets a bad press. Yet as an old idea held widely across many cultures, it cuts deeply into the issue of our common humanity and should not be lightly dismissed.

On cosmopolitanism

Cosmopolitanism is often seen as developing through the West in three critical moments: the Stoical moment of the ancient Greeks (defined by Diogenes, Cicero and other Athenians as 'citizens of the cosmos'); the Kantian moment of searching for universal law and perpetual peace; and the post-World War II moment of human rights (often linked to Karl Jaspers and Hannah Arendt).

But this really won't do. For this is a classical 'Western history'; yet we can find ideas of a perpetual search for a cosmopolitanism and international dialogue across many cultures and cities around the world throughout history. Muslim cultures are notably marked by their own struggles with cosmopolitanism: along the Swahili coast, the Ottoman Empire/Turkey, in Iran and in Indo-Pakistan. The long historical encounter between East and West suggests many attempts to bridge Muslim and Christian cultures. It is famously widespread as a form in the medieval period in Islamic Spain, and was present in Istanbul (Constantinople) as an early harbinger of East–West relations (and remains a hub today). India has always been 'an argumentative culture', and in China and the East there have been debates on connections with Asian values. So there are many intimations of cosmopolitan thought across a wide range of religious cultures, often envisioned in various 'Cities of God'.[1] But there are also limitations to this: it is really only under conditions of modernity and globalization that cosmopolitanism becomes an actual possibility for many – as the communications paths across the globe increase.

So just what might cosmopolitanism be? Holton (2009) manages to catalogue more than 200 meanings of the idea, but his study is far from complete and misses out the idea of cosmopolitan sexualities entirely.[2] So many people have tried to answer this question that it may help briefly to hear what just a few of them have to say. This is a small selection taken from many. Thus, for the Ghanian-American philosopher Kwame Anthony Appiah, it is a 'universal concern and respect for legitimate difference'. For the Swedish anthropologist Ulf Hannerz, it is 'a mode of managing meaning . . . a willingness to engage with the other . . . It entails an intellectual and aesthetic openness toward divergent cultural experiences, a search for contrasts rather than uniformity . . . an ability to make one's way into other cultures, through listening, looking, intuiting and reflecting.' For the German sociologist Ulrich Beck (1945–2015), who was at the forefront of sociological writers in this field, we have arrived at the 'cosmopolitan moment' as an emergent and distinctive feature of modernity: 'The human condition has itself become cosmopolitan.' For Beck, we live with the *mélange*, where 'local, national, ethnic, religious and cosmopolitan cultures and traditions interpenetrate, interconnect and intermingle – cosmopolitanism without provincialism is empty, provincialism without cosmopolitanism is blind.' He examines the need for boundaries, the growing sense of 'boundary-lessness' and the importance of common bonds and collective life in a world of individual differences. For the British sociologist Robert Fine, cosmopolitanism is bound up deeply with international law and human rights. Indeed, cosmopolitanism is both 'a determinate social form' that 'reconfigures' a whole sphere of (potentially contradictory) rights, as well as a 'form of consciousness that involves an understanding of the concept of cosmopolitanism and a capacity to deploy this concept in imaginative and reflexive ways'. Fine sees it as both an outlook (a way of seeing the world) and a condition (an existing form of the world). And finally, for the influential US liberal international, Jewish, feminist philosopher Martha Nussbaum, it raises the issue of a 'decent world culture' and a world moral community.[3]

So many speak of cosmopolitanism, even as they disagree about what it is. At base, they raise questions of differences and solidarity: of both human belonging and living with strangers. It asks how we can live with *our* closest family, community and nation, while simultaneously recognizing and living with other *different* families, communities and nations. They ponder how we can live together with *our common humanity*, in spite of ourselves and in spite of *our specific local differences*.

And, as the definition that opens Part One of this book suggested, cosmopolitanism works on many levels. There is a sociology of cosmopolitanism which suggests a form of society, a social structure of social solidarity where a reciprocal inter- and intracultural awareness of differences can become enshrined in human rights, laws, institutions and everyday practices. There is a politics of cosmopolitanism that suggests plural, agnostic activisms around differences that connect local political struggles with global ones. It bridges world stages and global civic culture with local governance through ideas like international law, global human rights, universal values and grounded ethics. There is a social psychology of cosmopolitanism which studies human empathy, dialogue and the capacity and ability to live with differences through an ever-expanding 'circle of others' spreading across the globe. And with this comes a cosmopolitan imagination suggesting an attitude of 'openness' and 'tolerance' towards difference (including sexual differences), which will often be accompanied by a sense of irony, paradox, contradiction and contingency as a fuller appreciation of the different kinds of humanity is developed. It enables us to recognize multiple stances in the world and position ourselves in relationship to them. It tries to avoid outright condemnation, adopting an appreciative stance (even as they are our enemies). Above all, cosmopolitanism asserts our grounded shared humanities. It is lived through a myriad of everyday, practical little actions where we accept and live with the differences of others.

But cosmopolitanism is also heavily questioned, as we will soon see.

Constructing cosmopolitan sexualities in a global arena

So what is cosmopolitan sexualities? In short, it suggests answers to different sorts of questions. For example, how can we connect our distinctive sexual and gendered individualities with human solidarity and belonging? How can we bridge our plural sexual differences with collective values, our sexual uniqueness with multiple group coherence? The challenge is to dwell simultaneously as citizens of multiple communities – of our own local and particularistic group, alongside other groups and, indeed, to share a common humanity, warts and all, more generally. Cosmopolitan sexualities sets an agenda for legal and political change, as well as a utopian imaginary and a critical way of thinking. It can provide one of a number of utopian visions for 'forward dreaming' to help create a better sexual and gender world for all. It can bring hope to a world where there is often very little reason for hope. It can create imaginative horizons to foster a wider willingness to live with, through and across our differences. And it surely does provide an orientation and a plea to keep a wide-eyed openness to engage with different sexual and gender others. It is part of the wider project of building cosmopolitan imaginations.

The laying of the foundations for a global cosmopolitan sexuality stretches back some two centuries, and the movement has gathered pace in recent decades. For the first time in world history, the possibilities of a transcultural, polyvocal, global empathetic response to the varieties and conflicts of human sexualities has become clearer. Although it may seem that the West, with its own preoccupations, has led the way, in fact new languages, new networks, new hybrid and innovative cultures have appeared in many, albeit not all, parts of the world. Communities of sexual and gender difference have gained wider global connections that in turn have started to transform local populations. We have witnessed, through both state and non-state actors, the construction of a new global civic culture of the politics of sexual difference.

Many factors have helped shape this trend. At the most general level, cosmopolitan sexualities depends on the development of social structures – call them 'democracies' – that allow for diversities, autonomy and freedom to flourish. Certain kinds of social order – those that are authoritarian, closed, dictatorial, ruled by despots and religious absolutisms – are not easily conducive to cosmopolitan sexualities. More specifically, we have seen the development of a transnational civil sphere, of new global social movements and new global media and technologies, all of which foster global intercommunication. Alongside these has come the emergence of wide-ranging arenas of critical public discourses around sexuality and gender, and, ultimately, a global discourse on humanity, global ethics and global rights. Many of the broader features of multiple modernities – a new consciousness, new technologies, new markets, new technologies and new cities, for example – have also helped create conditions for these emerging spheres.

In what follows, I suggest how such factors are now shaping a fresh global public arena, and facilitating the possibilities for cosmopolitan sexualities, even as they foster potentials to develop it in conflicting and contradictory ways.

Creating international global movements and counter-movements

From at least the time of the French Revolution onwards, social movements have become an increasingly influential source of political change in many nations of the modern world.[4] Existing in a perpetually contested relationship with the state, they demonstrably have a major expanding role in social transformation. We have seen this most recently in the Arab Spring, Occupy Wall Street, the Russian Pussy Riots, the Hong Kong student protests and the wider Global Justice Movement (GJM).[5] Quite simply, social movements question existing orders. They invent or imagine new worlds, mobilize resources, make claims, tell stories, set up new practices, tactics and strategies though activist performance, negotiate the media and, ultimately, if successful, enable their message to diffuse into the culture and (possibly) change the wider social order.

Sexual politics enters many of the earliest movements through their focus on issues of gender, family and health. There is now a wide variety of such movements (along with their counter-movements) that typically start out being local, then become national and, ultimately, sprout international wings. Those dealing with gender issues would include the various women's movement, the contrasting men's movement, the transgender movement. Others deal with sexual rights and citizenship (e.g., women, gay and lesbian, transgender, sex workers, children, disability), health (e.g., reproduction, child mortality, HIV and AIDS), as well as the new religious social movements, the family protection movement (e.g., on children, divorce and gay marriage) and the wider social rights and justice movements. There is now a multiplicity of these movements across the world: Durbar in India, representing thousands of sex workers; El Closet in Mexico, working for lesbian empowerment; the Inner Circle fighting for LGBT rights within Islam – everywhere, new movements are appearing.[6]

The women's movement, for example, has a history spanning nearly 200 years, moving through various 'waves' (first-, second- and third-wave feminisms), confronting various schismatic splits (classically between liberals, socialists and radicals) and moving largely from being Western-focused to being international. In the mid-1970s a convergence of the women's movement, the human rights movement and the postcolonial movement led to the designation by the UN of 1975 as the International Year of Women. Following this, the decade 1975–85 became the UN Decade of Women; what this managed to do was bring women from all round the world together for the first time, especially from low-income countries. The women's movement then moved into the mainstream of UN activities with the passage in 1979 of CEDAW – the Convention on the Elimination of all Forms of Discrimination Against Women. Often seen as the International Bill of Women's Rights, this became a benchmark for global social change. 'Gender mainstreaming' was adopted by the 1993 Vienna World Conference on Women, reaffirmed at the Beijing World Conference on Women in 1995 and became a buzzword for the next decade or so. And now, in the early decades of the twenty-first century, the women's movement engages with a multitude of global issues from women's rights to education, health and work, to more controversial issues like female genital mutilation, child marriage, polygyny, reproductive rights, sexual rights and sexual violence, in countries as different as Zimbabwe, Poland and Mexico. Many new global movements have appeared to address specific problems – the International Women's Health Coalition (IWHC), The Global Alliance Against Traffic in Women (GAATW), and the Global Campaign for Violence Prevention (GCVP), among others. More than this, women's movements are now found in nearly all countries around the world, developing their own agendas.[7]

Same-sex politics developed a little later and in its earliest 'homophile' days it was a small and somewhat secretive move-ment: homosexuality was, after all, illegal and taboo. There is an early history in the Netherlands and Germany, where seeds were sown; and the modern Western gay movement is usually dated from the late 1960s and symbolized by the riots at the Stonewall Inn in New York. Soon there was plenty going on around the world. Argentina has probably the oldest movement in Latin America – founded by Héctor Anabitarte in 1969 (*Nuestro Mundo* – Our World), and closely aligned to the revolutionary left (as gay movements frequently were).[8] In Brazil, the gay movement developed a decade later in São Paulo as *Grupo Somos* (We Are a Group).[9] In India, the most prominent group arose out of the HIV/AIDS crisis. The Naz Foundation was formed in 1994 as an NGO based in New Delhi; it later became an international movement.[10] Today, gay movements (by whatever name) can be found in most countries across the world, though often covertly. Change is in the air; and to try to make widespread international connections on gay issues, the International Lesbian and Gay Association (ILGA) was established in 1978 in the UK, developing a European branch in 1986. ILGA is now a major global organization, publishing an annual report, *State Sponsored Homophobia*, which documents the situation in every country of the world[11]

There are other connections. A significant cluster of movements must be those found within the world health movement: initially with global family planning, with children's and women's health and reproductive care; later, from the early 1980s, with the crisis of HIV and AIDS, demanding responses from each and every country.[12]

Not all movements are progressive. Many seek a return to more traditional and more conservative orders: there are many pro-family, anti-feminist, anti-gay and right-wing movements here too. Despite their presence and their power, these social movements are rarely discussed, often not even mentioned, in studies of either social movements or civic society.[13] Yet they are omnipresent and act as counterforces to progressive change, being major harbingers of conservatism and traditional gender and sexuality. Here are organizations such as United Families International, Family Action Council International, the Howard Center/World Congress of Families Alliance for Marriage. The political scientist Clifford Bob (2012) claims that there is now a 'global morality market' with its own global 'merchants of morality', and within this there is a potent alliance formed between Muslims and Christians working in defence of the traditional gendered patriarchal family (the Baptist–Burqha Network as Bob calls it). This alliance sets up a major stumbling block for the 'cosmo' project. At the most extreme and violent end of the scale are movements such as Boko Haram, responsible for thousands of deaths.[14]

Building arenas of transnational governance and global civil culture

Although there is a long history of international attempts to govern the world, it is only since the mid-twentieth century that they have become prominent.[15] Institutions like the UN, NATO, WHO and the IMF are amongst the most well known of a vast number of international nongovernmental organizations (INGOs) of all kinds – like Amnesty International (AI), Coalition Against Trafficking in Women (CATW), Human Rights Watch (HRW), the International Lesbian and Gay Association (ILGA), International Reproductive Rights Research Group (IRRAG) and umbrella organizations like the World Social Forum (WSF). Many are regional (like the Arab League, African Union (AU), European Union (EU), Association of Southeast Asian Nations (ASEAN), and the Organization of American States (OAS)). We can also see the rise of a global interfaith movement. While explicitly working to promote social change, exchange ideas and develop policy agreements, these organizations also bring together a very wide range of different people facilitating intercultural communication between diverse groups across the world. As a result, more people than ever before have started to meet across the world to talk about sexual and gender differences.

Take the umbrella organization of the UN, established in 1945, and by far the most prominent. With a budget of US$5,152 billion in 2012–13 (derived from the 'relative capacity' of its 193 member states to pay), the UN has a colossal number of programmes to advance: on world peacekeeping and security, on health and poverty, on rights and humanitarian concerns. But since 1945, it has also been involved in such issues as the global status of women, the global response to HIV/AIDS (through UNAIDS, working together with affiliates like the WHO), the prevention and regulation of sexual violence, including tribunals on war and rape, and programmes of family regulation and birth control. Likewise, the EU has ratified many programmes of gender and sexual equality.

Crucial here has also been the development of international justice through bodies such as the Strasbourg Court of Human Rights, and International Criminal Tribunals in Bosnia and Rwanda, as well as the International Criminal Tribunal for the Former Yugoslavia (ICTY), which started in 1992 in the wake of the Bosnian war and Serb/Muslim ethnic cleansing. Here 'war rape' was identified as a serious problem.[16] This was not a new phenomenon, but the work of the UN has made it, at last, a global public issue.

Connecting transnational media, digitalization and global networking

The new social media increasingly shapes the new global sexual politics.[17] This media provides an impetus for fresh *information* routes about sexualities and generates new *political* practices and global networks of political connectivity that are helping to shape a cosmopolitan sexualities (along the way creating new imaginations, fantasies and pornographies of sexualities, new ways of relating and connecting, and even new pathways of academic research on sexualities). Social networking has greatly raised the intercultural awareness of plural genders and sexualities as different patterns of engaging with, relating to and envisioning future sexual worlds begin to emerge. Feminist ideas, queer radicalism and issues of rights are shared electronically around the world, even as they change in the process. Google and mobile phones become the new mode of global communication. It is true that many countries place restrictions, and a few (notably China, Iran, Syria, Vietnam and Bahrain – named the five enemies of the Internet in 2013) are intensely regulative. But to put it bluntly: for the first time in history, it has become possible for large numbers of people across the globe to readily speak politically across many different cultures about their varying sexualities, relationships and desires, to share information of all kinds directly with each other, and to make 'open' or 'fluid' contacts.

The new global sexual network of connectivity means that global sexual politics changes rapidly. Many of the old barriers to communication and action have collapsed; and people are open to new ways of gathering: there is talk of a new 'fluid' emotional 'choreography' – of a 'networked advocacy', of 'mass amateurization', of horizontal, leaderless 'swarms' who mobilize on key issues. There is also an emphasis on performance and emotions. It has been seen at work in places as far apart as Russia (the Pussy Riots and All Out), Nigeria (Jail the Gays Bill) and in the furore in Singapore over Section 377a of the penal code (which effectively formally criminalizes homosexuality).[18] In the world of sexual politics, the women's movement, and the gay, queer, and transgender movements (as well as their responsive conservative counterparts) have been mobilized. Most countries now have their own feminist and queer Internet connections (and have had so for several decades: they are well established), and even in countries where they may be deemed illegal, alternative and underground connectivity is made.

Establishing agendas for the international public debate on cosmopolitan sexualities

The cosmopolitan debate on human sexualities recognizes differences in human sexuality and gender, promotes dignity and rights for these differences, seeks justice and equality of genders and sexualities, and enables both the care and flourishing of human diversity of gender sexualities. It seeks an *inclusive sexualities* for all, while aiming to reduce the harm of what can be called *dehumanizing sexualities*. Support for such ideas can be found generally in many UN documents, and more specifically in an array of research agendas, conferences, websites, charters and manifestos being developed through the new armies of social movement activists, civil society organizations (CSOs), NGOs and INGOs, researchers, social workers, youth workers, sex workers, moral crusaders, media and coalitions of all kinds. These are all busy developing global and local practices. Together, they create a dynamic arena of 'public issues creation': identifying troubles, making them visible, giving documentation and narratives; organizing activities, imagining solutions, making claims; finding resources, negotiating arguments, shaping public arenas of debate; identifying enemies, renegotiating arguments, and so on. Some of the debates are highlighted in Box 3.1. Out of nothing, significant structures and cultures have been created around many areas. In some ways, these can be seen as the hallmarks of cosmopolitan sexualities. One hundred years ago none of these public arena debates existed as concerns on an international agenda. Now, each of them has generated its own arena, animating global fields of action, structuring new claims, discourse and argumentation and new political practices. In a short book like this, I can hardly deal with all of these issues in detail. They are all now the subject of a growing body of research and analysis.[19]

The creation of global human rights regimes

At the heart of much of this activity is the idea of dignity and 'rights'.[20] These are old ideas, given a new global depth in the late twentieth century. For most of recorded history, world religions have laid the seedbeds of rights in their rulebooks, codes, commandments and 'ways of living' for societies to observe. Although these may not be 'rights' as we know them today, they do hint at the rights to come.[21] Likewise, historians have highlighted modern rights as unfolding in various waves: rolling through the Enlightenment, through socialism and the industrial age, through the world wars with their crimes against humanity, and now into the global age. Nevertheless, although ideas of rights may be centuries old, the twentieth century has become known as 'the century of human rights'.[22] It is certainly the time when human rights became big business, proliferating into major organizations and educational programmes and developing critics from all sides: feminists, conservatives, neo-Marxists, postcolonialists, and on.

Two key crises have precipitated this concern over humanity and rights. First came the concern over crimes against humanity in 1914, when more than one million Armenians were slaughtered by the Turks; and the second was the adoption by the UN in 1948 of

3.1 *Cultures of public sexual problems*:
Sampling a multiplicity of global debates

1 The debates on gender equality, rights and an enhanced global status of women throughout the world. This is animated largely through the global women's movement and its opponents, and has led to a gradual increase in women's equality in work, health, education, politics and life chances in many parts of the world. It also raises issues around masculinities and what it means to be a man in the modern world.

2 The debates on gender pluralism (or third sex rights) across the world. It is animated largely through the global transgender movement, the schisms within it, and its enemies.

3 The debates on the rights and equality of sexual minorities, but especially those engaged in same-sex relationships. This has also been connected to the movement for gay marriage in certain parts of the world, and the fights against global homophobia, gay asylum and migration, etc.

4 The debates on reproductive politics, leading to changes in reproductive practices, infant mortality and population structures in many countries. It includes debates on the multiplicities of sexualities that link up with procreation, motherhood, birth control, reproductive health care and education, alongside more controversial issues such as abortion and coercive sterilization. It has been animated by birth control agencies, the women's movement and by many nations (for example, China).

5 The debates on sexual violence, abuse and the right to a 'safe body' – which includes issues of rape, rape in war, FGM, honour crimes and the like.

6 The debates on diversities of family, including issues of child marriage and polygyny animated by the world family movements and their links to world religions, especially Christian and Muslim groups who often become allies.

7 The debates on sexual practices and care linked to health rights and various sexually linked diseases, but especially HIV and AIDS, animated by world health groups.

8 The debates on international trafficking and sex work, animated by sex worker groups concerned about rights, in contrast to trafficking anti-crusaders, who see it as a different form of violation of rights and a 'slave trade'.

9 The debates on education, children and youth rights, animated by child welfare groups and educational groups.

10 The debates on representations, imagery and regulation of cybersex, etc., animated by porn groups, anti-porn groups, censorship and freedom of speech lobbies; and now Internet regulation bodies and watch groups.

Note: By putting together four fields – health, sexuality, reproduction and gender – some have come up with the umbrella term 'sexual and reproductive health and rights' (SRHR). This is sometimes used as a political strategy to include sexuality (the least popular) in a wider claim.

the Universal Declaration of Human Rights (UDHR), in the wake of the holocaust. Grounded in the sheer scale of the horrors of the twentieth century, the necessity of global human rights became an urgent issue. Indeed, in the midst of the aftermath of the holocaust, World War II and the rest, Hannah Arendt made the important claim that: 'the right to have rights, or the right of every individual to belong to humanity, should be guaranteed by humanity itself'.[23] The abiding idea here is that of global human dignity and personhood, and 'rights' became ever more central to the global political project. There had been some international attempts at sexual and gender cosmopolitanism before 1948, but it is really with the arrival of the UN and the passage of the UDHR that the global stage was ultimately set for a debate on the common grounds of personal life.

The idea of sexual rights has slowly become part of this debate, together with notions of sexual citizenship and intimate citizenship.[24] Sexual rights (as well as gender rights and sexual orientation) were already being pioneered in the late nineteenth century, but, in its earliest days, the UDHR was never explicit on such matters. Instead, issues were raised obliquely in debates on health, family, children and, eventually, 'equality between the sexes'. Gradually, ideas of rights moved across a range of contested areas and were consolidated both in women's reproductive issues and women's concerns with violence. And, as these rights themselves had to confront sexual issues, so sexual rights moved onto the agenda. By the 1990s it was, as Petchesky famously remarked, 'the new kid on the block'.[25] It became an organizing focus for social movements both conservative and radical; and, as new alliances were made, new zones of conflict and arguments on the nature of human sexualities entered the public global stage at the UN and elsewhere. A stream of debates around women's rights, reproduction and fertility and abortion (which became known as 'reproductive politics'), children's rights, sexual violence and HIV/AIDS gradually established a space for a language of sexual rights. Espoused initially by women's groups, then by HIV/AIDS groups and gay and lesbian lobbies (mainly ILGA, ARC International and the Sexual Rights Initiative (SRI)), and latterly by human rights movements such as AI and HRW, the main antagonists have always been the conservative wings of religious and family movements, creating strange 'unholy alliances' between the Holy See and the traditional Mullahs through the Organization of Islamic Cooperation (OIC). By contrast, a broad programme of gay, lesbian and transgender rights have been more readily put into place through the EU through the Treaty of Amsterdam in 1999, the Strasbourg Court and Article 21 of the Charter of Fundamental Rights in 2009.[26]

Developing international law and 'cosmopolitan' legal systems

It is international law that ultimately frames the cosmopolitan sexualities project. Since the mid-twentieth century, there have been numerous treaties and covenants, principles and laws that have started to establish a framework for the global structuring of both human rights and also the lives of women, families and children, and personal relationships. Having established the UN Charter in 1945 and the UDHR in 1948, the International Covenant on Civil and Political Rights (ICCPR) and the International Covenant on Economic, Social and Cultural Rights (ICESCR), both very wide ranging, were adopted in 1966 (often collectively referred to as the International Bill of Human Rights), and a raft of legislation has followed. This has dealt with rights and discriminations concerning: race – the International Convention on the Elimination of All Forms of Racial Discrimination, 1965 (ICERD); women – CEDAW, 1979; children – Commission on the Rights of the Child, 1989 (CRC); and disability – Convention on the Rights of Persons with Disabilities, 2006 (CRPD). Other treaties have dealt with genocide (1948), refugees (1951), apartheid (1973), torture (1984), 'enforced disappearance' (2006) as well as the involvement of children in armed conflict, the sale of children, child prostitution and child pornography. Much of the legislation concerns rights, but also works towards harm reduction: for example, setting regulations against sexual violence and sex trafficking (e.g., the 1993 Declaration on the Elimination of Violence Against Women). This legislation operates as 'soft law': although there is much principled activity, such principles are not enforceable.

CEDAW was an early example and has become progressively established. Likewise, the Yogyakarta Principles, focusing on sexual rights, were developed by 29 world human rights experts on sexual orientation and gender identity issues in 2007. These affirmed binding international legal standards that all states must 'gradually', 'progressively' comply with.[27] And in 2012, discriminatory laws encouraging homophobic violence were condemned by the UN.[28] But a great many states still do not recognize these standards, and many are positively opposed to them. The problem then is whether the jurisdiction of a particular state, for the purposes of human rights, can be applied differently in different parts of the world. It is a complicated legal mess.

Creating the monitoring and debating apparatus for cosmopolitan sexualities

The law does not stand on its own, but is accompanied by a wide range of monitoring practices that have developed alongside it. Thus, for example, human rights are now monitored regularly through the Universal Periodic Review (UPR), and issues about sexual rights are specifically taken up by the global SRI and ARC International. Wider issues of social justice are monitored through the Millennium Development Goals (MDG) Indicators and the state of women in the world through Womenwatch and the Gender Inequality Index (GII), although such devices are always being 'improved' (and this often means changed and renamed). At the same time, many such organizations produce a cascade of reports of their own. (Box 3.2 gives one example and in Chapter 6 a wider list is provided). What these reports all imply is a significant machinery of monitoring and feedback in which the state of sexualities across the world, and the injustices that surround them, are

---

3.2   *Tracking human sexual rights*:
The Sexual Rights Initiative (SRI)

One example of monitoring is the SRI, which regularly engages in monitoring across all UN countries on a wide variety of sexual rights issues, linking to the UN's UPR. The SRI gathers information and issues regular reviews on all member countries and their policies concerned with:

- maternal mortality and morbidity
- rights-based sexuality education
- reproductive rights
- sexual orientation rights
- empowerment of women and girls
- universal access to sexual and reproductive health information, education, supplies and services
- the rights of sex workers
- the rights of transgender and third gender persons
- violence based on the exercise of one's sexuality, including sex outside marriage
- HIV/AIDS and human rights
- rights of young people
- rights issues arising from early and forced marriage

Other monitoring systems are discussed in Chapter 6.

now being regularly monitored (with the all the attendant problems of both surveillance and validity that this brings). Many of the reports coming from such monitoring will often leave the observer pessimistic, and many of their recommendations are rejected. Despite this, important structures are in place.

Mainstreaming the global discourses of a common humanity

Out of all this global activity, almost unwittingly, a new normative global order has appeared. Whether successful or not, the languages of human dignity and rights, of child protection, of women's equality, of reducing world poverty and misery, of peacemaking, of human development, of security, and so forth have surely become part of the routine everyday language of bodies like the UN, the International Court of Justice (ICJ) and many international conferences. They have been *mainstreamed*. In just half a century we have seen the formation of a global discourse for a common humanity, a world aiming to give people their dignity. None of this is binding; many do not like it; it flies in the face of much history; it is often a sham and riddled with problems; but its presence and influence cannot be in dispute. And it spreads out: it can be found across many global social movements: the education movement, the global interfaith movement, the global music movement. At the highest level it may even now be possible to speak of reaching out for a common human global ethics on which many have already started to agree. And a growing part of this has been the language of human sexual rights, human sexual justice and human sexual flourishing. A cosmopolitan sexualities is clearly in the making.

Troubles ahead: the contradictions and limits of cosmopolitanism

But just as meanings and structures for cosmopolitan sexualities are surely being globally developed and refined, so we find many continuing problems. Some are practical, but others go really quite deep. Cosmopolitan sexualities brings a utopianism in the face of more pragmatic and practical politics; it brings internationalism in the face of major local claims; it brings elitism when confronted with grass-roots politics; it brings a tendency towards abstractions and theory in the face of grounded sufferings. Above all, it brings into focus a tension between a cosmopolitan spirit of pluralism and openness tolerant of human variety, and a simultaneous belief in absolute universal values of truth and ethics. Here, and all the time, we walk a fine, fine line of contradictory tensions between the general and the specific: between particularism and universalism, the local and the global, the relativist and the absolutist, the abstract and the grounded, the essentialist and the constructionist, the utopian and the realist. On top of this, we have to confront the inevitable limits of any idea. Cosmopolitanism does not always confront the limits of the market and justice, the limits of tolerance, the interminable problems of fanatics, the sheer nastiness[29] of both some religious movements and even some specific people. There are indeed troubles ahead for anyone who wishes to use theories of cosmopolitanism, and it will require developing ingrained critical habits and a balancing of these tensions to move ahead. In what follows, I briefly examine a few of these troubles.[30]

Troubled global governance

First, and most straightforwardly, there are practical and down-to-earth problems. As we have seen, cosmopolitan sexualities depends a great deal on the workings of global and glocal governance and, critically, the workings of the UN.[31] The troubles with this are formidable. To take just the UN: it is hugely expensive, regularly fails and is often not just ineffective symbolically, but also practically – wars and strife rage on around the world in spite of protestations from the UN. We are talking about mega bureaucracies, often 'not fit for purpose', and in need of major overhaul. At the simplest, it comes with all the well-known problems of such big organizations: self-interest, schismatic ideologies, dysfunctional formality, impersonal scale, sluggish organization, cumbersome bureaucracies, overlapping duties, wordy unreadable documents written by committees, squandered yet limited funding, and corrupt or stagnant careers. Much of this governance has simply become Big Business that reinforces only the US business hegemony – with the United States refusing to follow many of its edicts, and countries walking out and displaying their own belligerent intolerances. So although the structures are there, they do not work very well. In addition, they cost a lot, are often ineffective and are highly prejudicial. Quite what can be done about this is not clear, although there are endless proposals for reform (indeed this may be one more of its problems).[32]

A differentiated universalism

At a quite different level, the major political problem of cosmopolitan sexualities lies in the tension between the universal and the local. As we have seen, cosmopolitanism champions the search for a common humanity with universal values, while at the same time seeking an empathic openness to the uniqueness of the differences of local human life. It makes strong claims for universalism in the face of the particular and the unique. But this brings major problems. Most famously there is the well-known problem of whether and which rights may be universal. How, for example, can it be possible to blend universal claims about sexual rights with the specific challenges of local cultures that are directly at odds with them? How can the Ugandan hatred of homosexuals be made compatible with UN dictates on the human rights of homosexuals? How is it possible to live with one God and his universal laws, while living differently in a local subculture? How can local honour be commensurate with universal value?

The list of questions goes on. How can the equality of women across the world be championed when some local cultures devalue their legitimacy and claim honour in local patriarchal and religious belief codes that dehumanize and degrade women? How can women's education be advanced in the face of local terrorist groups like Boko Haram that will slaughter those who support it? Indeed, 'are women human?'[33] – given that they are often not afforded rights at all. And how can child marriage and forced marriage be justified if we hold to an ethics of human rights, freedom, justice and human flourishing? How can we reconcile the fact that FGM was condemned by the WHO in 1950 and yet is still routinely practised in some 29 countries, affecting more than 125 million girls and women?[34]

Many universalistic claims favoured by cosmopolitan theorists regularly come from the rich North or the 'advanced' West, who then become imperialistic over the poorer South and East. Cosmopolitanism easily becomes a symbol of the West's hegemony. The so-called 'universal' just becomes another colonizing version of neoliberalism specificity, the white Western-centric middle-class manqué. It becomes a new homogenizing view that co-opts and dominates 'the other', rather than being an attempt to create innovative human bonds and belonging through difference. It can readily become a racializing tendency to suppress a 'savage', racial or ignorant other. Thus, Muslim women come to be seen as victims brutalized by their religion and Africans are seen as homophobes failing to understand homosexuality or gay rights. Ultimately, much cosmopolitanism in the past has been like this: suggesting progress towards a Western liberal citizenship and disavowing non-Western cultures (i.e., most of the world). It is not surprising that many of these countries have made strong arguments against the UN and its rights models as being too Western.[35]

Consider the example of gay rights, which is now on its way to being accepted as a global human right by the UN since the creation of the Yogyakarta Principles. Pro-Palestine Middle East academic Joseph A. Massad, examining the history of same-sex relations in Arab culture, has argued forcefully that 'gay rights' actually amount to claims made by a Western movement, orchestrated by what he calls 'the Gay International', to universalize the specific case of Western gay rights to the rest of the world. These may not be at all applicable to Arab cultures coming with a very different history and background (one that he claims has historically accepted same-sex relations organized in a very different way). Indeed, the issue of 'gay rights' has itself caused a backlash as Western gay movements work outside Muslim frameworks. Massad says:

What is emerging in the Arab (and the rest of the third) world is not some universal schema of the march of history but rather the imposition of these western modes by different forceful means and their adoption by third world elites, thus foreclosing and repressing myriad ways of movement and change and ensuring that only one way for transformation is made possible.[36]

Massad has a point; but recently it could be claimed that the lead in promoting gay rights and challenging laws around homosexuality has moved from the West to the South. Many Latin American and Asian countries are now taking a positive lead in challenging the oppressions of people with different sexual lives, drawing a little from the West, but moving ahead with their own arguments and original political claims. (We can see this clearly in Brazil and Mexico and, to some extent, in the unusual case of Signapore.)[37]

Some take these arguments further, suggesting that the US gay movement has fostered a growing Islamophobia within its global queer organizing. Through this, it cultivates a form of 'homo-nationalism' that marks out the 'properly hetero', and now 'properly homo', US patriots from the 'other': And this 'other' becomes the dangerous racialized terrorist and the sexualized enemy.[38]

And there are parallel problems with feminism and women's rights. The rise of a global women's movement has long posed many dilemmas about just how far the claims of Western women can be linked to those of non-Western cultures and the responses of a 'third world female subject' (often a victim). In Chandra Talpade Mohanty's words, it has led to a feminism that is beyond 'Western eyes' – a 'decolonizing feminism'. Here, the very ideas of care, justice, or rights come to mean very different things in different cultures. Indeed, looking at the work of women's movements in many cultures suggest the obvious: there are some things they work for in common and yet there are many very specifically different tensions. The history of the Iranian women's movement is a classic case.[39]

So where might this lead us? It is far from a new problem. Ruth Lister seeks what she calls a 'differentiated universalism' – 'a universalism that stands in a creative tension to diversity and difference and that challenges the divisions and exclusionary inequalities which stem from this diversity'.[40] A *differentiated universalism* seems a useful concept. It suggests moving between very detailed, local, unique and differentiated knowledge of specific cultures and making a linkage with their wider contexts: of general awareness, common grounds, universal principles, abstractions. Cosmopolitanism needs a globalization that creates diversification and heterogeneity rather than pushing for homogeneity and essentialist categories.[41]

There can be neither a 'centre' nor a core to cosmopolitanism; and yet it is very hard to work form a position that is 'nowhere'. Still, many ideas are currently being developed to help us move beyond the fixed one-stance view and keep a sense of flux and movement: we do not have just a 'differentiated universalism', but also shifting positions, multiple stances, contested tensions, mobilities, mobile knowledge, hybrid views, scattered hegemonies, diasporic belongings and rhizomes.[42] A whole new language is in the making to represent the struggle to capture the diversities of multiple voices at work together.

These changes are important and constantly serve as a reminder of the potential arrogance of that small part of the world known as 'the West' that persistently claims itself to be best or right. Cosmopolitanism must knowingly challenge this arrogance, asking questions about the ways in which narrow Western (largely Anglo-American) ideas ooze through the world, shaping an intellectual hegemony. These are everywhere challenged by the differences of other cultures. Yet these other cultures also harbour troubles, and the need is to search critically and, paradoxically, simultaneously for the common grounds of our humanities – those slender golden threads that tie human life together – even as we accept the deep world of differences.

A sceptical universalism

Linked to the universal–local tension is the longstanding argument over relativism and absolutism. In a series of outspoken speeches between 2005 and 2006, Cardinal Joseph Ratzinger (to become the short-reigned Pope Benedict XVI) claimed: 'We are moving towards *a dictatorship of relativism* which does not recognize anything as certain and which has as its highest goal one's own ego and one's own desires' (my italics).[43] Tracing this to the communist and sexual revolutions, Pope Benedict saw it as a pervasive scourge of the modern world. His attack on relativism is joined by many others and, indeed, has a long history.

Cosmopolitanism, once again, takes the dual stance of recognizing local differences (which pushes it towards relativism), while also searching out the bigger picture (the universal values we started to examine in Chapter 1). It will be very clear that an understanding of cosmopolitan sexualities has to start with the recognition of the universal significance of sexual cultural variety and difference. This lies at its core and is central to the argument of this book. But it is not in itself a relativist stance, even though it can be mistaken for one. It is, rather, a self-aware and sceptical one. Likewise, modernity itself also brings with it a relativization stance – a self-awareness of these differences that can generate its own absolutist and fundamentalist backlashes. Fundamentalism, with its extreme absolutism, may itself be seen as a product of modernity and a response to an extreme relativism. This is why we hear so often of the conflicts of multiculturalism, of postmodernism, of the clash of civilizations, of terrorism. The struggles with relativization are built into the modernist dilemmas.[44]

The problems of relativism come in many forms: cultural relativism, methodological relativism and moral relativism are just three prime examples. I will briefly look at each.

Culturally, we can readily demonstrate the existence of a wide variety of sexual experiences across the world and how a modern 'transforming world' seems to be cultivating even more. We know that there exists a wide range of biological and cultural differences; that there are divergent 'patterns of sexual behaviour' across cultures; that there is 'evolution's sexual rainbow'. These are empirical 'facts', well researched and documented.[45] Yet in the midst of all this unique diversity, human universals can also be found. Common features of human social life can be found across cultures, countries and continents; and many of these suggest universal features of sex and gender.[46]

Methodologically, there are many major controversies about relativism and knowledge, as any review of the contemporary state of the philosophy of science will reveal.[47] Pure objectivity and scientific truth can only be a straightforward matter for the most naive. People come to believe different things in different ways in different times and places while working from different standpoints. Across cultures we can soon find a multiplicity of human wisdoms: aesthetic, pragmatic and practical, imaginative, hermeneutic, personal and subjective, spiritual and, of course, scientific. We need aesthetics to help us see the beautiful; pragmatism to help us see the consequences of our ideas; imagination to help us push horizons and break boundaries; reflexivity to locate and ponder our own relation to it all; spirituality to help us foster wider connections to nature and to the pluriverse; and science to help us see 'the real'. In all cultures there are 'wisdoms' that help us tie it all together. The debates from postmodernism and the challenges from cognitive science and cultural anthropology over relativist knowledge are hardly new: Herodotus, Pythagoras, Thrasymachus and many other ancients were aware of this. So too were the religions, especially Buddhism. Cosmopolitanism has to recognize all this. But at the same time it seeks the bigger picture – ways of mapping together an understanding of all these differences. This is not an easy task: it needs theory, conceptualization, rationality, questioning, objectivity, systematic evidence – and perpetual doubt. It needs, in fact, the search for a universal realist science that incorporates diversities in its understanding.[48]

Probably what concerns cosmopolitan sexualities most are *normative value differences*. All human sexualities are bound up with values. Being concerned with how people relate to each other, sexualities are often at the heart of ethical systems and, indeed, all religions make strong moral declarations about sex. Even in the modern world of sexology and the claims for a scientific study of sex, values are never far away. As soon as we talk about rape or incest, same-sex relations or sex outside marriage, of multiple wives and genital mutilation, of child sex and animal sex, we confront values head on. And much sexuality brings heated responses: anger, disgust, outrage, contempt, cruelty, shame, honour. Cosmopolitanism, celebrating difference and unique variety, hurls us into debates about absolute and relative values; and how human differences are often seen as necessarily relativist. But I want to claim this is not necessarily so, and cosmopolitanism is rarely relativist. To help us, Isaiah Berlin made a crucial distinction between 'value pluralism' and 'value relativism' and it is one that debates on cosmopolitanism should heed. That human beings establish multiple values is unmistakable, and indeed they may not be commensurable. But this does not make us relativists. The challenge for the cosmopolitan is to grasp this value pluralism, and to then proceed to weave out of it a wider sense of universal value. This is what I started to do in Chapter 1 and will continue in Chapter 6.[49]

There are, then, identifiable diverse facts of sexual experience (cultural studies), diverse ways of finding the truth about them (contrasting epistemologies) and diverse values over them (the so-called sex wars). All raise tensions: can we make choices between them? The trouble lies with any extreme positions of relativism and absolutism. Strong absolutism allows for no plurality; strong relativism allows for no foundations: both are untenable and dangerous. To hold strong absolutism is to close down the world and its possibilities, and maybe to create worlds of terror and violence and hatred of unbelievable dimensions. To hold strong relativism is to totter into the chaotic anarchistic view that 'anything goes', we can say anything; there is no truth. Both are so dangerous. Yet great minds have been known to hold such views.

My own view, as ever, is linked to humanist pragmatism. Thus, these problems cannot be readily resolved on a grand scale. Each situation has to be examined, matching universalist and relativist claims in concrete detail, being sceptical of each. There will always be differences and conflicts. Out of this we need to look for the common grounds: of culture, of truth, of value. We always need to navigate a careful movement between extremes – to be pragmatic about it.[50]

A grounded universalism

The philosopher Seyla Benhabib has posed a further linked question: 'Is Cosmopolitanism the privileged attitude of globe-trotting and world-hugging elites, removed from the concern of ordinary citizens?'[51] After reading a great many writings on cosmopolitanism, there is little doubt that much of it does indeed rapidly soar to the academic heavens of a few cognoscenti. So this is a problem. My argument is that cosmopolitanism needs to face in two directions: keeping its feet firmly grounded in the local everyday, it also needs to stretch out intellectually to the universal, abstract heavens. What do I mean by this?

Moving in one direction, we find the need for serious, critical and abstract thinking, enabling us to compare a range of situations and bring analytic ideas forward. But if we are not careful, this brings a high-minded prescriptive, normative abstractionism, typically embedded in systems of Western power. We may need some of this; but getting right down to the everyday particular struggles of people must always counterbalance it. Hence, and moving in another direction, a more banal, people-based cosmopolitanism from the ground upwards is also needed.[52] In the face of real and deep problems, there is sometimes too much of an abstract touch in cosmopolitan theory that suggests easy solutions while neglecting the brutal and obdurate realities of human suffering and the deep agonizing pains of people which really need to be faced. People are being shot and abused, left without rights, put through war rape, while philosophers and academics fiddle.

And in being grounded, we can readily see how in many parts of the world different lives can frequently live well together – in schools and universities, in streets, in places of work, in communities. Of course, many do not; and we are regularly told about prejudice, hostilities and conflicts. But that is the bad news. The good news is that many people do live quite happily alongside their different neighbours: 'being cosmopolitanism' is a daily fact of many lives. 'Getting on with your neighbour' and 'living with differences' are quite simply ways in which many people around the world exist practically much of the time. More than this, people create solidarities as they work with each other on different projects – and these often cross over differences and boundaries. Politically then, there is a 'cosmopolitanism from below'. It can be seen as pragmatic action, enacting practices, doing things. And not just theory.[53] We need to keep this in mind and learn lessons from this much more banal, bottom up, grounded cosmopolitanism; even as we remain aware of the analytic arguments being generated in academic cosmopolitanism.

A paradoxical tolerance

Cosmopolitanism takes tolerance to be a key idea to be celebrated; but this in turn brings its own paradoxes and limits. Tolerance, as an idea, has a very long history in pluralistic thinking (some claim it goes back to the Greek idea of conversation and on through Erasmus to Voltaire). It directs us to at least three critical problems. First, it raises 'the paradox of toleration': should we tolerate the intolerant? And more, if we did not think the beliefs were wrong in some way, then the issue of tolerating them would not arise. Hence, to be tolerant may always actually presume and reinforce a position of superiority.[54] Second, and following the critique of political scientist Wendy Brown, we may need to distinguish between tolerance as a (cherished?) virtue and value, and toleration as an ideology and practice. While a personal ethic of tolerance may be valued, toleration can also easily be used as a political discourse to invalidate other positions. Very specifically contemporary theories of tolerance are 'entwined with postcolonial, liberal and neoliberal' ideas encoding 'the superiority of the West'.[55] Finally, there is the issue of 'the limits of tolerance': we cannot live with all differences, not all should be tolerated, and where are the boundaries to be drawn? People who champion tolerance often do not like such searching questions.

With each of these difficulties, we are led to ask the same question: what is the stance we are taking from which we tolerate? Applied to the fields of sexuality, tolerance normally means the validation and superiority of the heterosexual gendered reproductive matrix. It serves the function of reinforcing one major norm. Tolerance is surely better than violence and intolerance; but it does bring its own problems and may not act as real advance.[56] We have to be doubly wary of the strength of our own normative base line and its prejudices.

Pushing the boundaries of cosmopolitan sexualities

Human progress can never depend on just one idea, and the consistent argument of this book is the need for plural values, diverse ideas, multiple pathways and contingent vulnerabilities. One of our major follies is to deal with the singular; so let's be clear that cosmopolitanism cannot be expected to handle all concerns, and must live, sometimes in tension, with other ideals and ideas. Even though it cannot be exhaustive, cosmopolitanism has to be inclusively aware of some of these wider issues, touching on them whenever it can. These surely include the following:

Justice Most apparently cosmopolitanism can so easily neglect wider critical issues of social justice and inequalities in favour of issues of differences and recognition.[57] It can give little focus in itself to *divisive, pauperized, colonized, exiled sexualities*. Most cosmopolitan analysis really does not begin to work with the problems of the overarching power of the markets, the inequalities that this generates and the way this often militates against cosmopolitanism. Cheah (2006) makes clear the 'inhuman' imperatives of capitalism and technology that are distorting humanity. He finds that the global division of labour compromises any true global solidarity, ravaging and excluding certain groups. This in turn makes something of a mockery of cosmopolitan ideals and, indeed, the idea of Western human rights. Likewise, many close-up studies of sexual life – for example, in the now numerous studies of sex work – reveal only too clearly how sex is deeply structured by class, race, gender and age, with poor low income and their sexuality being at the bottom of the heap. A cosmopolitanism that fails to take on board such issues would be a poor cosmopolitanism.

Brutalizing conflict One background to much cosmopolitan debate has been the Kantian ideal of 'perpetual peace'. This ideal, of peace being permanently established across the world, has been a major force in recent peace studies as well.[58] Yet cosmopolitanism often focuses too much on belonging and sharing, while neglecting the real horrors of war and armed conflict. Every night as I watch the world news, I see more desperate faces of lives grieving loved ones who have been brutally killed in conflicts, and I worry how those lives could ever get over this and live in harmony with their assassins. Cosmopolitanism sometimes holds a somewhat naive belief in 'conflict resolution', which all too frequently fails and is often not remotely possible. Conflicts and differences are just too historically rooted and too emotionally deep-seated for ease of change. As we will see, the world of sexualities is stuffed full of conflicts – often linked with sexual violence of all kinds that leave wounds. One of the major challenges for cosmopolitanism is surely how to learn ways of handling it.

Dangerous religions   Another weak spot for cosmopolitanism can be its relative neglect of the deep and pervasive influence that religions have in most societies, most of the time. Often, intellectuals and cosmopolitans veer towards the secular end of the continuum of ideas. They fail to grasp that religions generally have a tremendous grip on cultures, dwelling deeply in the everyday lives of many people. And yet the briefest look at the world will show that religion lies behind many world conflicts – and many of the absolutist claims. So although, of course, cosmopolitans can embrace the pluralities of religions, they have major problems when those religions turn out to be closed and violent – and actually a key source of anti-cosmopolitanism.

Today, as ever, religions have a way of putting sex on the agenda: birth control, 'women's position', same-sex relations are still the hot topics. And the religious response has sometimes been hysterical, even violent: they become the harbingers of monologic terrorism. And cosmopolitans are in a deeply antagonistic relationship with such closed religions; this poses real problems. Indeed, cosmopolitanism has real practical problems dealing with what have been called 'closed minds' and this issue, as we will see, stretches way beyond religions.

And so on: the problems do not stop here. Often, cosmopolitanism can head us to the dustbin history of wonderful utopian ideas that frequently don't work and can bring much harm. It also has serious problems in dealing with the ever-present danger of the fanatic. Whatever we do, there are likely always to be extreme people – such as the Norwegian mass killer Anders Behring Breivik.[59] Cosmopolitanism and its allied humanism needs to confront inequalities and injustice, resist simple grounds for tolerance, be very aware of the deep conflicts that people are willing to die for, the profundity of religious lives and deeply held convictions of difference, and even confront and somehow live with the case of individual fanatics. We are not on an easy journey.

The (very) long walk to cosmopolitan sexualities

Given these deep criticisms, I wonder who in the end can take up a position of cosmopolitanism? Indeed, given these problems, some readers may even think that I have 'done cosmopolitan in': killed it off before I even got started. Indeed, in writing this book I did often think of junking the word, so many difficulties does it pose. But to junk it would mean leaving a gaping void. One collection of writings, called *After Cosmopolitanism*, does indeed pose this question: 'Is cosmopolitanism still useful?'[60] It provides many critical debates, and although the authors find cosmopolitanism to be severely lacking, as I do, they manage in the end to conclude that, while it needs serious revisions, we still do need it. And that is my view. These many challenges are important: they need to be grasped and worked with. The idea of cosmopolitan sexualities comes drenched in trouble. It brings tensions, limits and practical problems that need to be confronted perpetually. But overall I believe that the idea of cosmopolitanism is too good a one, too grand an ideal, to be jettisoned by these problems. We need to work to overcome them and that is partially what this book is about. We may need a better word eventually for all this, but for the time being it seems that, a bit like the word democracy, it is the best we have. But, unlike democracy, the idea of cosmopolitan sexualities is far from being a familiar or accepted one. In this book I want the idea to at least breathe a little.

So in conclusion, here are six lessons, a mini mantra if you like, for a critical cosmopolitanism to keep in mind perpetually. They caution us from easy or quick responses.

1 Be cautious of any colonizing universalisms that are insensitive to difference. This even includes the notion of universal rights (the problem of universality-specificity).
2 Search for the bigger picture while always recognizing multi-plicities of standpoints (the dilemma of absolutism-relativism).
3 Use critical abstract theory for vision and understanding, but then always bring it down to earth to people's everyday practical con-cerns and practices (the dilemma of abstraction-groundedness).
4 Be aware that 'tolerance' always works from a 'superior' posi-tion: and that this often brings a patronizing stance (the tension of tolerance and arrogance).
5 Try to keep your hopes and dreams alive, while remaining practical and aware of inevitable failures and the dark side of life (remember the inevitability of disappointment; yet the impor-tance of hope).
6 Always simultaneously keep your eyes on wider visions of justice and inequalities, of the dangers of religious dogma and of violence; and beware of fanatics (the dilemmas of limits: we can never do it all).

With all this in mind, we can conclude that over the last half-century the growth of cosmopolitan sexualities has been a partial success story: there have been real changes in gender and sexuali-ties on the ground that only the most fanciful utopians could ever have dreamed about in the past. With new institutions have come new languages, debates, networks, practices, beliefs and hopes that have emerged from and been diffused through many differenti-ated cultures. Not all cultures, for sure, and with very differing impacts; but there is much more than could perhaps have ever been imagined just a little while back. There are now Muslim women debating their subordination and conservative Christians debating gay marriage rights. That said, the change has also been slow and falteringly uneven, and the future brings many problems. Some are quite philosophically and politically profound; others are more practical and local. The future of cosmopolitanism sexualities cannot be an easy or guaranteed one; in the next part of this book I consider some of these problems.

Part Two

Inclusive Sexualities: Nudging Towards a Better World

> You got to have a dream,
> If you don't have a dream,
> How you gonna have a dream come true?
>   Rodgers and Hammerstein, *South Pacific*
> (Used by permission of Williamson Music, A Division of Rodgers
>   and Hammerstein: An Imagem Company, © Imagem CV)

Inclusive sexualities are those that can embrace sexual and gender complexity and variety. They humanize sexualities through an awareness of the following:

1 *Cultural sexualities*: Appreciate the varieties of cultural sexual and gender differences and complexity, and the struggle between the local and the global.
2 *Contested sexualities*: Recognize the ubiquity of agonistic conflicts and look for peaceful resolutions.
3 *Dialogic sexualities*: Know yourself, recognize the sexual other, identify power and move towards a common mutual horizon.
4 *Empathic sexualities*: Understand others – appreciate and maintain dialogue with your sexual partners and their worlds.

5 *Caring sexualities*: Be kind – care for the sexual other as well as your self, and work to reduce violence.

6 *Just sexualities*: Seek justice – create free, fair and equal sexual and gender relations.

7 *Dignified sexualities*: Foster human rights and dignity – respect others, their sexual dignity and their sexual and gender rights, being aware of their fragility and vulnerability

8 *Flourishing sexualities*: Encourage lives to flourish – foster relational flourishing for all across gender and sexuality.

9 *Pragmatic sexualities*: Stay grounded and be practical – keep at it: it's not easy!

10 *Hopeful sexualities*: Be positive and work for better worlds for all – keep hopeful in sexual relations. Reduce sexual harm and foster peace.

4

Cultural Sexualities:
Cultivating Awareness of Complexity

> Culture is ordinary: that is the first fact. Every society has its own
> shape, its own purpose, its own meanings.
>
> Raymond Williams, *Resources of Hope* (1989)

In this part of the book I ask how we might deal with some of the
dilemmas of cosmopolitan sexualities. And I start in this chapter
by showing how there has been a vast and significant growth
in documenting and understanding contrasting and conflicting
sexual cultures in every nook and cranny of the sexual globe. At
the outset, this means approaching the problem of different sexual
cultures.

Cultures, in general, are the (often cherished) 'ways of living',
the 'webs of meaning', the 'stories and dialogues' of a people. They
provide solutions to everyday problems and help focus on our
ordinary everyday values, religions, languages, identities, dress and
rituals, even as they may be 'internally riven by conflicting narratives'.[1] Cultures flag the 'taken–for–granted worlds' of people.
Underpinned by material and power relations, they are really the
creative tools that come to be taken for granted in resolving our
ordinary problems of daily living. Neither 'high' nor 'low', they are
ordinary, capturing the basic flows of everyday routines in all human

societies: they are 'the scraps, patches and rags of daily life'.[2] There may be dominant cultures, but if so, such cultures are always changing and contested, multiple and moving. Never uniform, stable or consensual, they are always fragmented and multilayered. They are hybrids.[3] And this means that multiculturalism, so often discussed as a social policy of specific societies, should really be seen as a widespread feature of the organization of most, if not all, societies.

Following from this, *cultural sexualities* are the routine ways of sexual life of a group. They provide the embodied and emotional tools and narratives that help make sense of the complex sexual contradictions and tensions of our lives. They take us to the heart of the ways in which people routinely work out these difficulties of their desires, genders, reproduction, relationships, embodiment, emotions – and pleasures. Sexual cultures harbour contrasting solutions to the sexual and gender problems of living (and their failures.) Ultimately, they provide the sexual stories we tell, the sexual rituals we make and the sexual values we develop. And although sexual cultures are found everywhere across the world, and usually have dominant (hegemonic, heterosexual, patriarchal) forms, they are never monolithic, unitary, self-consistent, tight, fixed or agreed upon.

The most widely known explanation of these sexual cultures comes from the evolutionary biologists who highlight the problem of sexual selection and suggest how culture (and its 'memes') is built out of the survival of the fittest and the search for the ideal mate. Darwin's theory of sexual selection claims that: 'amongst almost all animals there is a struggle for the possession of the female . . . [T]he strongest and . . . best armed of the males . . . unite with the most vigorous and better nourished females – to rear a larger number of offspring than the retarded females.'[4] This view has many celebrants and critics. This book is not designed to discuss this abundant and well-trodden path; indeed, I ignore it.[5] What can be simply said here, though, is that the range of diversity I raise in this book (from masturbation and chastity through homosexuality and transgenderism – and on to various fetishes, digital sexualities and sexual violence) does not fit easily with this grand sociobiological schema, even though many do try to find a link.[6] A great deal of research from biologists themselves suggests that many of the claims of the evolutionary psychologists do not match the findings of biological researchers and suffer from being seriously overstated. It is, at the very least, contested. Thus, for example, the leading and world-renowned biologist of sex and gender Anne Fausto-Sterling (2000) finds there is a much wider range of male and female behaviours than evolutionary psychologists would allow us to believe.

Here, then, I take a broader view, which starts by standing amazed at the complexity of sexual cultures, seeing them as environmental as well as biological, and with a sense that sexual cultures grow out of historical battlegrounds and contingencies, enabling us to deal with a wide range of problems – like handling our bodies, fulfilling pleasures, creating identities, providing legitimations and accounts, and so forth. Questioning global sexual cultures means a persistent nagging awareness of cultural multiplicity and complexity.

Global sexualities and research

The history of examining sexual cultures is now quite rich and varied. Perhaps the first 'modern' sense of our global sexual variety came with a Western gaze: from the tales told by Western travellers, colonialists, traders, historians, philosophers, anthropologists and diarists of 'exotic' other lands. Many such accounts have drifted to us from the past, but they are riddled with what today we would see as traces of divisive prejudices, colonial power and subaltern oppressions. In this chapter I look briefly at this early drift and pose the question of how we can fruitfully learn to grasp the wider range of our different world sexual cultures.

Still the most widely read essay on this topic is 'Of Cannibals' by the French nobleman memoirist Michel Eyquem de Montaigne (1533–92).[7] He wrote about the South American Tupinambá, detailing the classic problem of how to approach very different, strange cultures. Confronted with this so-called 'barbarism', Montaigne claimed: 'I do not find that there is anything barbaric or savage about this nation, according to what I've been told, unless we are to call barbarism whatever differs from our own customs.' The problem is set: how to remain neutral about other people's desires. And many people have been puzzling over this problem ever since.

Three centuries later, one of the most celebrated examples of this interest was the travel writings of Sir Richard Francis Burton 1821–90. An exotic Victorian explorer, translator, cartographer and diplomat, he travelled widely in Africa and India, translating the *Kama Sutra* from Sanskrit and the *Perfumed Garden* and the *One Thousand and One Nights* from Arabic. But his writings display an anomaly: an infatuation with exotic sexualities born of his estrangement from his own puritan and Victorian culture.[8] Later, the anthropologists started their task of creating a cornucopian catalogue of the cultural differences of human sexualities. The titles alone of such studies now suggest that something intriguing but suspicious was afoot: Malinowski's *Sex and Repression in Savage Society* (1927) and Mead's *Sex and Temperament in Three Primitive Societies* (1935).

Not surprisingly, many of these brilliant and original studies have been open to heavy critique, and now seem a little limited and naive to the modern reader. This whole period of early work culminated in the landmark broad statistical survey of some 200 mainly traditional societies, published in 1952 by Clellan S. Ford and Frank A. Beach as *Patterns of Sexual Behaviour*. If we ever needed evidence of basic sexual and gender differences across the world, by the 1950s it had surely been accumulated. As we have seen before, the existence of widespread human sexual and gender variety is not really now in dispute.[9]

Still, none of this early research really helped very much when AIDS arrived in the early 1980s. For the earliest global research into HIV/AIDS used the simplest biomedical models of human sexuality derived from traditional sexology and 'rational' psychological (cognitive-behavioural) research – mainly developed in the sexology of the United States. In the understanding of this global pandemic, there was a mainstream failure to recognize that many of these 'essentialist' ideas, binary frameworks and languages (including the language of biomedicine) that were taken for granted in 'the West' could not really be applied straightforwardly to the rest of the (colonized, subaltern) world. For essentialist ideas take categories to be 'there in nature', often telling clear, unitary, fixed, unproblematic accounts. By contrast, subaltern worlds see languages more problematically: created through the oppression of dominant groups. The challenge then is to contextualize and not essentialize these 'other' worlds.[10]

So, by the early 1990s, much of this early work was being challenged. Through the research of sociologists, historians and anthropologists, a greater awareness developed of the deep cultural significance of differences around gender and sexuality. We began to see the emerging analyses of critical medical anthropology (CMA) and critical sexualities studies (CSS) – as well as the rise of queer theory; of emergent groups like the International Association for the Study of Sexuality, Culture and Society (IASSCS) from 1997 and Sexuality Policy Watch (SPW) from 2002;[11] and in journals like *GLQ* (formed 1993), *Sexualities* (1998) and *Culture, Health and Sexuality* (CHS, 1998).

Recently, then, there has been something of a sea change in the study of sexualities. Sexualities must now be seen in the multiple; differences are socially organized, shaped by intersecting religions, class, race, gender, etc.; and desire is embedded in body and language.[12] A new phase of global research has emerged, often initiated through the need for both AIDS and reproductive research. Increasingly, local and regional groupings have appeared, such as the Africa Regional Sexuality Resource Centre (ARSRC), the Latin America Centre on Sexuality and Human Rights (CLAM) and the Asia Pacific Forum (APF), all of which, while learning a little from Western debates, claim their own voice. Inspired by the need for local political actions, and drawing upon local ethnographic fieldwork, often accompanied by oral testimony, fiction, official records, fiction and film, and memoirs, these insider accounts have challenged Western ideas.

Substantial research is emerging, then, from within different cultures around the world. We now find research being conducted by, with and for the people themselves – not simply being studied by some dominant outsiders. Sylvia Tamale's fine collection *African Sexualities* (2011), for example, provides African voices that 'seriously challenge Eurocentric approaches to African sexualities'. With essays coming from 16 of Africa's 54 countries, the book shows different sexualities speaking from within these diverse cultures and displaying a new African scholarship that 'defies categorization'.[13] Here we find the importance of polygamy rather than monogamy, the widespread acceptance of intergenerational sexualities, and the omnipresence of HIV on all lives, but especially the young and women. There is evidence of new research centres, conferences, journals and publications, etc. At the same time, many of the contributors also recognize the importance of learning from Western work – otherwise the wheel may just be reinvented. Similar significant volumes have also emerged that look at Latin America, Muslim cultures, East Asia, Thailand and 'the global South'.[14] They contain enormous knowledge of wider sexual cultures. More and more, the stories of human sexualities are coming from places far removed from the previous Western hegemony and are challenging both Western assumptions about gender, family, identity and sexuality, as well as the assumptions of their own local cultures.

We have reached the stage where an understanding of cosmopolitan sexualities can be developed by looking at very specific, local sexual cultures as well as at the broader, wider sexual frame. Cultural research is charged to move between the broadest trends of a constraining sexual culture and the immediacy of the uniquely active embodied sexual encounter. In what follows I explore this a little.

World cultures and macro sexualities

Cosmopolitanism is a global vision of the world, so it is wise to start by looking at the big picture. To help us grasp this broadest of analyses, I want to recruit the concept of *meta-sexualities* to capture the wide and deep historical world structures and cultures that encircle human sexualities. They function a little like global tectonic plates, moving slowly and organizing all around them. I see four of them as significant.

The first concerns *world religions*: the monotheistic Abrahamic religions (Judaism, Christianity, Islam), the Hindu, the Buddhists, the Yoruba and the rest – all have made long, historically changing claims on how to live the sexual life. Some, like Christianity and Judaism, have been largely negative in their prohibitions of sexual life; most have been misogynistic and have been a major source of women's subordination throughout history; all come in a wide range of varieties. The second concern lies with *civilizational regions*: different states and economies throughout world history. This is a much-contested scholarly field. Huntington (1996) notoriously suggested that there are nine major civilizations. Others flag at least the Sinic (the configurations around China), the Indic, the West Asian or Arabic, the European and the sub-Saharan Africa. There are others (Japan, Latin America, Nordic . . .). Each has an evolving, cultivated and distinctive set of beliefs, rituals and institutions around families, gender and the sexual, often divided again by a multiplicity of regions.[15] A third concerns *migratory human groupings* that form diasporas (people leaving their country and dispersing) and colonization (people establishing new settlements and taking over the rule of those already there). When European cultures invaded the world (the Dutch in Indonesia, the French and English in India and North America, the Spanish and Portuguese in Latin America), they created *hybrid sexualities*, mixed and matched from different places on the earth. And finally, there are the deep structures of global *social divisions* (notably, economic, ethnic and gender) that cut across societies. The vast and shockingly deep inequalities of the human world provide major structures and cultural forms in which sexualities get organized: issues of sexual slavery, global poverty and transpatriarchy, for example, are raised.[16] Each, as we will see, have their own multiple splits and divides.

These are big stories: complicated, global, wide-ranging, historically deep, and yet also easily open to crude stereotyping and dangerous universalizing. Their study is a vast emerging field of enquiry, the scope of which goes way beyond this book. But to give the briefest sense of the issues I am raising, let me just simply introduce three sample meta-sexualities from Africa, China and Muslim cultures.

Africa – the word itself is dangerous – is the second largest and most populous continent in the world; any account of sexuality that ignores it has to be very limited. But it is hard to grasp and is mired in misinformation.[17] With 54 countries rooted in very diverse histories of tribal conflicts, slavery, Ubuntu philosophy, Muslim divides, Christianization and missionaries, and postcolonial struggles, alongside the decimation by HIV/AIDS, economic marginalization, war and civil conflict, corruption and, most recently, colonization by the Chinese, sexual life is complex. On the Human Development Index (HDI) scale, most of Africa's countries are at the lowest end; it has the 10 poorest countries in the world. Many people suffer from what I have called *pauperized sexualities* and *colonized sexualities*. Nowhere is the background of inequality in shaping human sexualities clearer, as people daily confront poverty, disease, drought, debt, violent civil war, forced migration and poor public services. And nowhere are the ravages of colonization and the desire to civilize the savage natives of the 'dark continent' more apparent.[18] And it is in these contexts that sexualities are shaped.

Across the continent, there is a multitude of different responses to global cosmopolitan sexualities, from both within and across the different countries. Often, matters of sexuality are far from a priority, yet everywhere AIDS is an issue. In 2011, Africa accounted for 70 per cent of the world's AIDS deaths (although only 15 per cent of the world's population); and there were an estimated 23.5 million people living with HIV in sub-Saharan Africa, with around 1.2 million people dying from AIDS (in 2005, the figure was 1.8 million). In South Africa alone, there are 6 million people with HIV, the largest number in a single country in the world. Since the beginning of the epidemic, 14.8 million children have lost one or both parents to HIV/AIDS. That said, recent studies do suggest that a significant change is taking place – there are fewer new infections, deaths are in decline and use of antiretroviral therapy (ART) is increasing.[19]

There has also been an increase in religious fervour: Muslim and Christian faiths are growing in strength and size, usually bringing a claim for more patriarchal family and gender structures and sex negativity, often fundamentalist, with them. Polygyny is widespread, causing many problems both for families and for women. And attitudes towards homosexuality are mainly negative, if not openly hostile. Altogether, 38 of Africa's 54 countries have criminalized consensual homosexual sex, some with the death penalty, even as more negative laws are being proposed in Malawi, Uganda, Nigeria and elsewhere. And at the same time, traditional African sexual rites and rituals can be found.[20]

For African societies, some of the debates conducted about sex in the West must seem a little odd, to say the least. Intricate discussions about the nature of lesbian culture or the politics of BDSM, so prominent in the West, hardly sit well with those experiencing the everyday pauperization of sex or the ravaging of rape and sexual violence in tribal wars. Yet at the same time there is ample evidence of a great deal of social movement politics across Africa.[21]

Consider too the sexualities of *China*. By 2010, China was the world's second leading economic state and the twenty-first century is tipped to become the Chinese Century. One of the oldest and biggest societies in the world, how can it not be included in discussions of world sexualities? Its population of about 1.3 billion is the largest in the world and increasing by about 14 million a year, despite its policy of controlling family size. The 1979 One Child Policy has led to a serious gender imbalance: the 'bare branches', whereby millions of men have no wives, and the power of the family is threatened. Sexualities are broadly shaped within frames of so-called Asian values – collectivist, family centred, more authoritarian – alongside the harmony of Yin and Yang, where families, the veneration of bloodlines and the power of the father lie at the heart of the culture. Most people are influenced by these traditions, embedding belief rituals like ancestor worshipping in local communities and economies.

Over its history, sexuality in China has moved in permissive–repressive cycles. Richard Burger's popular account, *Sex in China*, shows how, for many centuries, it was a 'society of extraordinary openness';[22] but in Mao's time, only marriage, monogamy and chastity were acceptable. While modern China is ruled by an intensely regulating centralizing government (making sure the Internet is strictly under control, even as citizens find ways around it), it is moving rapidly from a 'socialist citizenship' into a new 'market citizenship', bringing major rapid changes and uncertainties. The Chinese now live at the interface of the authoritarian Chinese state and local cultures. It brings a mélange of sexualities that range from Confucian patriarchal ideals to Taoist pleasure-seeking sex manuals, through Communist planned single families to the capitalist 'sexualized cities' and widespread modern markets of sex work. The sex industry is expansive.

Homosexuality has been part of this openness: Cuncun (2012) shows how male homoeroticism played a central role in the cultural life of late imperial Chinese literati elites. At the same time, although half the Asian countries still criminalize homosexuality, the situation seems to be changing quite speedily: in China, homosexuality has been decriminalized and there are thriving gay bars in the big cities.

Finally, consider the issues of *Muslim cultures*, which include around a quarter to a fifth of humanity. A billion and a half people live in Muslim cultures across some 60 countries, mainly in Arab (e.g., Iraq, Egypt), Asian (e.g., Malaysia, Pakistan) and African (e.g., Algeria, Morocco) societies – with large and growing minorities in Europe and America. For Muslim cultures, religion defines gender and sexuality. At its heart lie the teachings of the Quran, tradition (hadiths) and the codes of customs (fiqh), though, just as with the Bible and other traditions, there are many problems of interpretation here. According to Abdelwahab Bouhdiba 'sexuality [in Islam] enjoys a privileged status'. Even so, it is accompanied by many purification systems, and 'male supremacy is fundamental in Islam'.[23] There is the distinct separation of men and women: an unmistakable system of patriarchy and male power. For women's sexuality is seen to be more powerful than men's and hence needs more regulation and control. As we see throughout this book, this does pose a pivotal stumbling block for the development of cosmopolitan sexualities. That said, in many Muslim countries today, there are now women's movements fighting against this orthodoxy from within Islam.[24]

Some historians also suggest the existence of a long and complex history of sexual relations between men. With the cultural diffusion of negative Western ideas about homosexuality into some Muslim cultures, attitudes were changed.[25] Today, Muslim cultures in general treat homosexuality with little tolerance: the very worst situations are to be found in certain Arab Muslim states and in many African states.[26] Across parts of Muslim Asia, however, there are some signs of change. In Indonesia, for example, the largest Muslim culture, there have been many new 'progressive' developments.[27]

Once again, it is necessary to recognize multiplicity: there are many different categories of Muslim. The key and most well-known difference is between the Sunni and the Shi'ite. Sunni Muslims, the largest group, are orthodox, following the customs of Muhammad: they base their lives on his sayings and actions. In contrast, the Shi'at Ali – the party of Ali – thought Muhammad's nearest relative should become their Imam. Sunni Muslims see Islamic leadership as being a result of consensus in the community rather than coming from the religious and political authorities. In general, they have more tolerant views, based on the Quran (sometimes a parallel is drawn with Protestants in Christianity, as being a more flexible and less traditional approach). But politically too there are major splits across Muslim cultures. There are, for example, many radical groups that have appeared to fight the jihad (or holy war) across the world: the Muslim Brotherhood in Egypt, the Islamic Revolution Front in Algeria, Hezbollah in Lebanon, Hamas in the West Bank, and Al Qaeda in Afghanistan. These more militant paths all have their own distinctive cultures – language, worldviews, identities and knowledge. Further, the Arab world is very conservative and different from that of Southeast Asia, where things are changing. FGM is common in some Muslim societies (Egypt, Somalia, Sudan, the Gambia) but not others. Honour killings are found in some (Pakistan, Arabia) but not others. Difference is once again the rule.

In addition to the three just outlined, there are many other 'meta-sexual cultures' and a valuable study awaits us that would bring them all together in detail. Nordic cultures, for example, are small and highly successful: they are also notably less religious, have fewer conflicts, the best gender relations and the most open sexualities: in many ways, they may be the harbingers of cosmo-politan sexualities. Likewise, in both the Latin American continent (with some 600 million people and 22 countries, usually Catholic and poor) and Southeast Asia, many of the countries are moving towards economic modernity and displaying an accompanying transformation in sexualities. All these cultures, of course, display great diversity. Much more needs to be said on all this.

Impure cultures and subterranean sexualities

So there are 'macro cultures' and the 'big picture'; and these dominant (or hegemonic) cultures reproduce dominant sexualities and genders. Most people have to work within the sexual cultures into which they are born. (Western social science commonly calls this a 'hegemonic consensus', as cultures exert a definite pressure to conform).[28] But there is always a lot going on in a society that stands outside this 'dominant' form. To start with, all cultures are also built out of the contingencies of critical variables such as age, or class, or ethnicity, leading to the impurity of cultures (as Box 4.1 suggests).

Human social life is always active: people are born into particular cultures. Then, in myriad ways, little and major, most peoples around the world are always actively modifying and mocking, resisting and rejecting the realities in which they live. And as complex modern cultures develop systems of regulating human sexuality, so they also generate alternative marginal cultures that simply do not fit into these dominant sexualities. Human actions generate new *subterranean sexual cultures* with submerged and less visible patterns, distant from the *hegemonic sexualities*.

The heterodoxy that strains against the orthodoxy comes in many varieties, and there are many histories of the sexual outsider: from the Dionysian and the dissident to the deviant and dispossessed.[29] These anomic, marginal and subterranean sexualities bubble just below the surface of any culture. They are emergent cultural forms, ways of life, modes of politics and even forms of study that approach sexual differences from a different angle from that of mainstream ideas. But their very existence is symbiotically dependent upon a dominant culture – without it, they would not exist. And sometimes the subterranean tradition of one generation can become the orthodoxies of the next. Some become future 'homes' for cosmopolitanism as they often live on what might be called the margins of differences. Here are all those people who, standing in an ambivalent position to the dominant world, necessarily come to take on a different view of it. And here too, to paraphrase Durkheim, the pathologized always hangs around

4.1 *The impurity of cultures*:
Sampling a multiplicity of contingent and intersecting sexualities

The classic research by Kinsey in 1948 and 1953 introduced the important idea that human sexualities are contingent upon various key social variables like class, gender, age, ethnicity, rural or urban living. A little later, the idea of intersectionality was introduced to suggest their dynamic interrelation in any life – how dimensions interconnect. In all sexual cultures, human sexualities can thus be seen as lying at these intersections.

- *unequal sexualities* – where sex gets shaped by economic and status differences like class, caste and slavery;
- *gendered sexualities* – where sex gets shaped by being man, woman or 'third sex';
- *racialized sexualities* – where sex is shaped by ethnicity and race (ethnosexualities);
- *theocratic sexualities* – where sex is shaped by religions and religious splits;
- *generational sexualities* – where sex gets shaped by rune and age cohort;
- *urbanized sexualities* – where sex gets shaped by the city rather than rural life;
- *disabled sexualities* – where sex gets shaped through health and disability;
- *national sexualities* – where sex gets shaped by nation and state;
- *intersecting sexualities* – how these all work together.

with the normalized. We have long been aware of this world of outsiders.

I want to suggest, then, an important imagery of society that is made up of micro worlds in which sexual lives are conducted at a distance from the dominant hegemonic order. Around the world, there is a lot of literature, film and drama depicting this seething 'sub-reality' quite vividly. A really popular (and now classic) film of the mid-1980s – David Lynch's *Blue Velvet* – captured this well, starkly showing the nestling together of the extraordinarily conventional with the extraordinarily fetishistic and violent underworld adjacent to it. The message sent out was that while sexual lives on the surface may seem to contain 'normality and consensus', underneath there is a seething world of desire and deviant alternatives. And this is the case all around the world – there is plenty of evidence to suggest that there are a lot of people who work against the grain in many Chinese, Muslim and African societies.[30] Today, some of these hidden worlds have become more visible, but other new subterranean modes, still largely hidden from sight, are doubtless shaping up too. (The arrival of the Internet does seem to be making them more visible: have a good look around!)

These subterranean sexualities are not all cut from one cloth. There are multiple differences in practice, in legitimacies, in visibilities; but for my introductory purposes, I sort some of these diverse cultures into four basic social types: the *sexual retreatist*, the *sexual ritualist*, the *sexual rebel* and the *sexual innovator*. Clearly, there are others.[31]

Retreatist sexualities are those that withdraw and disengage from sexualities, mildly, episodically or completely. The expectations of a dominant culture for a sexual life are left far behind, and we encounter the chaste, the celibate and the asexual. It might also include those who retreat from society in other ways (as drug users, hermits, prisoners, priests) or those who retreat to institutions – such as a monastery, a home, a prison. Withdrawal from the routines of life can also often mean a withdrawal from sex. Indeed, this may become the unspoken widespread practice of partners, married or not, who are tired of the whole damned thing! Throughout history many women have seized on it as a way of removing themselves from the drudgery of home and the relentlessness of male sex (often retreating to the cloisters, the nunnery). And some celibacy movements created by men can be seen as early forms of anti-feminism.

Retreatist sexualities are notably widespread across most global religions and the centrepiece of many. Three of the world's major religions – Christianity, Judaism and Buddhism – actually foster another worldliness and a withdrawal to a monastic or celibate life. Celibacy is at Christianity's core, linked with the Virgin Mary and the ubiquitous imagery that surrounds this. Catholic priests are all supposed to be celibate under the dictate of God and the Pope.[32]

Likewise, the Buddhist monastery, with its 'precepts' to be followed, makes chastity a prime condition. Theravada Buddhism proclaims it is 'better . . . that your male organ enter the mouth of terrible and poisonous snake, than it should enter a woman'. Elizabeth Abbott's study of celibacy reveals how it permeates 'ancient history, from the celibate shift workers of the Oracle of Delphi and the virginal trio of Athena, Arthemis and Hestia, the Greek World's greatest goddesses, to Rome's majestic vestal virgins'.[33] Her list goes on and on: the Incas required perpetual virginity from their *acllas*; there were the Eunuchs in Byzantine and Ottoman Empires, often attached to harems; Mother Ann Lee's Shakers; Father Divine's Peace Movement; Mahatma Gandhi; Elizabeth I of England; Florence Nightingale; Italy's operatic castrati and the opera mania.

But retreatism also has its distinctively modern forms. In recent years there has been much interest in asexuality – someone who does not experience sexual attraction – along with new social movements for the asexual. The movement AVEN (Asexual Visibility and Education Network) holds international meetings. In the United States, Evangelical chastity movements have arrived with their chastity pledge rings, which ironically work to make chastity the new 'sexy' amongst the young. There is, then, an emerging 'politics of celibacy' and 'asexuality'.[34]

Ritualistic sexualities are those that engage with a sex, often fully and regularly, that is heavily symbolic and ritualistic. This can mean several things. For psychologists, sexual rituals are repetitive behaviour to reduce anxiety; for anthropologists, they serve as symbolic rites; for sociologists, they are formal ceremonial activities.

Ritual sexualities come in two major forms: active and passive. Passive rituals suggest withdrawal through routine: ritualists have sex, follow the rules, but lack engagement or engulfment.[35] There is a hive of regular and repetitive sex, sex that goes on and on, but without much sense of fun or satisfaction. It just happens. Here we might find a lot of routine marital sex, where passion is replaced by boredom, or is coerced; or much routine and perpetual masturbation and solo sex. Masturbation is possibly the most common of all sexual activities across the world – and the least discussed. Yet it is surely a universal act; even if the meanings it raises are not. In a stunning history of solo sex, the historian Thomas Laqueur has suggested an unusual key moment in history. Before the early 1700s, Laqueur argues, masturbation was not a subject of great interest or speculation. But since then, it has evolved from being the terrible disease of *Onania or The Heinous Sin of Self Pollution, and all its Frightful Consequences* (the title of a major work published in 1712) to becoming more recently celebrated as therapy in masturbation workshops and 'buddy jerk off' groups. It has moved from a passive ritual to a more active ritual.[36]

Active rituals, by contrast, suggest a much fuller engagement with sex. The symbolic features provide enhanced meaning: the symbolic side of sex, always present, is now made manifest. We can find it in the world of gay men who celebrate femininity (the Faeries) or masculinity (the Leathermen). Centrally, their sexuality is defined through symbolic ritual. Nowhere is this perhaps clearer than in the stylized sexuality of fetishists and those engaging with BDSM, where the practices take practitioners into the realm of the transcendent and the spiritual.[37]

Rituals are also clearly found in 'carnival sex'. In the Egyptian parades honouring huge phalluses, in the Dionysian festivals of Athens, in the Bacchanalian orgies in ancient Rome, sex is often found in the carnival space. Today, we can find them all round the world: the Amazonian carnival Boi Bumba in Parintins; Mardi Gras in Sydney, in Trinidad, Olinda, Rio and New Orleans. And they all bring a hint of the sexual and often a lot more. Rio de Janeiro's carnival alone drew 4.9 million people in 2011, with 400,000 being foreigners.[38]

Rebellious sexualities are those that seek to reject the existing order and transform the world. Some are expressive and romantic: they want to change the world through their own actions. Others are reformist: they seek piecemeal change in the sexual world through reform and assimilation. And still others are explicitly radical or revolutionary, wanting to change the sexual world at its very roots. There is a very long history of these varieties of dissent. Much could be said.[39]

One example must do. The key contemporary Western version

of this rebellious subterranean tradition is the Nietzschean-inspired queer theory and queer activism. This developed towards the end of the 1980s in the US academy and through the politics of AIDS, and can be seen as linked to poststructuralism, postmodernism, multiculturalism and lesbian and gay studies. Some claim a genealogy back to certain strands of anarchistic thought. Queer 'is by definition whatever is at odds with the normal, the legitimate, the dominant. There is nothing in particular to which it necessarily refers.'[40] It deconstructs discourses and creates a greater openness and fluidity by suggesting that very few people really fit into the straightjackets of our contemporary gender and sexual categories.[41] Claiming to be 'anti-normative' it seeks to subvert all 'normativities' (especially hetero-normativity) and challenges all sexual categories to become open, fluid, unsettled and non-fixed (which means that modern lesbian, gay, bisexual and transgender identities are fractured and dissolved along with all heterosexual ones). It 'queries' any stable sense of gender, sexuality, identity or 'the normal'. It frequently celebrates gender transgression, sexual fetishes and the social worlds of the so-called radical sexual fringe.

'Queer' provides a critique of mainstream, neoliberal or 'corporate' homosexuality, shunning all 'normalizing processes' including 'homo-normativity'. It is critical of the old radical languages of liberation, identity politics, rights and citizenship, giving way to practices of transgression and carnival as a goal of political action – a 'politics of provocation'. And it is internally critical of the gay movement itself – as a limited, parochial, nationalist, Western movement.[42] Often characterized by cleverness and flamboyant intelligence, in some recent versions it has suggested there can be 'no future' – casting a dark shadow on the possibilities of progress, positioning the queer as anti-child, fostering the antisocial, anti-normative and anti-future, celebrating the importance of failure, the dismantling of time, the arrival of the posthuman. It can even take Lady Gaga as a glimpse of worlds to come.[43]

Queer theory may be the latest manifestation of a very long radical tradition of subterranean sexualities. It has been around for a quarter of a century in the pockets of Western academia, although some now claim that the theory is exhausted.[44]

Finally, *innovative sexualities* are those that explore the many diverse creative potentials of sex: the sexual experimenters, sexual adventurers, sexual explorers and sexual cultivators who bring new forms of sexualities into being. One clear example of this happened with the arrival of HIV/AIDS in 1981. Only a few months into the epidemic, a group of distraught and grieving gay men in New York and San Francisco were busy organizing and campaigning for 'safer sex', a programme of sexual behaviours where body fluids would not be transmitted. For a while, with irony, it was adopted by the WHO. This gave a whole new twist to sexualities – to 'outercourse', buddy masturbation, telephone sex and fetishistic desire.[45] More: amidst a flurry of controversy in the mid-1990s, a contrasting culture of 'barebacking' was invented, where men, in the wake of the HIV crisis, turned unprotected anal sex into a new innovative erotic reality. The virus now became a focus of the sex, the men became 'bug chasers' who wanted the HIV in their bodies, and a 'breeding culture' centred on viral exchange was created. In this world, gay men made HIV infection central to their meaning: they were driven by the bug, even wanting it, giving 'no limits' to their range of multiple pleasured ejaculations. Sex takes on the meanings of an abundance of hypermasculinity and a spiritual force. Gay men here are certainly not sissies: they are more men than men. This is *real* sex and *real* danger. And of course it raised an abundance of controversies.[46]

Whenever any new technology arrives, it is speedily inspected for its innovative sexual potential. The camera was immediately turned into a pornographic eye; the hoover became a masturbatory adjunct; the telephone led to phone sex. J.G. Ballard's controversial but influential 1973 novel *Crash* (made into a film in 1995 by David Cronenberg) tells the tale of a man turned on by car crashes (and this is linked to the idea of sexual fetishes with disasters – and a new term coined by the late sexologist John Money, *symphorphilia*). Likewise, most new materials lead to new fetishes: there are *plastic* fetishes, *leather* fetishes, *rubber* fetish, *PVC* fetishes. Above all, the Internet has created a veritable smorgasbord of new sexual delights, where a florid array of fetishes can be tracked down with relative ease. It seems likely that the arrival of technologies has significantly increased the range of innovative fetishistic desire.

Local cultures and micro sexualities

Understanding sexualities, then, requires a broad mapping of dominant (meta) cultures and their resistance. But the core of any cultural analysis must concern itself ultimately with how people live unique everyday lives alongside other people. It requires a close familiarity with the complexity of people's actions in local situations. This focus on micro sexualities asks how people create different sexualities and genders: how they develop and move with different bodies; embody different emotions; perform contrasting identities and roles; confront different choices and constraints; assemble different sexual meanings; enact different sexual scripts and practices; use different languages; tell different sexual stories; experience different sentimental structures and subjectivities; evaluate their lives and worth differently; become attached to different beliefs, cosmologies and religions; and dwell in different material and power-based worlds. It starts with the person and is concerned with the doings, accommodations, negotiations and resistances of everyday sexual life.

All this has been a crucial arena for much contemporary 'ethnography of sexualities'. Over the past few decades, there have been hundreds of small research projects taking place in many parts of the world that give little glimpses of this complexity. Box 4.2 suggests some of this. Starting with individuals with everyday troubles and local situations, we hear their voices, confront their problems, face their personal sufferings and joys. In making sense of cosmopolitan sexualities, this is what has to be grasped: that it is necessary to listen carefully to what individuals have to say and to dig deep down to seek out micro sexual cultures. From this we can start to isolate the power in everyday lives of languages, relationships, symbols, scripts, meanings, bodies, emotions, identities, rules, interaction rituals, social worlds and, ultimately, politics. And in doing this, over and over again we find that values are contradictory, languages are ambiguous, embodiments are plural, choices are constrained, identities are multiple and fluid, subjectivities are in tension, and emotions are ambivalent. We are living with sexual complexity.[47]

4.2   *Learning about sexual life*:
Sampling a multiplicity of ethnographies of sexualities

Cosmopolitan sexualities thrives on an awareness of cultural complexity. Ethnographies of sexualities provide the materials for the close inspection of everyday-grounded sexual worlds, showing how people live their sexual lives. And over the years, I have learnt much from some of these ethnographies. In the earliest days, I learnt from Margaret Mead that gender is constituted in very different ways across different cultures; from Gil Herdt that boys can commit oral sex with each other en masse as a status passage into adult heterosexuality; from Laud Humphreys that there are interaction rituals that enable same-sex activity to take place in public toilets by men (men who were subsequently – unethically – traced and found to be married 'heterosexual' men); from Esther Newton that there were fine distinctions and much humour to be found in the worlds of drag bars and 'female impersonators' (and just as I was starting to visit these very bars myself as a young man); and from Raewyn Connell, I read the stories of men that revealed just how 'hegemonic masculinity' can be resisted in a myriad of ways.[48]

Later I turned to ethnographies of sexualities to help me grasp worlds of sexualities around the world. In *Indonesia*, the fourth most populous country in the world with the most Muslims and the third largest democracy, I learnt from Tom Boellstorf that *gay* and *lesbi* Indonesians come to an understanding of their sexual subjectivity through what has been called a 'dubbing culture'. Here, men and women having same-sex relations learn about themselves through Westernized media representations that, in turn, are then played within their own culture to inform an understanding of themselves as islands (of non-*normal*) selfhood in an archipelagic unity of differences. A complex process allows them to see themselves as 'being same but different'. In *China's* post-Mao landscape, James Farrer introduced me to a new generation of Chinese young people in Shanghai who had reinvented the disco as a capitalist sexual hot spot; while Tiantian Zheng showed me what happens to karaoke bar hostesses in the city of Dalian – what goes on in the club, the kinds of roles that the girls have to play, and their lives outside. Susana Peña showed me just how exiled Cuban gays have actively created a new vibrant gay Cuban culture in Miami; while Martin Manalansan introduced me to the lives of Filipino men confronting the prejudices of New York city as they create an innovative transnational gay and life style.[49] In an array of Arabic and Latin America cultures, I learnt about 'passive' men who are seen as homosexual and the 'actives' who are not: the Nicaraguan *machistas*, for example, who have sex with other men but do not consider themselves homosexuals. And I learnt too that radical movements take on very different cultures too. Thus, the women's movement may exist across the world, but the active cultures of women surely vary according to their different languages and values: the battles of women and sexual 'rights' in India, for example, are different from post-revolutionary Nicaragua or Iran, which, in turn, are different from those in Indonesia.[50]

Getting close to local cultures always shows the creative, complex, contingent and changing worlds of sexualities that people inhabit from within, revealing once again the aleatory, agonistic and ambivalent nature of social life. Learning about the vast multiplicity of these created cultures and active unique people is a very good starting point for grasping the significance of diverse sexualities.

Ethnographies of sexualities reveal the importance of the very language people use and the problems with translation. It is hard to make any sense of sexual and gender cultures without grasping the linguistic complexities behind them. Even seemingly simple English words, like 'sex', 'gender', 'masculinity', 'femininity', 'love', and all kinds of sexual categories, like 'lesbian' and 'homosexual', 'gay' and 'straight', 'feminist', 'transgender' and a host of others, cannot be readily transplanted from one culture to another. Scholars of 'homosexuality' have had a field day with this problem. The modern word 'homosexual', invented in Europe in the late nineteenth century, does not travel well across either time or space. The word 'homosexual' was and can really only be used for a limited range of Western experiences in the mid-twentieth century: there are hundreds of other terms for allied phenomena across the world and across history but *they are most certainly not the same*. Even in North America and the UK, the word is now rarely used and has been followed by a succession of debates about what term to use, even as the experiences themselves change: gay, queer, LGBT and linked variants, MSM, WSW, same-sex relation, and so on. Today, we know that each local culture brings its own terminologies and that political debates ensue as to the most appropriate terms to use. But once we have moved beyond these limited 'Western cultures', we find that each one has generated its own multiplicities of languages. One study of sexual language in Thailand, for example, shows varied, multilevelled sexual vocabularies of literary style (*phasa khian*), spoken Thai (*phasa phut*), formal language (*phasa ratchakan*), slang and marketplace language (*phasa talat*) and academic vocabularies (*phasa wichakan*), all of which shift across many different situations and groupings, from transgender to women who love women.[51] In a huge litany, we have, for example, 'toms' (masculine Thai lesbians), 'dee' (feminine-identified women who have relations with other women), 'kathoey' (males who dress like women and wear make-up), or 'lady boys' (transsexual or transvestite males). The words make little sense out of their culture and need to be grasped before any sense can be made of Thai cultures.[52]

A further key concern lies with the critical issue of *human agency and creativity*. People across the world may create their sexual lives but not in conditions of their own choosing. They act with *constrained choice* and we need to see both what these constraints are and how people handle them. Sex workers/prostitutes reveal some of these difficult (and not so difficult) circumstances that just might lead women and men into selling sex, but which also show how these are often decisions taken because of wider concerns (making money for their desperate families, getting a job when there are no other jobs available, etc.).[53] As we get close to individual lives, questions have to be raised about the range of choices confronted in lives that are often lived in impossible circumstances. Opportunities arise and sexual activity becomes one of a drifting pathway of choices.

Another issue concerns what we might call human dignity-making. Here, the idea of self-value (self-esteem, self-worth, honour and dignity), so basic to humanistic psychology, becomes central: from where do people get their valued sense of sexual and gendered self? Or fail to get it? Issues of belonging and significant others become critical, as they highlight the degree to which the human self depends on others and their evaluative codes. In many cultures, this in turn is linked to an honour code.

For example, studies of female genital mutilation (FGM) soon show how the valued self is bound up with traditional values and cultures – important to mothers as well as to daughters in establishing who they are. Ellen Gruenbaum spent five years in the Sudan, where FGM is widely practised, and in getting close to the women involved she could soon see just how important the process is for different generations in creating a sense of who they are and how they belong.[54] A simple hostility to FGM, so common from the West, will not do because it often denies these important issues of self-worth. But change is certainly needed – and indeed is on its way. Even more controversial and complex is the way in which 'rape cultures' are bound up with the significance of a hegemonic masculine self-worth across the world: not only in tribal conflicts, war rape and terrorism, but also more locally in boy gangs, in college fraternities and even the linked gang rape – all are bound up with strong cultural norms and networks that actually use sexual violence to help frame a man's sense of worth. This sets a severe problem and one that is not easy to resolve. Sanday (2007) has shown the cultures of brotherhoods on campus which legitimate violence and even gang rape: boys find their sense of self in their peer group. Controversial as it is, this closely grounded dynamic of self-worth needs to be critically grasped. Somehow, this kind of bonding for a self needs to be worked with. The issue here is not only normative belonging to groups – and the degree of integration that can provide a sense of positive self – but also those who fall outside, who do not belong and become cut off and isolated. The lack of integration can generate low self-esteem and self-value, causing yet further problems.

All this links to another critical issue: of body and identity. While bodies are universal, their shapes, forms and meanings are not. A very wide range of 'masculinities' and 'femininities' can and do become attached to a very wide range of different bodies, acts and partners: there is no automatic linkage between bodily acts and senses of gender; and in each local culture this needs to be unravelled. For example, in a much-celebrated study, Don Kulick described living with a group of young Brazilian drug-ingesting, female-looking male prostitutes (called *travestis* in Portuguese) in the city of Salvador. Despite irreversible physiological changes, virtually no *travesti* identified 'herself' as a woman; and they saw their modified bodies as a positive experience. Kulick's study brims with first-person accounts from the young men whose bodies and identities defy what many might take for granted. Bodies, identities and gender are complicated. Likewise, in India, Gayatri Reddy studied the lives of Hijra closely to show the range of new identities and roles they come to experience under conditions of great local oppression. They occupy a unique 'liminal' space that places them between man and woman, sacred and profane. And in Hong Kong, London and Shanghai, Travis Kong traced how Western body styles 'had a profound impact upon the Chinese gay male body' of men travelling from East to West. He showed that while these men have the identities of 'Chinese' and 'gay' from their local colonized home culture, they also have transitional bodies: some go West to become 'Golden Boys', and others East to become 'tongzhi'. New words and worlds are shaped out: feminized 'golden boys', the 'tongzhi', the 'money boy', the 'memba', the 'potato' and 'rice queens'. These new worlds have meant 'the creation of different hybridized gay identities'. Increasingly too, we now learn about a 'transgender China'.[55] Just how we define who we are, as gendered, as sexual beings, moves in different ways through our bodies. But there is no automatic or essential state here. A wider sampling of this plurality of gender and sexual identities is suggested in Box 4.3.

4.3   *Gender pluralism*: Sampling a multiplicity of genders

The complexities of sexual and gender cultures become really clear through research on the 'third sex' (Herdt, 1993), or what Michael Peletz (2009) has called 'gender pluralism'. While most cultures make elementary divides between men and women, there are always many people who do not fit into any category. Naming this global phenomenon is itself an issue. I have encountered a bewildering array of terminologies, which have kept changing and adjusting since my first research and personal encounters with the issue in the works of Virginia Prince (who focused on *transvestism* and favoured *femophilia*), and Harry Benjamin (who favoured *transsexual*).[56] Ideas of intermediate sex, third sex and third gender abound. People whom I interviewed in the 1970s strongly contested just what they should be called. Today, we have an extensive glossary, which can be found online, ranging across: androgyny (bioguy, biogirl), transvestism, cross dressings, transsexuality, transgender (true or not), MTF, M3F, MF, M–F, female masculinities, shemale, transmen, transwomen, masculinities, multiple crossings, hermaphrodite, inter-sex, typologies of Cisgendered Variance – and so forth. All can have quite specific meanings and most bring their own conflicts and politics. Just how these categories are imagined and constructed has become a field of research in itself.[57] People quite rightly get very excited and agitated about what they are to be called.

Variants of third sex and transgender have also become a popular theme for television programmes, autobiographies and films. A short listing of the many films captures something of the pervasiveness of interest in all this – and the variety: *Some Like it Hot, Women in Revolt, Cabaret, Dressed to Kill, The Rocky Horror Picture Show, Tootsie, Victor/Victoria, Yentl, La Cage aux Folles, Mrs Doubtfire, Priscilla: Queen of the Desert, Orlando, The Crying Game, Ed Wood, Boys Don't Cry, Paris is Burning, Ma Vie en Rose, All About My Mother, TransAmerica, Trans Generation, Beautiful Boxer, Normal, Hedwig and the Angry Inch, Wigstock* – and on and on.[58] Even if often fictional, these titles capture a very wide-ranging sense of the gender differences within the narrow confines of the Western world.

But looked at more globally, gender pluralism has become a key site for investigating gender complexity. Thus, we find: the Indian *Hijras* ('not man, not woman') a special social role that involves performance, prostitution and spirituality and necessitates self-castration (Nanda, 1998; Reddy, 2005); the Thai *kathoey* (Jackson, 1999); the Filipino *bakla* (Garcia, 1996); the Afghanistan *Bacha Posh*, the Malaysian *mak nyah*, the Indonesesian *waria/banci*, the Samoa *Fa'afafine,* the Nigerian *yan daudu* (Murray and Roscoe, 2001); the North American 'two spirit' Indians – the Zuni, the Navajo, the *Berdache* (Roscoe, 2000); the *Takatāpui* of New Zealand (Murray, 2003); the *Travesti* of Salvador, Brazil (Kulick, 1998); the *Vestidas* of Mexico City (Prieur, 1998); the *Xanith* of Oman (Wikan, 1977); the 801 cabaret drag queens of Key West (Rupp and Taylor, 2003). And on . . .

The performing of identity, gender, sexuality and body across the world is never a simple thing.

Conclusion: complex cultures

Sexual cultures, our sexual ways of life, are indelibly multicultural, bringing together layers of meanings, stories and languages to make sense of perpetually changing diverse bodies, identities, habits, values and emotions. They exist in both big (state) and small (face-to-face) ways, and are always being negotiated. We may like to look for simple harmony and unity, and politically it may be expedient to do so; but the world is never like that. Simple views of monocultures will never do. Cosmopolitan analysis demands a persistent, nagging awareness of cultural multiplicity, contradictions, conflict and complexity. It is to these tensions that I now turn.

5

Contested Sexualities: Inventing Enemies, Making Boundaries

> Having an enemy is important not only to define our identity but also to provide us with an obstacle against which to measure our system of values, and in seeking to overcome it, to demonstrate our own worth. So when there is no enemy, we have to invent one.
>
> Umberto Eco, *Inventing the Enemy* (2013)

Across history and culture, conflict is ubiquitous. Umberto Eco's succinct insight is a long-established wisdom that suggests why human life is full of tensions, enemies and wars. Conflict can be found both across and within religions, tribes and nations and within classes, races and the genders (the so-called 'battles of the sexes'). But conflict can also be found in much more specific matters: we have seen there can be disagreements over some 200 meanings of cosmopolitanism. And we can easily find contestation even in the long struggles over the nature of 'human rights'. In the West alone, the term has been contested as rights to 'security' (Hobbes), to 'life, liberty and property' (Locke), to 'freedom' (Kant), to 'life, liberty and the pursuit of happiness' (Paine) and so on.[1] Think, if you can, of any area of social life where there is no conflict. Wherever cosmopolitan sexualities live, there also dwells the potential for perpetual conflict. So the challenge will always be to handle this well; to keep a 'peace' where a 'bloody war' may rush in.[2]

I first became really aware of conflicts over human sexualities when I sat week after week in the London School of Economics in the earliest days of the Gay Liberation Front in the late 1960s. Of course, the movement was set up in conflict with the outside straight heterosexual world; it was built out of conflict and it organized campaigns and protests. We marched and picketed in the London streets for the first time ever as visible gay men and lesbians. But it was also a site of perpetual conflict *within* itself. One week, the liberal reformer Anthony Grey, who pioneered the Sexual Offences Act 1967, would come to speak and would be almost booed out. Another week, the passionate transgender lobby would trash us all for excluding them. The next week, the whole women's movement would walk out accusing gay men of being more sexist and misogynist than straight men. There was also a generation tension: between young and old (the younger men would be suspicious of the older men eyeing them up). And then the paedophiles would speak up – and, being rejected, create their own splinter groups: PAL (Paedophile Action for Liberation) and PIE (Paedophile Information Exchange) and both of these in disagreement. And all the time the old battle lines between right, left and middle were being drawn up again. The whole movement came and went within three years, as we swung from one exciting extreme to another. It was a sharp learning curve in sexual politics.

Since then, conflicts have rushed into every area of sex research and sex politics that I have ever engaged with. I have witnessed bitter conflicts over homosexuality and lesbianism (these very 'modern' words subsequently contested out of existence by some), AIDS, transgender, pornography, sex work and prostitution, paedophilia, BDSM, the nature of sexual violence and exploitation. Famously, the women's movement has a long history of conflicting positions – the divides between liberal feminists, socialist feminists, Marxist feminists, radical feminists, postcolonial feminists and cultural postmodernist feminists are but the well-known iceberg surface of deep conflicts. And it is sometimes a very personal conflict, creating major animosities amongst the women themselves. The debate, as we have seen, over those who see sexuality as violence against women and those who see sexuality as pleasure for women has created a longstanding historical split that creates camps that will not even speak to each other. The landmark modern example was the Pleasure and Danger Conference in 1981 (captured in Carole Vance's 1984 collection with that title), but this is but one symbol of it. It is so very alive today in debates about the sex industry, pornography, transgender, religion, body surgery, etc. Sheila Jeffreys articulates a contemporary no-nonsense coherent view of the strong feminist radical position.[3]

Latterly, as I have moved more into thinking about the global politics of sexualities, rampant new conflicts – between and across religions, ethnicities, states – become instantly visible and vicious. Here we find conflicts over genital mutilation, child marriage, honour crimes, dowry murder and war rape. Schisms and suffering abound. Deep worlds of human sexual differences soon become deep worlds of rage, anger and contestation. And these conflicts can be found everywhere, from the grandest global level down to the tiniest face-to-face tiffs, family disagreements and personal enmities: with everything in between. Ubiquitous, they exist within and across cultures, within and between groups, and within and between people, caught up in the dynamics of nations, religions, social movements, international agencies and moral crusaders. The battles over sexual and gender differences will not vanish under cosmopolitanism, but they may well be handled in a more benign way than in the past.

Scaling the battlegrounds

Box 3.1 (see pp. 83–4) suggests some 10 arenas of conflict around sex and gender; and in an earlier study, I documented five arenas of conflict: 'family wars', 'the battle between the sexes', the 'erotic wars', reproductive politics and 'the politics of the body', introducing the idea of intimate citizenship as one tool for handling these conflict zones.[6] However the conflicts are designated, all these contemporary conflicts can also be seen as layered, from the most global to the most specific and local (from macro to micro), arising from both *within* and *between* groups (inter-conflict/intra-conflict).

Thus at a *global* level, we can speak of 'global sex wars', where core schisms can be found between nations, religions, regions (North/South) and, sometimes, even civilizations.[7] Here are the big debates over 'modernity', the 'clash of civilizations' (Huntington, 1996), of 'Jihad versus McWorld' and the clash of world religious values. The global conflicts over human rights are all instances that raise issues of sexual, gender and family change on a global scale.[8] Much of this gets linked to *national* conflicts, where we find a continuing tension between traditionalists and radicals (with many positions in between). Recent examples could include the battles over abortion laws in Poland, the problem of adultery as a crime in Turkey as it tries to enter the EU, the routine tensions over 'honour crimes' and 'adultery' in Pakistan and the so-called 'sex wars' and 'culture wars' in the USA, which can split communities to the roots.[9]

Strident disagreements are also routine in social movements, where deep schisms can be found within as well as between them. It is perhaps centrally exemplified by Muslim women's conflicts with various Muslim states – for example, the mobilization of and conflicts over women's rights in Egypt and Iran.[10] Multiple tensions usually exist between conservatives, assimilationists and radicals. To take a few examples: some transgender activists seek to demonstrate that transgender radicalizes the fluidity and variety of genders, showing how people choose to radically break gender norms and live different lives; but they are soon shouted down by large numbers of transgendered people who claim they had no choice over their gender at all and have no wish to play or 'perform' with it radically. Likewise, some gay movement leaders argue assiduously for gay marriage in their countries (and have been increasingly successful), while other gay people are very critical of such a move, claiming it is a move towards normalizing. The Muslim women's movement is split over the Quran, with many internal 'schisms' amongst women, from Iran to Indonesia.[11] And many sex workers marching the streets to claim their legitimacy and rights across the world find themselves confronted by a 'feminist rescue industry', set up to rescue them from their plight![12]

Yet, ultimately, and independently of world issues, nations and movements, conflicts permeate everyday relationships. In courting, in sex relations, in the daily skirmishes between men and women – we all know about conflict. Most of us live with it everyday. At its worst, it ends in sexual violence or 'honour crimes' – and much unhappiness. Taking conflict seriously is part of the cosmopolitan sexualities project.

Divisive sexualities, agonistic politics

It might help if we look at some of the many deep sources of this ubiquitous entanglement of conflicts around human sexualities. They flow from the intersecting divides over gender, ethnicity, class, religion, age and nation. Each can be seen as a fissure that splits the organization of societies and groups. In the languages of some recent politics, they are agonistic.[13] They are part of a necessary conflict in the world, where debates have to be organized around core schisms for change to be possible. The challenge for cosmopolitan sexualities is to see how these conflicts can be used creatively for the good. Here I just highlight a few of these schisms.

Gender schisms

In the most straightforward terms, most societies have been, and still are, patriarchies. (In another interminable conflict over terminology, social scientists nowadays often call this a gender regime or gender order, or male hegemony, or whatever – and the language is regularly reworked and contested.[14]) Nearly every aspect of sexuality discussed in this book suggests the omnipresence of male power hovering over women. We dwell in patriarchal sexualities. Even though there are many signs of change,[15] and there is much interpersonal variation, there is now a very substantial documentation of these gender divisions around the world and the conflicts generated (see, in particular, Chapter 2).

It is clear that the history of sexualities is deeply shaped by gender inequalities and conflicts. Marilyn French's four-volume *History of Women in the World* (2008), as Margaret Atwood puts it in her Foreword to the first volume, describes 'the bizarre customs, the woman-hating legal structures, the gynaecological absurdities, the child abuse, the sanctioned violence, the sexual outrages – millennium after millennium' (p. x). Deprived of human rights and organized through patriarchy, today we find that women are the prime 'victims' of war rape, of female genital mutilation, of pornographic violence, of child marriage, of bride money. Women's place in both the public and the private worlds is usually defined by men, and the same is true of their sexualities. Much of this has been orchestrated by religion. Even today, in most religions, the subordinated position of women is the deep structure behind much conflict.

Under the challenging conditions of modernity, some women have started to gain more of a voice and a presence: women's historical powerlessness and invisibility is starting to break down. But this is deeply threatening to many trans-patriarchal states and groups who see women's education, their changing role in the family and their public visibility as serious threats to the old order. Deep and bitter conflict ensues. Just how women are silenced and how battered voices can break though to herald a cosmopolitan civility is now a central problem for the future. In many contexts and in many ways women are still completely silenced and not even allowed an education. To a considerable extent, the future of sexualities hangs on this conflict.

Ethnic schisms

Human sexualities are also embedded in worlds of race and racism, generating an eroticization and exoticization of ethnicity that can turn into the basis of major 'ethnosexual' conflicts. There are conflicts over sexual relations that cross ethnic borders ('mixed marriages', 'mixed blood', 'miscegenation') like the controversies in South Africa (in the Apartheid era, 1949–85), in Nazi Germany (from 1935 to 1945 via the Nuremberg Laws) and in the USA (from 1691 to 1967 in some states). Sex racism is also fostered in many religions – the caste system of Hinduism, for example, forbids congress across caste. Sexualities are also prone to ethnic stereotyping, casting the racial 'other' as exotic or dangerous people, 'racializing the other' as an extreme object of disgust, discrimination and even sexual violence (as in slavery and rape in war). Such hostility can feed into nationalism and, ultimately, genocide. Floating behind all this is the presence of a dominant group's power and the ubiquitous deep fear of strange others.[16]

Religious schisms

Conflict, ironically, abounds in religion. And this is not just the well-documented history of religious wars with *outsiders* (like the eleventh–thirteenth-century Christian crusades, or the Muslim Caliphate conquests), but also the striking history of divides with *insiders*. Religions regularly excommunicate or banish those who do not follow their own religious rules, and new schisms proliferate. The Catholics battle the Protestants and the Sunni slaughter the Shi'ite, who in turn slaughter back. And more: many others have so vividly documented religious history as also being one that, for centuries, has been the cause of perpetual misogyny, exclusion, subordination and violence towards women.[17]

The pluralization of religion is very important for cosmopolitan debates, because some versions of each religion are kinder and more compatible with cosmopolitan difference than others. There are some 'open' religions that can participate in interfaith dialogues, which is a form of religious cosmopolitanism. There are many who now seek 'religious pluralism', 'polydoxy and divine multiplicity', along with 'interreligious solidarity'.[18] Others, by contrast, foster absolutism or fundamentalism with no tolerance or acceptance of diversity at all. Despite the great varieties of religions, monotheistic religions in particular are all grounded on the one absolute (Hinduism and Buddhism can be more multiple and flexible). It is this absolutism that is the enemy of cosmopolitan sexualities and for which there are no easy solutions. And an interesting 'backlash' alliance between these major monotheistic religions across the world (Conservative/fundamentalist versions of Christianity, Islam and Judaism) emerged during the latter decades of the twentieth century to establish what might be called a 'natural family agenda'. One key organization, the Howard Center, puts it well:

> The World Congress of Family's coalition model represents the final opposition for an effective pro-family model worldwide. All coalition members, usually orthodox religious believers, are asked to set aside their own personal theological and cultural differences and agree on one simple, unifying concept: the natural family is the fundamental unity of society, If coalition members can agree on this concept, then all of their other disagreements may take a back seat.[19]

This includes such organizations as the Catholic Family and Human Rights Institute, The Howard Center itself, Human Life International, the Family Research Council, Concerned Women for America, the World Family Policy Center and, of course, the Vatican. The Vatican has not only decreed in various encyclicals, but also has 'permanent observer' status at the United Nations. The 'Holy See' is the official face of the Vatican at the UN. It has led to the World Congress of Families (WCF). They also produce what Buss and Herman have called 'Christian Right Social Science' (2003: xxxiii).

At the broadest level, Norris and Ingelhart (2011) have claimed that a major world divide now lies between the religious and the secular. They show how advanced industrial societies have become more secular over the past half century, yet in the world as a whole, there are more people with traditional religious views than ever before. Religiosity persists most strongly among vulnerable populations, especially in poorer nations and in failed states. This brings ongoing possibilities for more tensions.

Colonial schisms

We still live with the human consequences of those many European and Western countries that went out to the rest of the world from the sixteenth century onwards with a sense of their own supremacy (and a passion for violence) and proceeded to colonize, imperialize, Christianize, exploit and ravage native peoples.

The contingencies of these bloodthirsty invasions also left the sexualities of these countries marked. Colonial governments regulate sexual arrangements, policing the sexual margins and attending to marriage and the family so that they may suit their needs. Voices of non-European sexual cultures are not expected to be heard, and are deliberately, if not always consciously, suppressed. Of course, this was a complex process that is crudely summarized here. But it is one more pathway of schism. Jeffrey Alexander talks about cultural traumas: when the colonizers depart, they leave a scarred culture or a traumatized culture[20] – it can take generations to work through the problems.

In rebuilding, cultures become a mélange of past, colonized and future elements – struggling to rediscover the past, deal with legacies and traumas, and look ahead to contemporary concerns and issues. Often this marks a battle with 'modernity'.[21]

Generational schisms

One more example of conflict is that of schismatic generations. Family demographics will typically show five generations of potential conflict alive at any one time (you, your children and grandchildren and your parents and grandparents); and more distant ghosts of past and future may accompany these. Historically, generations form cohorts symbolically organized around key traumas, conflicts and events – for example, Tiananmen Square, World War I, 1968, the 1979 Iranian Islamic Revolution, the Arab Spring or even the 'Twitter Generation' – providing symbolic solidarity for groups that can then move through the world together. Generational conflicts highlight the 'clashes between systems of aspirations found in different periods'.[22] They become 'immigrants in time'. And as sexualities change, so different generations bring both nostalgia for remembrance of sexualities past, lost or denied, and anticipation of fresh sexualities to come. These generate tensions that must quietly infuse much of the sexual generational order, often breaking out into direct hostility: panic, generation attack, scapegoating of all kinds. In the current moment, much of this anxiety is focused on the changes that are happening because of differing knowledge, skill, use and awareness of 'digital natives' across generations, a lot of which is also accompanied by a new form of 'sexting' and digital sexual activity amongst the young (see Box 5.1).[23]

5.1   *Generational sexualities*:
Sampling a multiplicity of modern Western gay generations

As one illustration of differing sexual generations, consider the interesting case of just six gay and lesbian cohorts forming in the UK and the USA during the twenty/twenty-first centuries, and sense how these differences can work to generate possible schisms at any given moment, as memory traces linger and coexist from each generation. These phases are:

1 Criminal, sick, closeted worlds. For a good two-thirds of the twentieth century, between at least 1900 and the early 1960s, there were different generations that could be seen as criminalized, closeted and 'sick', with several subgenerations linked to World War I, the Depression, World War II and its aftermath. All these generations, as the books put it, lived 'in the shadows'; their diversities are revealed in the accounts of lives in that period.[4]

2 Coming out of closeted worlds. These are the early coming-out generations. Between the late 1950s and 1970s, homophile movements were slowly gathering strength and there were the beginnings of visibility. With intense stigma, homosexuality was inching open the closet door.

3 Gay liberation worlds. This is the gay liberation generation of the late 1960s and the 1970s, when gay men and lesbians came out publicly and were both proud and political about it. This explicit and public politicalization of gays, lesbians, bisexuals and transgenders certainly worked to transform the experience of 'downcast gays' into a more positive and much more visible one.

4 HIV/AIDS worlds. The AIDS generation, which started in 1981 and dominated much of life in that decade. The death

and dying of notably young men became a central feature, as homosexuality became oddly remedicalized and activists started to become highly professionalized (through AIDS work and academic work). To give a personal example, it changed the way I moved about in the gay world and generated grief as friends died.

5   What might now be called 'Queer Generation Two' started to arrive in the late 1980s and aimed to deconstruct any stable sense of gender or sexual category. No longer criminal, or sick, or even clearly categorized, gayness became queered. Some of this was academic (queer theory) – identified with Sedgwick (1990), Butler (1990), Warner (1999) and Halperin (1995); and some was activist – identified with organizations like Outrage and ACT UP.

6   Cyber-queer worlds and the post-closet world. The Internet generation gets going from the mid-/late 1990s onwards; here, gay/queer websites (like gaydar) start to play a major role in gay men's lives – for meeting, sex, social and other activities – and become increasingly prominent in lesbian life too. Lesbian and gay life starts to get produced and reproduced through Internet activity. At the same time, the new generation finds less and less difficulty in coming out or, indeed, even the need to come out (Seidman, 2003/2010).

Cohort worlds of gay and lesbian life are now starting to be documented. A number of writers have made brilliant starts on building our understanding of these differences.[5] I have discussed all this more fully elsewhere (Plummer, 2015). But note: this is an ideal type, a diachronic linear analysis, and it only makes sense of some pockets of Western male gay life in the twentieth century. It cannot be applied universally.

The fault line of contested sexualities

There is, then, much divisive sexuality rooted in conflicts. And standing above all these divides, I want to stress just one core problem, which can be found at work in all these schisms. It is cosmopolitanism's key 'enemy' and it is *the fault line of absolutism*. Here is the standpoint of the singular monologue, the absolute truth, the 'one and only way', be it the man, the white man, the white Christian man. Here only one voice can be heard: difference and conflict are suppressed, dialogue is excluded, 'the other' obliterated and cosmopolitanism thwarted. And it is in this suppression of our human differences, and the conflicts that come with it, that we find the suppression of our core humanity. There can be neither cosmopolitanism nor humanism amongst people who deny the multiple and fragmented voices of others.

We have been here many times before; we face *the paradoxes of cosmopolitanism*. How can we tolerate the intolerant? How can we speak to those who would ban our right to speak (to paraphrase Voltaire)? How can we have an open society with closed minds? How can we dialogue with those who will only monologue, or speak openly to those who only want to close things down? How can 'the one' live with 'the multiple'? And how can we 'belong' to one group and still appreciate others? Sociopolitically, it raises the problems of totalitarianism and despotic systems; discursively, it raises issues of monologue systems and fundamentalist beliefs; personally, its suggests authoritarian personalities, dogmatism and the closed mind.[24] In none of these systems can difference flourish; all are antithetical to the cosmopolitan imagination.

The key problem for cosmopolitan sexualities is most surely that of absolutist (or even fundamentalist) sexualities. By this I mean those who (a) reject pluralistic views of sexuality; (b) promote conservative and traditional beliefs about sex in an absolute way, often critiquing all those aspects of modernity that foster diversity; and (c) often pay homage to a time-honoured (often sacred) text that is given a strict and single interpretation of what sex is about (for example, the Bible, the Quran). At its most blatant, it calls for maintaining the power of men over women, the overwhelming superiority of the heterosexual, and the extermination of all diversities and perversities. Just as we have seen the rise of sexual cosmopolitanism in recent decades, so we have also seen the continuing journey of sexual absolutism or fundamentalism. This tension is a long historical one and it is not likely to go away or be easily resolved. It may indeed be a feature of social life that needs dealing with in each generation. It is the background horror story generating massive human suffering that haunts this book. And it is clear that, although cosmopolitan sexualities really has to engage in dialogues with such positions, this will never be easy.

On boundaries, belonging and the vulnerabilities of normativity

Human sexualities may be wildly diverse and passionately different; but in all societies and at all times, they are put under normative regulation. For when they are working in their full glory, human desires can be well and truly disruptive of both the personal life and the social order. They can spread diseases, destroy relationships, generate extreme violence; they can also create transcendence, extreme pleasure and sublime worlds that, in turn, can threaten the routines of everyday life. Human sexualities may indeed be wildly diverse and different, but they are always put under control. Oddly perhaps, even the wildest of orgiastic sadomasochist gatherings will eventually develop rules, orders and outsiders. (I studied BDSM many years ago, and soon discovered the highly scripted expectations within such encounters.[25]) Ironically, this very control may also help shape some of the key features of these differences, even heighten the experience. Control and desire have a symbiotic relationship.

Simply put, then, we know that: (a) all societies have rules and norms about the sexual; (b) they develop moral regulation and moral boundaries that mark sexualities off as the normal and the pathological; (c) whenever this moral order is created, there will be stuff – sexual 'disorder', 'dirt', 'danger' – that falls outside it; (d) this stuff, 'deviants', 'outsiders', *'homo sacer'*, are dealt with by society that either swallows them up and makes them their own, or vomits them out, expelling and excluding them. In what follows, I explore some of these issues, to make sense of this 'sexual order'.[26]

Boundary sexualities

Much has been written on the problem of boundaries and borders. Some key ideas on the normal were developed in the work of the founding sociologist Émile Durkheim (1858–1917), who saw the problem of 'normativity' – of the normal and the pathological, the good and the bad – as twin processes, bound up with the very conditions for social life. For him, the classification of the normal and the pathological served to mark out moral boundaries and unite people against common enemies, as well as innovating and changing societies around the edges. It established that there is a 'we' and the 'other', and it is hard to find instances of societies that do not do this. Indeed, many have subsequently demonstrated the inevitable need for classification grids and symbolic frameworks to provide coherence and order at both the personal and the societal levels.[27] Thus it is that the liberal sociological critic Alan Wolfe is compelled to write: 'It is impossible to imagine a society without boundaries'; the philosopher Charles Taylor wants to defend 'the strong thesis that doing without frameworks is utterly impossible for us . . . stepping outside these limits would be tantamount to stepping outside what we would recognize as integral, that is undamaged, human personhood'; and for the sociologist Ulrich Beck, the boundary debate shows the social need for enemies. As he says, 'enemy stereotypes empower'; enemies ('others') galvanize animosity, strengthen ones own self and identity.[28]

There may, then, be some who like to believe the social can be run without norms and who search for 'non-normativities'. But this is wishful thinking: a curiously asocial view. Normativity abhors a vacuum, and when old norms die, new ones rush in. Sociologically impossible, politically impractical, nor even humanly desirable, neither societies nor people can live without borders. And so the question is raised of just how these necessary sexual borders and boundaries might be made that can coexist with cosmopolitanism.

This starts to become possible if we recognize a different kind of border: one that is more fluid, flexible and porous. This means that while always in need of sexual boundaries, we also can recognize these as persistently moving, changing and even sometimes dissolving. Sexual borders become key locations for conflicts about social change. But this change is endemic in the nature of society, and especially 'modern' societies. Such borders will always generate ambivalence, contradictions and tensions – and modern societies, being more complex than earlier ones, may well generate even more. A feature of them becomes the growing need to live with ambivalence in modernity. Sexual borders become more workable to the extent that they are kept open, porous, mobile: there will be a perpetual flow of boundaries across cultures, across histories. And sexual borders can surely have playful horizons: while there will always be boundaries in the distance, these can be played with imaginatively, playfully, 'lightly'. Visions of living societies move on. In short: cosmopolitanism and regulation can live together as long as the boundaries are recognized as flexible – and capable of being reworked, redrawn, reshaped.[29]

Normative sexualities

All societies (and groups) come to have negotiated boundaries. They develop norms and institutions that regulate sex, producing armies of people whose task is to police, control and stigmatize sexualities (moral entrepreneurs), simultaneously creating groups of people who are stigmatized by such processes.[30] These shifting regulations flow through all social orders, and our lives and our sexualities cannot but help be touched by them: either directly (we are shamed, arrested, treated, banned, exterminated) or indirectly (we are deterred, monitored, controlled by them). This very control, usually contested, also comes to shape the very sexual variety we live with.

All societies, then, have their emergent rulebooks, their flowing 'normativities', about what is acceptable and unacceptable sexual conduct (usually based on their religions). There are lists of 'do's and do-not's' which come to form a hierarchy. Varying across history and society, some are explicit, others tacit. One much celebrated and discussed account of all this comes from Gayle Rubin, the pioneering theorist and activist in feminist, lesbian and gay/

queer studies since the 1970s.[31] For her, societies come to build imaginary lines of 'good' and 'bad' sex, which she depicts as a sex hierarchy or even a charmed circle. In the USA when Rubin was writing (early 1980s), the 'good' was depicted as 'hetero-sexual, marital, monogamous, reproductive and non-commercial. It should be coupled, relational, within the same generation, and occur at home.' 'Bad sex', by contrast, was depicted as 'homo-sexual, unmarried, promiscuous, non-procreative, or commercial. It may be masturbatory or take place at orgies, may be casual, may cross-generational lines and, may take place in "public" . . . it may involve the use of pornography, fetish objects, sex toys, or unusual roles.'[32] Rubin's listing was, I suspect, quickly constructed and it can be found wanting. Clearly, such listings can change (already sex outside marriage has become much more acceptable and much homosexuality has also become legitimated in Western societies) and it is certainly not universal (in Africa, for example, polygyny and bride marriage may often be the norm). But the general point was very well made: it is not always the specific prescriptions, but the fact that such hierarchies always seem to exist. They work to make some sexuality normal and normalized, and others abnormal and deviant.

Put very simply, here are some of the major modes of hierarchi-cal sexual regulation found across societies. They are not all found equally across all societies. We have regulative flows of:

- *religious regulation* – different religion systems impact sexual lives;
- *gender regulation* – men, women and others are polarized and shaped in different ways;
- *symbolic regulation* – classificatory systems of the sexual emerge and become ritualized;
- *medical regulation* – science and medicine create systems of pathology and sickness linked to the sexual;
- *material regulation* – economies, bodies, populations organize dif-ferent patterns of the sexual life at different historical moments;
- *government/state/legal regulations* – 'governance' shapes sexual codes;
- *stigmatizing and shaming regulation* – often 'honour codes';
- *discursive regulation* – the languages of sex shape sex.

Violating these various systematic regulations creates pathologies – or, in Mary Douglas's famous term, 'dirt': 'Dirt is the by-product of a systematic ordering and classification of matter, in so far as ordering involves rejecting inappropriate elements. Dirt . . . appears a residual category, rejected from the normal scheme of classification.'[33] Sexual order will always bring the existence of 'dirt'. And this can lead to the zeal to classify more and more, and expunge and annihilate the dirt that this may leave. This 'expulsion' takes a multitude of forms. People can be simply silenced, face stereotyping and discrimination, or be segregated and ghettoized. Ultimately, it may lead to violence of all kinds, including genocide and extermination.

The earliest of societies, and most still today, depend heavily on religion for casting out rule breakers as sexual sinners, sexual devils, sexual witches, sexual heretics. A process of cultural and social purification is at work. As secular laws became increasingly important (and the split between religion and state occurred), so a litany of sex legislation became critical for the shaping of sex crimes: sexual miscreants were increasingly punished and cast out as sex criminals and sex offenders. A process of legal and penal segregation has come into being. And in the Western world, since the late nineteenth century, sexual deviants have come increasingly under the orbit of medical regulations, becoming in various guises the mentally ill, the sexually pathological, the sex addict. A cultural process of medicalization, pathologization and surveillance takes over. In modern societies, the media gets to play an increasing role in generating fear by creating the sex panic (which is the little brother of the moral panic) and the making of various sex monsters. The modern world goes into a perpetual state of fear about sexuality, even as recent history documents a long line of such fears and moral/sex panics (see Box 5.2).[34]

Purity crusades exist across both time and space. They have been used to highlight race issues (such as in lynching rapists in the USA) and in colonial Southern Rhodesia (interracial sex). In India, gang bang rape has resulted in an enormous outcry. In many Muslim countries, moral panics are deeply connected to 'the honour code', highlighting the honour of being a man and a woman. In Iran, a notorious case of sex murder in 1973 produced enormous public

5.2   *Sex panics*: Sampling a multiplicity of moral purity crusades around sex

There is now a very long history of ideas of *moral purity crusades* accompanied by *mass hysteria* and *moral panics*, which show how sex can be used as a symbolic boundary-marker event. The terms are often overused and pose many critical problems; but they do suggest there are moments and acts when responses to sex are disproportionate, unfair and irrational. Sometimes they may even create and provoke the very thing they speak about, as in the witchcraft hysteria of the sixteenth century that is so well documented. For Roger Lancaster, sex panics often 'give rise to bloated imaginings of risk, inflated conceptions of harm and loose definitions of sex'.[35] They generate fear and anxiety and often may be used to deflect issues. In earlier times, they were linked to McCarthyism; today, they can be readily linked to terrorism surveillance and the rise of the punitive city.[36]

Moral panics have been widely studied in the UK and the USA. Here is a list of some of the 'objects' of moral or purity crusades: abortion, AIDS, 'black sexuality', various 'celebrities' like Michael Jackson, children in danger – the 'imperilled, innocent', child sex abuse, contraception, cross dressing, female genital mutilations, homosexuality, Internet abuse, masturbation, paedophilia, perverts, premarital sex, pornography, prostitution, rape, satanic abuse, serial sex killers, sex addiction, sex crimes, sex fiends, sex trafficking, sexualization, slum sex, teenage sex, terrorism, transgender, venereal diseases/sexually transmitted disease, Vatican abuse, veiling, video nasties, women – all kinds but usually 'bad'.

Masturbation, for example, was the object of mass hysteria from the mid-eighteenth century till the mid-twentieth century; prostitution and sex trafficking have long histories of being the objects of moral crusades, well documented since the nineteenth century when the fear of white sex slaves was the precursor of the modern fear of sex trafficking. Homosexuality has been a popular focus, and the showcase UK trial was that of Oscar Wilde in the Victorian period. Sex crimes became major

> panics from the 1930s onwards; teenage sex hit the headlines in
> the 1950s; AIDS became a major global epidemic of the 1980s
> (syphilis had been an earlier focus). These days, 'paedophilia' has
> been orchestrated as public enemy number one.[37]

debate; in Pakistan, the 'tribal' murder in 2008 of a young woman
over a 'love marriage' (suggesting female autonomy) was a threat to
the 'safety of an orthodox male order'.[38] Indeed, in many Muslim
countries, moral panics have also recently developed around the
breaking of the changing dress code. In Africa, such panics have
been shown to have direct links to the Christian Right in the USA,
which funds, campaigns and colonizes 'African values'.[39] Moral
panics, it seems, are going global. But in turn this raises new problems of misappropriation, as Western cultures use these stories for
their own ends, often to stigmatize other religions and cultures.[40]

   Despite their global topicality today, the purity crusades of
modern times do go back a long way: there is nothing new about
them. Jeffrey Richards's study of 'persecuting societies' looks at
sexual minorities in the Middle Ages (homosexuals, prostitutes,
Jews, lepers, witches, heretics), finding them all to be the objects
of sex fears; Richards claims that history may be characterized by
'recurrent periods of seismic change' when dominant values are
challenged. 'All', he suggests, 'have involved the idea of rebellion
and rejection of the dominant ideology and all have been followed
by periods of repression and retrenchment.'[41] The great American
sociologist Barrington Moore Jr. (1913–2005) takes an even wider
historical span. He spent the latter years of his life studying moral
purity and persecution to show that purity wars have occurred
throughout history. Manifestly, they can be found in the Old
Testament; Moore claimed that the collective search for purity
shows a high correlation with Christianity as opposed to some
other religions like Buddhism, Hinduism or Confucianism, all of
which show less concern with moral purity.[42]

Vulnerable sexualities

In the making of these moral purity crusades and the drawing of 'sexual boundaries', a great deal is at stake. On the surface, conflicts seem to be *instrumental*: they are about achieving 'rational' goals such as resisting modern secular trends, stopping abortion, preventing contraception, regulating same-sex relations, controlling sex criminals, banning pornography or prohibiting sex work. But often these conflicts go much deeper, tapping into both *symbolic*, more personal matters and wider *structural* contradictions and traumas. Thus, despite the public accounts, there may also be hidden motives, suggesting scapegoating, moral indignation, *ressentiment*, panic, fear, or breakdown of honour (often these days such fears are given topical names: like homophobia – invented around 1973 – and Islamophobia – invented in the mid-1990s). They also have social foundations: defending class, gender or religious interests, for example.

Many studies of religious rebellion or modern terrorists have found people and groups to be 'fragile, vulnerable and under siege'. Often they found that 'the modern idea of secular nationalism had let them down'.[43] Overwhelmingly, terrorists are men. We are only at the beginning of coming to terms with the various vulnerabilities, anxieties and fears that underpin these panics, but if cosmopolitanism is to advance we need a better understanding of them. Box 5.3 suggests some pathways.

It will come as no surprise to anybody who studies human beings to sense the almost shocking fragility on which many lives are built: of our perpetual vulnerability, of a sense of an ontological self that is precarious and dependent upon others and the social world for its meanings and stability. Some theorists have suggested that this precariousness – this 'ontological insecurity' – is a feature of the modern world, but I suspect this is an error. Modernity will bring its own specific ambivalences; but insecurity is surely present in humans across all cultures and all history. This is a strong claim and this is not the place to develop such an argument fully. Suffice to say, though, that we now have hundreds of threads of ideas – from anthropology, psychiatry, history, sociology, literature,

5.3   *Life is not easy*:
Sampling a multiplicity of humanity's
perpetual vulnerabilities

The world is riddled with much suffering, fear and anxiety, which become the sources of widespread human conflict and panic. They pose potentials for disruption to human life and reveal our perpetual vulnerability. Amongst these sources are:

1 *Bodies*: our anxiety over natality and mortality – birth, death and illness.
2 *Material need*: our anxiety over brute 'bare' subsistence – food, shelter, clothing.
3 *Meaning*: our problems in the search for making sense of it all – religions, philosophies, wisdoms.
4 *Relationships*: our anxieties over balancing autonomy and individuality with connectedness and belonging (friends and love).
5 *Environment*: our anxieties over security – fears of fire, flooding, earthquake, tsunami, environmental/climate change.
6 *Change*: our fears of having to live with both personal change and cultural and social change, even as change is never ending.
7 *Hierarchy*: our fears of rank, status and position in the unequal 'pecking order'.
8 *Pasts*: our anxieties generated personally by a past life (bereavement, violence) and culturally through societies damaged (in war, slavery, financial crisis, holocaust, violence), both of which can generate 'cultural trauma'.
9 *Gender identity*: our anxieties in locating ourselves, of knowing who we are – which is especially (but not exclusively) linked to gender (being a man, being a woman).
10 *Complexity*: our fears of multiplicity, variety and difference and the preference for homogeneity and sameness.

Each of these has the potential for generating enormous suffering and anxiety.[44] To overcome many of them, we often deploy a very wide range of (often unconscious) personal 'defence mechanisms': we deny, we repress, we reject, we project, we displace, we sublimate. We engage in reaction formation. At the same time, society creates modes of handling them – and the moral purity crusade is one of them. Social science and research is ready for a full-scale account of these multiple vulnerabilities and their attendant defences. In the modern world, many are exacerbated through the rapidity, prevalence and ambivalence of social change: human worlds become very unsettled. Bodies are transformed, poor lives abound, meanings are questioned, new forms of relationships are in the making, climate change unsettles, inequalities are prevalent, and in many countries people are living with cultural trauma derived from past histories of violence – they live with 'ghosts' and the troubles of generational ancestors.

Notably, too, as gender is transformed, anxiety is heightened about what it means to be a man and a woman across the world. Michael Kimmel writes of 'angry white American men' who have developed an 'aggrieved entitlement'; others speak of a 'gender-based explosion' in violence and terrorism as the traditional masculinity and patriarchy of some Islam is put under great threat.[45] Amartya Sen (2006) suggests that many cling to simple, 'solitarist', unitary categories – and it is our inability to grasp the complexity of human categories and their rich multiplicity that underpins much of contemporary world violence.

Somehow, to reduce conflict, we have to understand the perpetual vulnerabilities of all human beings. Life is not easy.[46]

music, religion, philosophy, art – that, taken together, lead to this conclusion. We know that our vulnerabilities and the defences we develop around them are key issues of human social life, and we need to appreciate this as we grasp the nature of sex regulation and fears. Cosmopolitan sexualities will always be put at risk by the vulnerabilities created by our bodies and our cultures that create fears around sexuality.

And surely it is with our human sexualities and genders that we can reach very deeply into the heart of these vulnerable humanities. This is not news. For the French intellectual Georges Bataille (1897–1962) the key function of eroticism is to 'destroy the self-contained character of the participators as they are in their normal lives'; for the North American sociologist Murray Davis (1940–2007), sex brings the possibility of the 'destruction of the individual': the 'lascivious shift' into a 'sensual slide into erotic reality' that breaks up conventional worlds of time, space and bodies; and for the feminist Gayle Rubin, sex negativism is a fear of what sexuality might and can do to us.[47] It was probably the mad and imprisoned, brutalized and brutalizing Marquis de Sade who gave us the first clear modern documentation of its potential for danger. Of course, all civilizations have known this, which is why it is usually so highly regulated. Human sexualities can create a dangerous precipice.

These dangers from sex come from many directions. For sex lies at the core of human biological reproduction; it is the intimate bond to human child care; it raises the universal incest taboo; it reaches deeply into interpersonal relationships, making them full of potential joy, but also of pain and hate; it is a source of great human pleasure, but also so close to great human rage and violence; it is a source of disease and illness; it lies at the heart of gender regulation and social reproduction; it links into some of the basest fears of what it means to be animal-like and human at the same time. It can be psychologically frightening, physically disturbing and socially disruptive. For some, it provokes disgust, shame, dishonour. No wonder we have to control the anxieties that sexualities generate.[48]

Looking ahead

Cosmopolitanism, then, has to come to terms with this inevitability of human vulnerability and anxiety, even as it also has to come to terms with the deep, global inevitability of human conflict (including human sexual conflict) and the universal need for norms (including sexual norms). With gender and sexual conflict, we are rarely if ever speaking of simple rational debate, but rather, of embodied emotions, and even psychic rage, in the service of various anxieties and economic and status interests. Nor are these conflicts likely to go away; cosmopolitanism has to persistently understand the sources, shapes and complexities of these fears. Ironically, conflict, within limits, can sometimes also be functional and important for groups and societies: it can create bonds, maintain group identities, clarify arguments, channel stress and distress. But ultimately it is damagingly destructive and the challenge is to find ways of reducing conflict: of negotiating around it, of creating bridges of reconciliation, of enhancing the respect for different others, of developing universal peace processes. And all this, while at the same time recognizing the need for boundaries. None of this is easy, as any peace negotiator, reconciliation organizer or conflict manager will soon tell you. And so I go in tentative pursuit of all this in the next and final chapter.

6

Communicative Sexualities: On the Hope and Empathy for a Common Global Humanity

What most horrifies me in life is our brutal ignorance of one another.
William James, 'On a Certain Blindness in Human Beings' (1899)

Another world is possible and urgently needed.
Global Justice Movement

A key to living with human variety lies with good communications and relationships: their breakdown can lead to the squandering of much human social life. Through a skewing of power relations, communication becomes impossible, or at least one-sided, leading to the brutal ignorance referred to by James in the quote opening this chapter. People are spoken down to: there is no dialogue, no self-awareness, no empathy, no reflexivity, ultimately no compassion. There is only monologue, hostility, rage and often violence. As our communication falls apart, so our human vulnerability comes further under siege and we face broken-down human life, broken-down human sexualities and, indeed, broken-down cosmopolitan sexualities. My challenge in this closing chapter is to inspect the significance of this communication[1] – personally, interpersonally, culturally, ethically and politically – and to show how grasping its grounded dynamics can help us clarify complex cultures, move to some resolution of perpetual conflicts, generate some common grounds of humanity and sense a little ground for hope. There are no grand solutions here, but they can help nudge us towards a little more understanding of how to approach both cosmopolitan and inclusive sexualities as we struggle to make a better world for all.

Empathic sexualities

I start with empathy because it is the bedrock of communication. And in Harper Lee's classic story *To Kill a Mockingbird* (1960) we are taken to the heart of the matter. The lawyer Atticus Finch gives his tomboy daughter Scout some key advice for life: 'If you can learn a simple trick, Scout, you'll get along a lot better with all kinds of folks. You never really understand a person until you consider things from his point of view, until you climb inside of his skin and walk around in it.'

Empathy lies at the core of our humanity. It is this ability to 'climb into the skin' of another person and see the world from their point of view as deeply as we can that takes us to the heart of the cosmopolitan imagination. It helps link us to a family of connected ideas: the pluralities of human affiliations, the recognition of 'others', role-taking and sympathy. Ultimately, it can lead us to the compassionate life. Without these, cosmopolitanism simply can't work at all. Empathy becomes the closest companion of cosmopolitanism, humanizing us, civilizing us, making for a better world. And the same is true of our sexual lives: empathic sexualities means that we grasp something of the sexual life of those we engage with, we can see the sexual world from 'within their skin'. Again, this helps humanize our sexualities.

Much has been said about empathy, and its study straddles many disciplines and approaches.[2] The philosopher Michael Slote, for example, sees it as the foundation of social care; the therapist Simon Baron-Cohen places it in a 10-step neurological 'empathy circuit' at the heart of his understanding of human cruelty and kindness. Indeed, it is prominent in many strands of modern psychoanalysis.

Kohut suggests that 'empathy does indeed in essence define the field of our observations'.[3] The political scientist Michael Morrell links empathy and democracy to connect to a deliberative democratic reasoning; the psychologist Martin Hoffman discusses the implication of his developmental theory of empathy for social justice; and it is a core theme in Mark Haddon's hugely successful story and play *The Curious Incident of the Dog in the Night-Time*. The neuroscientists Jean Decety and William Ickes have edited a volume that suggests the biological centrality of empathy; and in bestselling blockbusters, Jeremy Rifkin and Steven Pinker claim boldly that as societies move forward they accelerate their empathic potentials. A lot, then, is being claimed for empathy.[4]

And so it should. While the idea is definitely a prominent one in current Western culture, it is far from just being a Western idea. We find comparable ideas with 'ren' in Confucian writings; with the Buddha urging an enlightenment that will bring wisdom and compassion; and key verses in the Quran describe Allah as empathetic (Surah Tawbah, 9:128) and compassionate (Anbiya, 21:107).[5] Perhaps we have here the elements for a major global ethical theory.

Being cosmopolitan requires practising good ways of enhancing empathy. As we have seen, the significance of empathy starts with the infant child developing an awareness of self and others. This grows through life into what Adam Smith (1758/2000) saw as the 'circle of others', an awareness and sensitivity to those all around, moving slowly outwards from the nearest and closest kin to the widest global circle of the world. (Following the philosopher Fonna Forman-Barzilai we might even talk of this nicely as the 'circle of humanity'.[6]) We need to empathize not only with our next-door neighbours, but also with strangers, across cultures, across religions, across social divisions, across generations, across politics, across honour groups, across all our multiple differences.[7] We can usually empathize with those close in the circle; but a full range of human empathy seems impossible to grasp. It is not easy and probably practically impossible.

The failure or breakdown of empathy is a critical issue and we are on our way to understanding it. Some psychiatrists have started to chart a continuum of empathy where, at the extremes, there are various pathologies ranging from benign (autisms of various kinds) to those that are pathological. Baron-Cohen (2011), for example, suggests factors that make for 'zero-tolerance empathy'; at the other extreme there are those who cultivate intense empathy and compassion for others. But there is another approach that asks not why individuals fail in empathy, but why whole groups of people experience 'empathy breakdown' – for example, in various mass killings, wars and, most famously, the holocaust. How can large numbers of people act in dehumanizing ways with little regard for their mass victims? This remains as pressing a question for our times as it was 60 years ago. (Hannah Arendt's meditations on what she calls 'the banalities of evil' – on how everyday people in Nazi Germany, but elsewhere too, do bad things – are as relevant today as they were when she wrote them.[8])

For some people, empathy is hard to achieve. Perhaps the starting task in developing empathy lies, curiously, with the fostering of a certain gentle self-awareness – to 'know thyself' is, after all, one of the oldest of all wisdoms in philosophical and religious thinking and a precondition of good communication. At the outset of any understanding, it helps to be familiar with our own 'prejudices' and 'horizons' (or limits of our thinking), those biases that might be shaping both the ways we live in the world and the outcomes of our dialogues. There are many helpful ideas like this across the world: mindfulness and awareness in Buddhism, self-awareness in both Judaism and Islam. These biases often arise out of our past vulnerabilities and experiences, creating current defences and weak spots. While it may be hard to function without them, it is very necessary to be aware of them.[9] And in communications about human sexuality, the backdrop becomes our own sexual lives, histories and fears. We need a 'coming to terms' with our own sexualities before we are really open and ready for good dialogues with others about sexual politics; and my hunch is that this very rarely happens, because it is so hard in itself. Indeed, it is very hard to imagine our world leaders – or our local terrorists – inspecting their stances and personal sexual lives with much critical acumen. Too passionate, too committed, too busy – the reflecting self is often absent. And the sexual self is rarely analysed. But if we are to move on, it is surely necessary to focus on this for a little while.

This said, the ultimate need is to go beyond all this and take very seriously the problem of empathy with our adversaries and enemies: with those who do damage, like the terrorist or the fanatic, or those who create dehumanized sexualities. How can we empathize with the intolerant, the rapist, the abuser, the sexual murderer? How can we empathize with honour crimes? Hard as it is, empathizing with adversaries is a necessary route to cosmopolitanism. It was Gandhi's thinking when he declared, 'I am a Muslim! And a Hindu, and a Christian and a Jew' (during the conflicts between Muslims and Hindus that led up to Indian independence in 1947). Much more lightly, Paul Knitter captures it in his 2013 book *Without Buddha I Could Not Be a Christian*. It has led me to ponder how the quiet contemplative worlds of 'Muslim women' could be connected to the sexualized transgressive world of, say, Lady Gaga. And how the radical Jihadist world of terrorists can be connected with the worlds of gay weddings. Some can make the journey of understanding across such worlds; most probably fail.

After 9/11, many in the West had to struggle to make sense of so-called Muslim cultures, which were so readily presented to us by our political leaders and media as an 'enemy other'. Sadly, politicians and media are often not to be trusted as leaders in these matters. I was friends with a few Muslims, knew a little about the diversity across some 50 Muslim nations and had visited some of them. But I really knew very little and so I embarked upon a short programme of reading 'good stories' about them. Here I found the 'ethnographies of sexualities' (see Chapter 4) very valuable. Conducted carefully by social researchers, they afforded me real insight into the diversity of Muslim sexualities and gender. Thus, Lila Abu-Lughod introduced me to the world of women in a Bedouin tribe, showing the struggle to uphold 'honour' (*'agl*) and 'modesty' (*hasham*) through poetry, resisting tribal hierarchy through rebellion in myriad quiet ways. I learnt that there were many pious Muslim women who resisted the victim model that had been forced upon them by the West. In stark contrast, Evelyn Blackwood guided me into a very different world of Muslim women in Indonesia: the Tombois, who are masculine females who identify as men and desire women, while their girlfriends view themselves as normal women who desire men. Both are contradictory practices that draw upon but subvert both conventional

Islamic and international notions of men and women. Meanwhile, I learnt from Marcia Inhorn's research on infertility amongst Arab men that many of these men are a long way from any violent and macho stereotype and struggle sensitively and caringly with their loving wives over problems of infertility. Here was the 'New Arab Man' who was developing new forms of masculinity in the face of a changing world. I learnt too from Momin Rahman – an English Pakistani Muslim queer – about active 'gay and lesbian' Muslims in the West confronting both homophobia and Islamophobia simultaneously: under attack from two fronts. I learnt of the struggles with modernizing sexualities from many Muslim voices.[10]

I even read interview accounts from terrorists that helped me to see the religious basis that inspired their killing sprees. Jessica Stern, a leading expert on terrorism, published interviews with extremist members from three religions around the world, coming face to face with people who willingly kill others with the passionate conviction that they are doing it for their God.[11] (Stern herself also comes under attack for even trying to do this research – why should terrorists be understood?) Her book is a vivid and important portrayal of empathy at work. And yet the modern terrorist she describes would stand against everything that cosmopolitan sexualities, and this book, is about: humanism, feminism, global governance, pluralism, open religion. Here is an extremist view built out of faith and religion that simply *has* to save the world from itself. And I have to understand it. I have to sense their grievances, their desperation, their alienation, their humiliation, even as I dislike their actions. Only then can we move on.

Bit by bit I was helped to see other worlds different from mine. The stories and narratives became the basis for the building of an emerging empathy. And I am reminded of Martha Nussbaum's much-celebrated book *Cultivating Humanity* (1997), which helped show the significance of 'the narrative imagination' that is found through reading great literature both in the West and in cultures around the world. Nowadays, we can see the development of courses on 'Education for a World Community' aiming to start a 'Great Civilized Conversation'.[12] Here, Islamic, Indian, Chinese, African, Japanese and Western sources start to be put together into a revised curriculum that privileges plural humanity and civilization over one culture. 'Reading global literature' (which includes global film, documentary, art and music) can become an ethical act: an imaginative way of building empathy and thinking through our relationships to others across the world. Global stories, including ethnographies of sexualities, can work to inspire a 'global moral imagination', foster dialogue, expand horizons and facilitate the cosmopolitan imagination providing 'world sympathy biographies' where we appreciate the moral dilemmas of global life.[13] Ultimately, as Robert Coles nicely claims, they help us in 'handing one another along'.[14]

Narrative sexualities

Narratives are the basic resource open to a group or a society for building understandings. They become the air we breathe. Human beings are born into narrative worlds and dwell in a 'grand conversation' from birth to death. Narratives become tools for the conflicts we face. They are restorative in our sufferings, as they become our memories, our biographies and our life companions. They create connections between our innermost worlds and the wider public worlds in which we live. They can constitute a feeling of belonging, of creating a sense of the history and the communities we inhabit. These communities can be local or national, ethnic and gendered. And they can be sexual.[15]

Sexual stories help give meaning to human sexuality, enabling us to be distinctively human. It links our feelings to our doings, our languages to our bodies, the personal to the political, and our being to our communities. Above all, sexual stories help us to bridge the local micro-sexual culture (of who we are and what we do) with the wider more abstract sexual meta-culture. So sexual stories provide one of the key pathways into cosmopolitan sexualities, creating ways of appreciating cultural complexities and making sense of conflict. Through them we hear 'different sexual voices' and gain a wider grasp of the moral and sexual universes in which we all live. They can lead us ultimately to develop *narrative empathy* (appreciating sexual lives through stories), *narrative dialogue* (understanding the interactive nature of stories), *narrative ethics* (grasping the dilemmas of ethical sexualities from the practical stories of people's lives) and *narrative politics* (activating the role of stories in sexual politics). More than this, they enable us to seek out the contrasts between *dominant stories* (told by the ever distorting dominant media, etc.), *counter-stories* (that resist these dominant tales), the *putative stories* (which could be told but are not yet) and *the silenced stories* (those not allowed to be told).[16]

Sexual stories can be found throughout history and across cultures, speaking to our different sexual and gendered worlds, enabling us to sense both our common humanities and our different worlds. They can be found in anything from folklore and fairy tales to great religious tracts; from literature and drama to pottery, music and dance; from life stories and diaries to photographs, film and video. And nowadays they are to be found through the digital narratives of world websites and YouTube videos, on global social network sites and tweets. The multiplicities of sexual story forms are now global, everywhere to be found as they weave their way through social life – plotting, shaping and ordering their vast complexities while connecting us together. Sexual stories now circulate the world.

Now, these sexual stories can lift what were once private tales into the public world, transforming and reorganizing the public knowledge and political awareness of sexual worlds. The creation in the late twentieth century of 'gay stories' and 'rape stories' made sexual stories into public issues in the West, and the question is whether they can travel well. There is some evidence that they can, as social movements across the world use similar stories suitably localized to create their own challenges. Gay stories developed in London soon find their way to Jakarta or Rio, where they will be suitably transformed.

For example, in India in 2012, the Delhi bus gang rape case became a major global public story. A 23-year-old woman, Jyoti Singh, was raped on a bus by six other passengers coming home from seeing a film. She subsequently died from the attack. It was picked up as a national story in India, and went digitally global. One feminist activist and writer, Eve Ensler, formed One Billion Rising, a campaign to end global violence against women and girls.

She writes, hopefully, that 'India is really leading the way for the world' in confronting this global issue. She comments:

> Having worked every day of my life for the last 15 years on sexual violence, I have never seen anything like that, where sexual violence broke through the consciousness and was on the front page, nine articles in every paper every day, in the center of every discourse, in the center of the college students' discussions, in the center of any restaurant you went in. And I think what's happened in India, India is really leading the way for the world. It's really broken through. They are actually fast-tracking laws. They are looking at sexual education. They are looking at the bases of patriarchy and masculinity and how all that leads to sexual violence.

In September 2013, Jyoti Singh's assailants were found guilty.[17]

Many such stories are now appearing around the world. Ten years earlier, in Pakistan in 2002, the case of Mukhtār Māʾīm also became a global story. She was the victim of a gang rape motivated by honour revenge and her story became iconic: with a biography (*In the Name of Honour*), a documentary film (*After the Rape*), and a social movement (Mukhtar Mai Women's Welfare Organization). The story is used as a case study in the works of many researchers.[18] In Africa, the story of David Kato (born 1964, murdered January 2011) has become emblematic of Uganda's struggles over gay rights. A Ugandan teacher and gay rights activist, he was murdered – after winning a lawsuit against a Ugandan tabloid newspaper *Rolling Stone* – which called for him to be executed. He became a cause célèbre around the world.[19] And across the world, many complications of plural gender regularly become a major focus of storytelling. Maryam Khatoon Molkara was a prominent 'transgender' case in Iran in the 1970s; Bülent Ersoy was a popular singer in Turkey who underwent a sex change in the early 1980s, setting in motion a debate and a change in laws; Dana International was an Israeli Jew with roots in Yemen who won the Eurovision song contest in 1998; and Caster Semenya was the South African athlete who won the women's 800-metre race at the 2009 International Association of Athletics World Championship in Berlin and was given 'the gender test', raising the global issue of what it means to be a man or a woman.[20] And the story of Malala Yousafzai has become a bestseller, bringing the plight of girls and education to millions.[21] Celebrity stories of sex and gender are now global stories.

But, again, along with this cultivation of empathy, we have to learn limits. Personal stories often fail to tell us about wider structural matters. Some stories reach well beyond our imaginative horizons, breaking boundaries we can't be pushed beyond. And many stories may not be readily translatable from one culture to another. Many devout Christians and Muslims reading stories or watching films about contrasting cultures, for example, can face enormous difficulties with all this.

Dialogic sexualities

With a focus on empathy and storytelling in place, it then becomes important to recognize the *power of dialogues*. The Russian philosopher and literary critic Mikhail Bakhtin (1895–1975) has (along with many others) put this well:

> Life by its very nature is dialogic. To live means to participate in dialogue: to ask questions, to heed, to respond, to agree, and so forth. In this dialogue a person participates wholly and throughout his whole life: with his eyes, lips, hands, soul, spirit, with his whole body and deeds. He invests his entire self in discourse, and this discourse enters into the dialogic fabric of human life, into the world symposium . . . Truth is not born nor is it to be found inside the head of an individual person, it is born between people collectively searching for truth, in the process of their dialogic interaction.[22]

Dialogue and dialogic sexualities suggest neither monologue nor simple debate. Rejecting 'one view only' or 'two sides to every argument' posturing, human social life is seen as a much more creative, reciprocal and collaborative affair. There can then be no immediate taking of simple sides. Dialogues flow together – a swaying to and fro, an indeterminacy, a subtlety, a complexity. It leads to establishing workable ways for communicating together across our differences, accepting the inevitability of conflicts while aiming to reduce them. And human sexualities are also part of this 'dialogic fabric' as people set into motion a conversation and reciprocity of emotions and bodies.

Dialogues are everywhere. Ironically, 2001 – the year of 9/11 – was designated the 'United Nations Year of Dialogue among Civilizations' (a term invented by the Iranian President Mohammad Khatami a few years earlier). And we can find dialogues of nations, interfaith dialogues and dialogues of genders and ethnicity. Dialogic sexualities focuses on the communications between people in sexual relations. All require recognition of the inevitability of one's own biases, respect for the other and attempts to fuse horizons. They also require empathy, an appreciation of stories, a common search for a common ground and an awareness of power. And often, when all seems to be failing, dialogues can require a light touch. Recognizing the inevitability of disagreement, the challenge is always to create some kind of dialogic civility. Box 6.1 summarizes some key features of this.

But many refuse to engage in dialogic civility with their enemies. A Hamas terrorist whose children have been killed by an Israeli cannot sit comfortably around the same table with the enemy. An orthodox Muslim male can hardly be in the same space as an unorthodox feminist. A queer activist might squirm in the presence of a Roman Catholic fundamentalist. A radical anti-porn woman would be outraged in the presence of radical sex worker sluts. A social worker who works with abused children would be uncomfortable with a paedophile. But should this always be so? To recall a comment cited earlier (Chapter 1) by Philip Kitcher: 'Ethics is something people work out together; and in the end the only authority is that of their conversation' (2011: 411).

So 'getting people around the table' to have this very reciprocal conversation is a key issue. We can see it happening in dialogues around the world – like the Regional Dialogues on Sexuality and Geopolitics held in Asia, Latin America and Africa in 2009–10, which brought together groups to map these complexities; but such dialogues do not usually bring strongly opposing views to the table.[29] The real challenge is not mere differences and variety, but

6.1   *Dialogues*: The twelve pillars for dialogic civility over cosmopolitan sexualities

1   Recognize all of the different voices engaged around this issue (and certainly not just the dominant groups or the polarized spokespeople).[23]

2   Avoid dehumanizing, degrading, mocking or silencing 'the other'.

3   Develop an awareness of the inequalities and the differences of power between speakers.

4   Appreciate the different social backgrounds and group belongings of participants – what religions, family, etc., means to them.

5   Understand the differences across groups in arguing: Western 'argument culture' does not travel well. Authoritarian cultures do not readily live with debate. Develop plural voices rather than 'oppositional views'.[24]

6   Comprehend language differences, being aware that some terms may be untranslatable and even incommensurable.

7   Reflect on your own personal prejudice and location in all this.

8   Grasp personal enmities: often there are personal likes and dislikes involved.[25]

9   Understand the emotional and embodied basis (and history) of much life and talk.

10   Engage in reciprocity and learn the skills of negotiating conflict transformation, trust and reconciliation.[26]

11   Maintain a sense of lightness: keep a sense of balance, humour, modesty, humanity.[27]

12   Search for common grounds that can be agreed upon. Often the humanist values of empathy, dignity, care, justice and human flourishing can serve as a starting point: start with what might be agreed upon before entering the conflicts and differences.[28]

hatred and enemies. Often this is of a very personal nature and is hard to manage.

Ultimately, though, the problem of power raises its very ugly head at the face-to-face level. The influential radical Brazilian educationalist Paulo Freire (1972) highlights how the invitation to dialogue and empathy is not really possible between people of unequal power. Cosmopolitan sexualities – and dialogic sexualities – need to work for the powerless, not for those in power. So dialogue for Freire is only valuable as a mechanism where those without a voice can be heard. The emphasis is placed on listening carefully to the oppressed and learning from them: the dialogue should not be used as a tool for continuing the dominance of the elite and their subject's silence. (Freire is especially critical of academics and professionals who persistently ignore this.) Dialogical sexualities minimally means recognizing power relations and taking the partner seriously.

Ethical sexualities

Cosmopolitan sexualities are engaged in the major search for the shared narratives of a common humanity of ethical relationships, where people can practically live together convivially and reciprocally with their many differences, including their sexual, gender, ethnic and other differences, bound together by threads of care, empathy, dignity, well-being and justice and tempered by rationality. Partially, and perhaps surprisingly, this means constructing and making visible and public what many people across the world already struggle to tacitly live by. For on an everyday basis in many parts of the world, people do indeed deploy basic routines and rituals that suggest a common humanity whenever they can; they live their daily lives in a complex conviviality of kindness, respect, care and fairness that is echoed in the writings of the more abstract – including religious – thinkers. I hope we may all have at least seen glimpses of such conviviality, and that some are fortunate enough to experience it for themselves. 'Humanity' is that curious thing that often brings us together to help each other in times of serious crisis. Rebecca's Solnit's elegant and important work *A Paradise Built in Hell* (2009), for example, shows very clearly the ways in which people living through disasters reveal kindness, resourcefulness and generosity in the midst of crisis and grief. It might involve the simplest everyday conversation, where a mutual bond holds people together. Maybe, just maybe, there are some common threads of value here. Maybe there is a common human dignity. I am suggesting that there are certain ways of being in the world, like treating each other with more or less equal respect in day to day life, and certain values like the Golden Rule (one should treat others as one would like others to treat oneself, or negatively: one should not treat others in ways that one would not like to be treated) that are fairly common in everyday groupings across most cultures.

And all this hints at a grounded cosmopolitan ethics that recall the values I have suggested before (see Chapter 1, pp. 32–6). To repeat: some of the common-ground humanist values we struggle with in daily situations include:

- *A common human caring* – of looking after each other, belonging to some groups and identifying with them, but also looking after others not so close, and even the environment. There is surely an affinity here to what is commonly called 'love'.
- *A common human struggle for empathy* – valuing the need to under- stand and dialogue with each other. There is an affinity here to what is commonly called 'compassion'.
- *A common human dignity* – the basic common human right to recognize human worth and to live a life without unique dif- ferences. There is a link here with rights, but rights alone will not do.
- *A common sense of human fairness* – of basic freedoms, equality and justice.
- *A common sense of human flourishing* - of enabling all people to live full, good lives.

Again, this is tentative. There are no grand claims here: we have to start somewhere.[30] As we live in little worlds of empathy, dignity, human rights, social justice, human flourishing and everyday care and kindness, can we work to enhance this more and more – and in the process also transform our sexualities? Can we stimulate a cosmopolitan imaginary for a better sexual world for the coming generations?

Caring sexualities:
global 'love' and violence reduction for all

William James once asked his uncle: what is a life for? And he was told: three things in human life are important. The first is to be kind. The second is to be kind. And the third is to be kind.[31] And this broadly is a key principle of humanism, suggesting that a guideline for human sexualities is to be a kind and caring sexualities. Highlighting a cluster of linked values, it focuses on the ways we look after each other and the world. It indicates the importance of kindness, embodied care, generosity, compassion, altruism, security, 'repairing the world', love. Centrally, it is concerned with the human bond: of how people interconnect with each other, care for – even love – each other. It is often compared with the Confucian concept of *jen/ren*. The Beatles, it seems, got it right: 'all you need is love'. And this care and love brings its own ontology, ethics, practices and politics.[32]

In Chapter 1, I argued that this ontology of care derives from the fact that we are born into dependency, have to be looked after and then learn as best we can to look after others.[33] At a wider level this means a kind of responsibility to the world, to look after it. In her now classic study of care, Joan Tronto claims that care is 'a species of activity that includes everything we do to maintain, contain, and repair our "world" so that we can live in it as well as possible. That world includes our bodies, ourselves, and our environment.'[34] Our sexualities are surely but a part of this needy, caring repairing ontology. This means getting people to sense the universal importance of treating each other well in sexual relationships. It makes sexual cruelty one of its prime enemies (along with the wider structures that promote this perpetual cruelty, violence, war and hatred). It claims that sexual kindness is morally superior to sexual violence. And it is really only in recent times that the battle to outlaw sexual violence in all its forms has become explicit and got under way across the world. Now we see campaigns, not just against rape, but against many other forms of violence (like hate crimes, genital mutilation and homophobic violence) coming to global attention. Often, they raise big issues about gender and the link between women and care and men and violence. For the province of sexual violence is heavily linked to hegemonic masculinities. And all this points to the need for new and more flexible versions of 'being a man'. These issues are now firmly on the agenda in a way they were not 100 years ago.

Global gender and sexual rights: dignity for all

Rodrigue Tremblay suggests that the first humanist rule is: 'Proclaim the natural dignity and inherent equality of all human beings in all places and in all circumstances.'[35] And this most surely must also mean proclaiming gender and sexual dignity and equality. There are many problems with both these ideas, as we have seen, but the right of every person on the planet to their valued humanity and their dignity just has to be a core common ground on which agreement has to be found; and sexuality and gender deserve the same treatment. This 'right to human dignity' might flow from our god(s), our nation(s), our social movement(s) or any other group we wish to list. But a claim like this must be made, for it is a strong and necessary claim. It is the bedrock of our humanity. It must not be mere rhetoric, but actual practice; and it does mean that movements against human dignity and rights have to be challenged as anti-human. That said, the good news is that this is indeed increasingly the claim most likely to be agreed upon by quite a few states across the world, and the one that is advancing, if slowly (even as it is resisted by horrendous death and slaughter). The language of human dignity and rights is the gestating world-wide *lingua franca* of much of humanity. Contested as it may be from many sides, it has nevertheless spread to the farthest corners of the globe. We now have the Universal Islamic Declaration of Human Rights (1981), the African Charter on Human and People's Rights (1981), the Cairo Declaration of Human Rights

(1990) and the ASEAN Human Rights Declaration (2012). There are of course major exceptions: there exist many ideological tensions and radical groups who oppose humanism and rights, as well as broad principles and conventions that fail to be put into practice.

Furthermore, battles have been raging in the United Nations since the 1990s over the very ideas of 'sexual rights'.[36] An uneven start was made across many countries of the world concerning the right to dignified sexualities. Twenty years later, in 2006, the Yogyakarta Principles were developed and unanimously adopted by a distinguished group of human rights experts, providing binding international legal standards with which all states must comply on issues of sexual orientation and gender identity. In a speech on Human Rights Day 2010, the Secretary-General also expressed his concern:

> As men and women of conscience, we reject discrimination in general, and in particular discrimination based on sexual orientation and gender identity . . . Where there is a tension between cultural attitudes and universal human rights, rights must carry the day. Together, we seek the repeal of laws that criminalize homosexuality, that permit discrimination on the basis of sexual orientation or gender identity, that encourage violence.[37]

Flourishing sexualities: actualizing 'good lives' for all

A further humanistic principle highlights capabilities and human flourishing: it takes seriously what people value as their own goals and ways of achieving such goals, hoping to create a world with good life for *all*. It looks for the development of social institutions and structures that create opportunities to help *all* members to realize their potentials. I stress '*all*' because historically this flourishing has only been for a few: the elites. Starting at least with both Confucius and Aristotle, this principle asks how a good life could be lived and what kind of society will produce it. All the religious traditions (from Confucius to the Dali Lama) pose this question and provide suggested answers to it, often in the form of commandments, from which we can learn. But the principle is also to be found in social science – in Abraham Maslow's (1943) 'self-actualization theory', in Eric Fromm's 'art of being' (1993), in 'positive psychology', in contemporary virtue philosophy and happiness theory, and others. The most recent and widely used modern Western version of this 'virtue' theory is to be found in the influential work of Martha Nussbaum and the prize-winning economist Amartya Sen (the work of both these authors has helped to shape the United Nations Human Development Index (HDI)). Here, we start to look for ways of developing structural or social opportunities to lead fulfilling lives. Moving away from this largely economic understanding that often dominates discussions, Nussbaum and Sen both ask about human capabilities and the social conditions under which they can flourish. Traditionally, 'capability theorists' ask 'What is each person able to do and to be?'[38] To this we might ask a linked question: how might each person flourish sexually – become the sexual person they are able to be?

I must be careful. On the surface, books on human sexual flourishing and exploration abound. A book search would soon reveal titles like *Good Sex, How to Have Great Sex, Supersex for Life, The Greatest Sex Tips in the World, How to Blow Her Mind in Bed, Pocket Sex*; or more specialist books: *Unzipped – How to Give the Perfect Blow Job, The Ultimate Guide to Cunnilingus*. There are hundreds of such books on the market. But of course this is not at all what I am talking about here. These books express a narrow view that focuses on limited behavioural sex acts; and I am much more concerned to pose questions about the ways in which human sexual relationships work their way into a flourishing life.

I am concerned that, for many, the worlds of human sexualities connect so readily with lives that are 'wretched', 'damaged', 'depleted' and lacking in any kind of 'quality' (even as some follow the 'greatest sex tips in the world'). I am concerned with the bridge between human well-being, 'happiness' and sexuality: of joy and suffering; resilience; what – even – might be meant by the good life and the wasted life; what are human capabilities and potentials; and what might be a 'virtuous' life. If we follow this line of thought, we face the biggest challenge of all and it would probably subsume the others. Working for good lives and flourishing lives for all takes some doing. This will never be easy – even as there are those who make it seem so.[39] Still, a partial utopian list may help a little. A good and rounded sexuality might include some of the following:

- *Bodily health.* This would include good reproductive and sexual health.
- *Bodily integrity.* This would include being able to secure one's body against assault, including sexual assault, marital rape, homophobic attack, genital mutilation, online harassment, media defamation and domestic violence. It would also mean the ability to have opportunities for sexual satisfaction and for choice in matters of reproduction.[40] This listing hints at the unacceptability of those groups and cultures that condone all kinds of sexual violence and coercive bodily violation. And in fact there are many of those around today.
- *Attachments and affiliations.* This would mean being able to bond and connect intimately with others, and to love those who love and care for us, as well as being able to grieve at their absence. Being human is bound up with this ability to form good close, intimate human associations and, in their strongest forms, to be able to balance autonomy and belonging: and '*to love*'.
- *Emotions.* This would include an ability to experience a full spectrum of emotions linked with sexualities without becoming blighted by them. It also means an ability to come to terms with anxieties, handling abuse and trauma, recognizing issues of honour and shame. In short, being able both to live with and handle emotional, sexual life.
- *Play.* This would mean recognizing that human sexualities have a range of goals and functions: pleasure, play, bonding and not just procreation.
- *Senses, imagination* This would suggest a need to bridge our animal-like sexualities into 'truly human ways' and to recognize the significance of fantasy in human sexual life – here is a distinctive sphere. We know humans engage in much sexual fantasy; but we know relatively little about this or how it connects to flourishing lives.

Ultimately, all this means the ability to have control over one's sexuality and body, to be able to discuss and debate different kinds of sexualities, and to help shape the freedom to associate with like minded people and to enter into meaningful and loving relationships with others.[41]

Just sexualities: gender, sexual and social justice for all

In Chapter 1, I suggested that a major principle of humanism directs us towards justice: the longstanding struggles over the centuries for social structures that promote a fairer, autonomous and more equal society, where people are valued and wealth is redistributed. Throughout this book I have shown how global inequalities – pauperization, sexual and gender divisions, ethnicity, violence, etc., – are manifestly linked to our sexualities. For example, with global prostitution and sex work, there is a widespread inequality between richer and usually older men buying the sex of poorer, younger and racially different women. With AIDS/HIV, the market allocation of drugs and prevention favours richer countries: the substantial inequalities of world health are brought to the fore. Global surrogacy shows how babies of the poor are being sold to the rich, along with body parts. There is stratified sex work, stratified AIDS, and stratified reproduction.

Ultimately, then, a broad focus on dignity and rights always has to be complemented with wider concerns over gender justice, sexual justice and a broader social justice. All this raises paradoxes. How we can we have a just sexuality in an unjust world? How can we make sexualities democratic in an undemocratic world? How can we make sexualities free in an unfree world? And how can we make sexualities equal in an unequal world? With great difficulty, is the answer. But it is a call for action. What is required is a focus on changing the inequalities of a wider social order; narrow reformism is limited. Some key areas of action and discussion here will focus on how human freedoms are restricted by intersecting social divisions across class, gender, ethnicity, health, age, sexualities and nationhood; how we can bring about a society with more social justice, redistribution, equalities and freedom – for all, not just the elite few.

Always contentious, often the principles of equality and freedom can move in opposing directions. Humanism has to critically examine both governments and economies to foster both freedom and economic redistribution alongside interpersonal equality. A goal of humanism is to create a just society and build an understanding of a gendered global political economy of cosmopolitan sexualities.[42]

Democratic sexualities

Cosmopolitan sexualities are Janus-faced. They certainly look inwards to daily empathy and interaction; but they must also look outwards to wider communicative political processes and the state. They need to create negotiable states and foster political communication. Cosmopolitanism is deeply bound up with politics and only really works well under certain kinds of political conditions.

A humanist vision of the political process has to be a relational and communicative one. Politics is about empowerment. Loosely defined, power becomes the capability to control one's life (while resisting the control of others). It works *materially* (through access to resources) and *symbolically* (through the words, languages and ideologies we are skilled in); and as a *process* (it flows and is not fixed in one place), it is *interactive* (recognizing minimally two people in interaction), *grounded* (in everyday situations and practices), *embodied*, *multiple* and *structural* (there are broad patterns that guide it). Power is diffuse even as it becomes habitual and congeals in many ways. Power regulates gender, sexuality and class in its congealed forms (as we saw in Chapter 5). Power can take many forms: as coercion, as violence, as exchange, as integrative, as discursive, as persuasion. Cosmopolitanism is, in part, a political theory that has to confront these various forms.[43] A cosmopolitics has to symbolically negotiate between differences, even as it has to confront multiple unequal voices. To put it bluntly: within the cosmopolitan political process, some will get heard, while others will be silenced or be less likely to be heard. The real practical challenge for a radical cosmopolitics is to ensure that voices are heard from the bottom up.[44]

Sexualities are organized through differential political opportunity structures that flow through everyday life. At the broadest social level, cosmopolitan sexualities can only flourish in systems of power that are 'open', not 'closed' or authoritarian. Many of the world's existing political systems have structures that do not encourage openness, so it is well to be clear about this at the outset. How this works in everyday living is what matters though – whether people are crushed and brutalized, or able to create negotiated spaces for their own empowerment. Once again, the journey to cosmopolitan sexualities looks like it is going to be a long, long struggle to achieve.

The most open political systems we know of so far are democracies. Even so, they regularly fail, bring many problems, are open to many corruptions and have certainly been hugely hostile to sexual and gender equality in the past. There is no guarantee here. But in their ideal form, democracies do suggest many wonderful humanist futures: freedom and openness, equality and justice, transparency and trust, citizenship, the representation and civic engagement of the people, recognition of pluralization, aspirations for 'perpetual peace', a certain civility and common grounds for living together, along with conciliatory ways of reconciling conflicts. But these are ideals, rarely achieved.[45] There are also many kinds of democracy beloved by political theorists: so as well as the standard liberal democracy, socialist democracy and participatory democracy, we also now have to reckon with agnostic democracy, deliberative democracy, discursive democracy, thick and thin democracy, digital democracy, radical democracy, even cosmopolitan democracy. Each of these, of course, has its own interminable followers and opponents often living in their own hermetically sealed worlds. Such theories are often poorly grounded in everyday life.[46]

The most widespread position these days is the clumsily called 'neoliberal democracy'. This highlights free markets and competition, personal profits and private ownership, above all else. Wealth flows upwards. For some, it symbolizes the horrors – even decadence – of the greedy, selfish and arrogant capitalist West. On the surface, cosmopolitan sexualities can develop well in these neoliberal democracies because of their emphasis on freedom. Gender equality is relatively greater in them, and their openness means that sexual differences can sometimes find a home there: the rhetoric of 'free speech' and 'freedom of choice' is widespread. Thus, for example, there can be little doubt that most of the 'advances' in legal and political issues on same-sex relationships to date have been taking place in Western democracies. The development of gay marriage can be seen as the strongest case, and it is most starkly revealed in the 'same-sex unions revolution in Western democracies'.[47] Indeed, whenever the claims for a widening argument for democracy are made, so activists frequently find it easier to make the wider claims for gay rights.

But it also suggests that profit markets mean that sex of all kinds carries a price: the commodification of sex discussed in Chapter 2 is rampant. Worse, it also means, as many critics have remarked, a very skewed freedom of the privileged. Neoliberal democracies bring acute problems: they generate vast inequalities, of nations, class, race and gender, which work to restrict and structure choices. Many are excluded, become relatively powerless, and can become part of an international division of labour that seriously disadvantages them. They also live with a media that infantilizes and trivializes their existence, providing them with little real information about the world in which they live. And this means they have fewer resources for making grounded choices, and less control over their gendered and sexual lives.[48]

Although there are surely troubles for cosmopolitan communication under neoliberalism, the prognosis for cosmopolitan sexualities is even worse in many contemporary societies that are today generally viewed as authoritarian, where unquestioned obedience to the state is required. In some of these, absolutist religious affiliations have taken hold and shape the life cycle. A map of the world shows these areas quite clearly: for example, the Middle East and North Africa (MENA) region[49] as well as much of Central Africa, where evangelicals from the USA can often be found. These are regions where political opportunities for gender equality or gay activism are restricted, and where cosmopolitan sexualities cannot easily thrive. In many countries where fundamentalisms are widespread (whether Muslim, Christian, Hindu or whatever), crusades against both women's rights and gay rights can often be found. China and Russia are difficult cases – these are two of the world's largest authoritarian states (China is also the most populous, at some 1.35 billion people), where matters of sexual and gender change are not faring very well. Both states are 'middling' on the Gender-Related Development Index (with Russia 61st and China 88th).[50] China has no anti-gay legislation, and in urban centres gay activism is flourishing. But in general China is a no-go area. Russia is a more negative case. June 2013 saw the adoption of a federal law banning 'homosexual propaganda', creating a thriving climate where human rights violations are frequent and go unpunished. Both Russia and China feature prominently as key 'enemies of the internet'.[51]

There are also 'broken or failed states' that experience chronic breakdown, small chance of any human flourishing, and little hope of cosmopolitan sexualities. Through genocide, civil war and strife, extreme poverty and famine or natural disasters, they become marked by trauma and damage, often having to live with a deep sense of loss and wasted life. These include countries engaged in major conflicts (like Syria, Colombia, Afghanistan), those frequently named 'failed states' (like Sudan, Somalia and the Democratic Republic of the Congo) and those that have suffered recent major 'natural disasters' (like Haiti and the Philippines). It includes large numbers of people who become refugees.[52] Such damage may be short term or long term; but it is clear that such nations provide little opportunity, structure or context for the advance on cosmopolitan sexualities. Indeed, there is a real sense that such issues are Western luxuries. Issues of gay activism and gender rights are usually pushed firmly into the background.

The good news is that some former authoritarian states do change (including even the so-called 'post-violence societies'). South Africa (under apartheid), much of Latin America – for example, Argentina (under military rule and Galtieri and Perón), Chile (under Pinochet) – and Spain (under Franco) have all developed more open approaches to gender and sexuality. The strong case here is South Africa, where the breakdown of the discriminatory and anti-apartheid situation led to the creation of a new progressive agenda of human rights, which included both gender and gay rights. Spain has also rapidly become one of the most progressive 'gay rights' countries in the world and figures well at 16th on the Gender Inequality Index.[53] Likewise, in much of Southeast Asia there have also been changes. As one commentator puts it: 'Asia is becoming more LGBTI friendly. Most of the time change is not dramatic. Bit by bit. Incremental. A burst here and there. Status quo elsewhere.'[54]

A brief mention must also be given to *colonized states* shaped by histories of subordination and repression and confronted with the traumas left by former dominating states (in the long historical span, there are very few countries this does not exclude). Postcolonial nationalisms are often defined in response to their former colonization, shaped, often traumatically, by these invasions of culture. While there are many different patterns, colonized sexualities imposed by a ruling group always leave their mark. Britain and its colonies can be seen as a key example: these countries inherited British legislation against homosexuality. Even though they are now all members of the Commonwealth, more than 40 of them retain their anti-gay laws. Indeed, they constitute half of the world's countries hostile to homosexuality. While they have had to deal with the 'alien legacies' of UK imperialism, and especially the notorious Section 377, which criminalized homosexuality, the decriminalizing of homosexuality seems not to be on their list.[55]

It is clear that this book has been written against a background of both dark times and hopeful times. There are multiple atrocities enacted against women and sexual differences all across the world every day, even as there are major pushes towards a kinder, more equal and dignified world for some. In bringing the book to a close, I start to address this balance sheet.

Bleak sexualities

I start with a quick 'horror checklist' of reasons why cosmopolitanism is being obstructed. Starting with what I see as basic humanist values, what we find in the early twenty-first century world is:

- *Empathy breakdown.* On all sides, people simply refuse to understand one another. Thousands of groups across the world do not engage with each other, and many live with murderous intent. Hence, we have a situation in which the world is stuffed full of conflicts both mild and major – wars, civil strife, war rape, genocide and failed states, with millions slaughtered.

- *Kindness killed.* Dreams of religions and philosophers are confounded by perpetual global cruelty and the serious misdistribution of kindness. Documents of wars and hatreds over time show that we face our problems by killing each other (or rather we often make our young and relatively powerless men kill each other). We are capable, over and over again, of dreadful atrocities. Currently, we find crises, often religious and/or sectarian, across countries such as Afghanistan, Burma, Colombia, Egypt, Israel, Iraq, Korea, Nigeria, Pakistan, Palestine, Somalia, Sudan, Syria and the Ukraine – and we also had the so-called 'Arab Spring'. There may be attempts to understand – and maybe alleviate – perpetual violence and conflict and to cultivate kindness and the peace process. But the record to date has not been promising. The fact that rape and sexual violence are often involved has only just started to be openly discussed.

- *Dignity denied.* Rights and dignity suggest a wondrous language that can be heard universally. But human rights are everywhere contested and common humanity and its dignity are transformed into dehumanization and hatred. 'Rights' and 'dignity' have become mere rhetoric to be used when it suits. Meanwhile, we deny dignity to millions of people across the world and continue to create 'others'.

- *Justice failed.* The world has demonstrably become more unequal in recent times. We live in the '1 per cent/99 per cent world', evidenced in slum cities, feral societies and the manifest differences in lives between the mass outcast poor and the elite super-rich, women and men, the ethnically outcast and the wealthy white.[56] The search is on to find the means to lift the poor out of their poverty and appraise just how much wealth a life really needs. There are *pauperized sexualities* and *super-rich sexualities*, rendering the world manifestly unfair. There is an obscenity on the planet when we live and ignore so much abject poverty of the many alongside the luxuriant and wasteful lives of the multibillionaire few. But worse than this: most of the inequalities are linked to inequalities between men women and the perpetuation of racial divisions.

- *Human flourishing depleted.* Human sexual flourishing can only be a small part of an overall cluster of human flourishing – of human capabilities being actualized by social conditions. Much of human sexuality is what I have called dehumanizing; and much of it occurs in societies that are themselves so brutalized and damaged – 'the failed states', which sit at the bottom of the Human Development Index. In terms of gender and sexuality, their situation is probably the worst in the world.

We can speak here of both a bleak world and a *bleak sexualities* shaped by the continuing failures of the modern world. This is not good news; and if you are looking for material to bolster a dark and pessimistic view of both humanity and the future, I have just helped you. And you would be in very good company: from both the political right (for example, Roger Scruton) through the middle (for example, John Gray) and on to the left (for example, Slavoj Žižek), pessimism is widespread.[57] I have to say that when I hear the daily world news, my own heart sinks too. What a mess we humans have achieved. Yet, important as pessimism may partially be, I am cautious of it and vigilant of its negativity. I do not want to become *miserablist* (espousing a sort of philosophy of depression), *misanthropic* (cynically always believing the worst of human nature and motivation) or *melancholic* (with my mind in deep depression, sadness and gloom). Nor do I really think that the intellectual fashion for negative dialectics and negative and endless critical thinking has really helped humankind that much. It is so very easy these days to slip into the darkness and limits of modern-day doomsayers and apocalypse forecasters.

My problem with these (often justified) negative values and pessimism is that they can leave very little hope for most people in the world today. Every serious thinker must surely know about the current awful aspects of social life (and its ubiquitous and long history); it stares us brutally in the face. So this really has to be only a starting point for all analysis. The real challenge is to move beyond, to live knowingly with dark times and pessimism while acting and moving positively to at least make the world a little better for a new generation. And to do this we have to sustain hope: creating 'potentiality' for the 'coming community', pushing imaginative horizons, engaging with 'democratic experimentalism',[58] developing new beginnings and better worlds. We have to engage with utopian visions, seeking collective progress and individual emancipation, despite all the problems that this will bring. Just because we have sometimes failed in the past, this is no reason to stop actions in the future. There are always new beginnings and new generations. And *hope* highlights understanding both the ways in which people have made better worlds in the past and how they can use them in the present and the future. We have to live with the inevitability of disappointment and the importance of hope.

Hopeful sexualities

So, dark and disappointing as the human world indeed is, this is far from being the full story. There are many who have cautiously charted more positive ways. In the mid-twentieth century, Norbert˜Elias (1939) foretold a promising agenda, and this idea has been more recently updated by Natan Sznaider (2001). Both Elias and Sznaider tell promising tales of a slow humanizing of the individual. More recently still, Pinker (2012), Rifkin (2009), Richards (2010) and others have looked back to the horrors of the past and suggested that, for all the modern world's terrible failings, it may actually be slowly but gradually getting better: certainly, many have tried to improve it.[59] Indeed, in Chapter 3, I outlined the partial 'progress' that has taken place in the global world of cosmosexualities since the mid-1900s. Here I parallel Jeffrey Week's elegant work (2007), which documents this progress in the world of Western sexual politics: his own life (like mine) has witnessed truly extraordinary transformations in the past half century in the possibilities for living with sexual diversities in a few pockets of the world. But we have been the lucky ones: it has not been so for many people. The fact that this 'progress' is now being noticed and monitored could itself, though, be seen as a small sign for hope. Box 6.2 suggests some websites now available to use for keeping an eye on what is going on. Alongside this brief review of available material, a current progress report could read: 'Much has been done but there is much more to do.' For example, in 2014 while some 113 UN members (roughly 60 per cent) have decriminalized same-sex relations, some 78 (roughly 40 per cent) have not. Progress is very uneven round the world. The smaller Nordic countries have long taken the lead on women's rights and are also generally the most progressive on lesbian, gay and other sexual rights (they are also the least religious); they have been at the forefront of the gay marriage transformation. Latin American countries have also become more and more active in gay rights and AIDS, shaping them to fit their own forms of nationality. South Africa in its post-Apartheid phase suddenly leapt forward to become one of the most progressive of countries on all aspects of sexual rights. Meanwhile, Europe is uneven – although much of Eastern Europe is now catching up.[60] But there are downsides: Russia looks increasingly like a dark prospect.

The little grounded everyday 'utopian' processes of global hope

It was Ernst Bloch (1938–47/1986) who provided the fullest history of hope to counterbalance the pessimism. In the final stages of a radical and critical life, after an appalling war and human atrocities, Bloch turned to writing three magisterial volumes on the possibility of hope and 'a better world'. His task was a critical one of examining past societies and their chance of better worlds: their hopes and dreams, how they worked or failed. His challenge was to engage in what he called a 'forward dream' of a 'better life'. He claims: 'This book deals with nothing other than hoping beyond the day which has become.'[61] Some key areas for action and discussion centre on the tools of amelioration and change, the maps of utopias – past, present, real and imagined – and the problem of balancing optimism with pessimism into a realistic appraisal of future worlds. Humanism follows a principle of hope, considering the idea of 'real utopias' and the strategies to achieve them. President

6.2   *Cosmopolitan and inclusive sexualities*: Monitoring progress on websites

More and more agencies monitor our 'progress' towards common global human values and inclusive sexualities. Many websites exemplify this and a good number can be found at the book website http://kenplummer.com/cosmosexualities/. Here is a select sampling.

General: Monitoring cosmopolitan values

Promoting care and reducing violence
'Care' is at present very hard to monitor, but its opposite – violence – is being monitored in a number of ways:

Look in general at the Vision of Humanity website and follow up the leads it provides. See: http://www.visionofhumanity.org (you will find both the Global Peace Index and the Terrorism Index).

Human rights, sexual rights and dignity
The UN monitors the responses of states across the world, while Amnesty International and Human Rights Watch produce regular nation-based comparisons and reports:

Map of United Nations Indicators on Rights: http://indicators.ohchr.org/
Human Rights Watch: http://www.hrw.org/
Amnesty International: http://www.amnesty.org.uk/

Human flourishing
The Human Development Index (HDI) was constructed to measure the wider capacities of a life rather than the simply economic: it incorporated education and health. Since its inception, it has been supplemented with attempts to measure happiness or well-being:

Human Development Index: http://hdr.undp.org/en
World Happiness Report: http://unsdsn.org/resources/publications/world-happiness-report-2013/

A new general measure is being developed, though it will not be published annually. This is currently called the *Human Security Index* (HSI). It asks how well people are doing at home, in their communities, their countries and the world. The HSI covers 232 countries and is in an early stage of development. Watch this space: http://www.humansecurityindex.org/

Inequality and social justice

The key database is the *World Top Incomes Database*, being developed at: http://topincomes.parisschoolofeconomics.eu/ Results have been published in Piketty (2014).

Global inequality is largely measured by the Gini coefficient. See also: http://www.globalissues.org/article/26/poverty-facts-and-stats

A more complex measurement is that of the *Inequality-adjusted Human Development Index* (IHDI). It does not just rely on income, but also measures inequalities in education and health: http://hdr.undp.org/en/data See also Hudson et al. (2012), which makes a major attempt to operationalize the security of women in all the countries across the world.

Specific: Monitoring sites of contestation

Women's rights

On the state of women in the world, see the UN Women website: http://www.unwomen.org/en and follow entries such as 'Women Against Violence'.

Gender inequality is measured by the *Gender Inequality Index* (which includes inequalities in reproduction, politics and health): http://hdr.undp.org/en/content/table-4-gender-inequality-index

Sexual rights

Sexual Rights Initiative (see also p. 87): http://sexualrightsinitiative.com/

Gay rights

Look at the ILGA website (http://ilga.org/) and search also for the Annual State Sponsored Homophobia Report:
http://ilga.org/what-we-do/state-sponsored-homophobia-report/.
See also ARC International:
http://arc-international.net/

CAUTION: The statistical reports listed above monitor global trends of social change. But they raise many problems, not only in their construction, their reliability and their validity, but also in issues of politics. They are increasingly becoming tools of global governance-shaping policies, helping to structure the world in which we live. Criticisms of these 'indicators' are many. See Davis et al. (2012). However problematic they are, they surely raise key agenda setting issues.

Obama also gave us a story of hope; but he has also shown how tricky that path is. Another example is Pope Francis, who speaks in a different voice from other recent Popes.

Drawing a little from the advocacy of H.G. Wells, that 'the creation of Utopias –and their exhaustive criticism – is the proper and distinctive method of sociology',[62] some recent sociology has made a plea for a return to the idea (albeit critically) of utopia, the long-held dreams of a better world so beloved of writers down the ages. Both Erik Olin Wright (2010) and Ruth Levitas (2013) have pioneered some key ideas about utopia that may also be of help in the cosmopolitan project. Both are long-time avowed socialists.

Wright's emancipatory project (2010) suggests the critical analysis of *real utopias*: mini projects that actually exist in the world today and which demonstrate a better world of emancipation at work – lives lived that are desirable, viable and achievable. (He uses Wikipedia and Participatory City Budgeting as but two examples.) For cosmopolitan sexualities, the challenge is to seek out direct current global examples where the gender and sexualities transformations that have been occurring over the past few decades can be demonstrably shown to enhance people's lives. For example, village projects that educate women; gay men developing programmes for AIDS prevention; transgender groups creating communities of support for each other; battered women's refuges saving lives all over the world; local community councils of various kinds: this is where the future lies.

Levitas's (2013) project suggests that 'utopia' might become a normative method of critique. First we have to assemble conceptions of what a good society might look like. Then we need to envision building an archaeology, architecture and ontology for a good society that can then be used as a basis for the critique and analysis of actually existing society as well as progress towards a better one. For the student of cosmopolitan sexualities, this means envisioning what *good sexual lives and communities* might look like (perhaps ones based on care, empathy, rights, flourishing and justice), and then using this as a basis for critiquing what we have.

In both Wright's and Levitas's useful accounts, there is an undisguised advocacy of the view that sociology should be a normative discipline: it must take sides and be of visionary value. Both argue that utopia is not seen as a place; rather, it is a process in which we can learn from the best of today and help carry this forward into future generations. I think these are potentially useful ideas that are worth exploring in the future. We need to learn from the best of our contemporary complex human communications, and to 'dream forward' to a world where more and more people can cultivate these skills. I want to suggest that these are 'utopian strategies of hope'. Hope, with action, is not fruitless.

In the end

My central concern in this study has been with the ways human beings can live globally and locally with gender difference and sexual variety while recognizing the need for boundaries. I have made an argument for developing both cosmopolitan and inclusive sexualities, even as I have identified a road littered with problems.

The heart of the book lays out the acceleration in human sexual variety in the early decades of the twenty-first century, shows how both a cosmopolitan and inclusive sexualities have made some advances over the past half century and then suggests grounded, everyday 'utopian' pathways ahead. This will be greatly helped if we are able to make global connecting narratives that work through education and policy to energize a global discourse of ethical sexualities. But there are disrupting factors – namely, the ominous presence of cultural complexity and ubiquitous conflict. I devote two chapters to these issues, which are also touched on throughout the book. I make it very clear that there will never be any easy solutions and there will be major setbacks. But, and equally, there may be gradual and fitful progress both through politics in the public spheres and through personal everyday activities. The many conflicts I raise briefly in this book are not likely to go away; but they can be contained. Enhancing our ways of communicating with each other would certainly help. Sharing basic human values of care, dignity and well-being will also help if we can incorporate them in our daily practices. We can learn from a myriad of little attempts where people build 'good worlds' in their everyday lives. We can learn from practical emancipatory projects where imagining better human social worlds are being attempted. We can look at the everyday little acts of care and kindnesses that people engage in across the world, each harbouring a mini process of everyday utopia. We can sustain hope in the face of all kinds of evils as we sometimes see love, justice and kindness before our very eyes.

Reaching the end of this short mapping of sexual variety and asking how we might live with it in the future, I came across two observations that made me smile. The first came from the influential philosopher and committed atheist Richard Rorty, who is reported as saying: 'My sense of the holy is bound up with the hope that some day my remote descendants will live in a global civilization in which love is pretty much the only law.' The second comes from Aldous Huxley, who purportedly said: 'It's rather embarrassing to have given one's entire life to pondering the human predicament and to find that in the end one has little more to say than, "Try to be a little kinder."'[63]

Love and kindness. I guess this is how I feel too.

Human beings necessarily inhabit a world of different others. We have no choice over that: people across the word living differently are a fact of our universal humanity. This creates inevitable conflicts and suffering, and often cruelty. Some of these differences are built around sexuality and gender.

But we are practical animals. We can, if we wish, continue to create a terrible world by spending our time trying to exterminate these differences (by either excluding or killing these 'others' or forcing 'them' to be like us). Or we can help make it a better world by trying wherever we can to live with these differences, and maybe learn and develop from our living with them. We can do this through fostering recognition, empathy, dialogue, fairness and human flourishing; and by creating utopian imaginaries of inclusive kind and loving structures that will help in this, while refusing any legitimacy to forms of government or state that deny human openness and heterogeneity or which foster violence and hate. And we have to multitask our plural values – not just one value, but many. We need to look after each, and even be concerned for our enemies: to engage in reconciliatory compassion. Our seeming 'enemies' are often trapped in systems not quite of their own making. It will never be easy; there will always have to be limits, borders and boundaries. I have suggested a global humanist baseline to help guide this. I know, of course, many will be critical of me for being so naive and simple-minded. Still, however simple, this still has to be said: we have to be reminded of important human things. The challenge remains to live with the differences wherever we can while working to cultivate values that foster common bonds and human solidarities of love, care and kindness.

Oddly perhaps, my deepest concern does not lie with world global politics and the deep structures of cosmopolitanism, which will always bring their problems. The transformation of the wider social structure and its tragic inequalities is a necessary but very long-term project. My more pragmatic concern lies with the wider and global practical fostering of the everyday humanist cosmopolitan imagination and its daily practices. For, despite how some may see this book and its claims, the days of big abstractions and dreams of large structures and revolutionary grand utopias are over. We have seen too much damage and horror come from this. We need instead a down-to-earth everyday loving pragmatism of empathy, fairness, kindness and care. These, indeed, are the little-grounded utopian processes of hope. We have to think very small in a very big way. So just as the spirit of William James haunts this book, let me end with him:

> I am done with great things and big plans, great institutions and big success. I am for those tiny, invisible loving human forces that work from individual to individual, creeping through the crannies of the world like so many rootlets, or like the capillary oozing of water, which, if given time, will rend the hardest monuments of pride.[64]

Epilogue:
Contingent Sexualities –
Dancing into the Sexual Labyrinth

Is that all there is?

When I was fifteen, I discovered homosexuality.
They said it was a crime.
And a sickness, a sin, a shame and a sadness.
And I said to myself: is that all there is?

When I was twenty-five, I discovered liberation.
It was GLF; we were out and proud; we made demands.
We were modern homosexuals out to change the world.
And I said to myself: is that all there is?

When I was thirty, I discovered research.
Transvestites and paedophiles and sado-masochists and more:
The conflicting meanings of the whole damn thing!
And I said to myself: is that all there is?

When I was thirty-five, I discovered AIDS and feminism.
I knew the tragedy of AIDS: twenty-five million dead and still
   counting
And the tragedy of feminism: its interminable divides.
And I said to myself: is that all there is?

When I was forty-five, I discovered the global and postmodern.
Queer had come around again;
And human rights was a world agenda.
And I said to myself: is that all there is?

When I was sixty, I nearly died: but I didn't.
Starry starry nights and the incorrigible plurality of snow.
The multiplicities of life, of death, of suffering.
And I said to myself: is that all there is?

So life goes on as I look to seventy.
The inevitability of disappointment,
and the importance of hope.
And I say to myself: is that all there is?
So let's keep dancing.*

Back in the early 1970s when I was reading the opening of a passage of Simone de Beauvoir's account of her ageing and her life, *All Said and Done* (1972), I was struck with words that have stayed with me ever since:

> Every morning before I open my eyes, I know I am in my bedroom and my bed . . . I wake up with a childish feeling of astonishment – why am I myself? What astonishes me . . . is the fact of finding myself here, and at this moment, deep in this life and not in any other. What stroke of chance brought this about?.. . It seems to me that a thousand different futures might have stemmed from every single movement of my past; I might have fallen ill and broken off my studies; I might not have met Sartre [the philosopher]; anything at all might have happened. Tossed into the world, I have been subjected to its laws and contingencies, ruled by will other than my own, by circumstances and by history; it is therefore reasonable for me to suggest that I am myself contingent. What staggers me is at the same time I am not myself contingent.

---

*   This little ditty can be sung along with Peggy Lee to the 1969 song by Jerry Lieber and Mike Stoller. The original was inspired by a short story by Thomas Mann, 'Disillusionment'.

So much to think about: 'every single movement of my past shapes the future', 'a thousand possibilities', all tossed by 'the contingent' even as 'I am not myself contingent'. And this was surely true of my sexualities? I have pondered on this ever since. Human sexualities, like lives, are contingent. They do not have a safe, sure inner coherence, but lead us tumbling into precarious worlds. Sexualities can be seen as flowing through vast mobile labyrinths, full of pathways and secret doors of great complexity through which human sexual lives fall, meander, energize, fizzle, stumble, sleep, bounce back, take wrong turnings and often get lost, becoming hurt, damaged – and delighted – on the way. There are traps and turning points and mysteries, thrills and heartbreaks. The great Argentinian storyteller Louis Borges (2000) knew all about this and it is his imagery I draw upon here. My overriding imagery throughout this book has been that of the multiplicities, the pluralities, the varieties, the different strands and threads of human sexualities that are constantly on the move.

That sexualities are contingent is far from being a simple idea. It suggests that human life – and all its sexualities – depends upon all manner of chances, constraints and tacit, drifting choices. It is shaped by many unforeseen events that then can have enormous social consequences. Small chance factors can have huge causal power. And equally, many contingencies can pile up into regular sequences and patterns to become almost unnoticed. Life is fragile and precarious. We all suffer all the time from the contingencies of time and history, space and culture, divisions and inequalities, bodies and emotions, rules and relationships. Chance happenstances are the stuff of our everyday lives. Yet we do not understand this very well – this fragility of the moments of life – even though contingency has been a persistent and popular theme of art and history, literature and music.

Most of the time – most days of our life – we stave off the wider possibilities of our existence and their shaping through chance occurrences because of our persistent tendency to make _social habits_. The huge potential and risk of human existence is turned into daily routine – narrowed by the flywheel of habit. The 'blooming buzzing confusion' of the world is channelled down so that most of our lives – most of our days – we follow well-patterned habits.

We cannot stand too much life and we have to restrict our daily potentials into well-formed routines – in behaviour, in thoughts, in feelings. Crudely, we become zombie-like. But this does not stop the many precarious moments from harbouring full-scale chance possibilities of change.

Personal tales

I close this book with just a tiny fragment of my own life, so you can glimpse a little of where this book started its life and the contingencies that have shaped it. I first 'came out' as a young gay man between 1966 and 1970, between the swinging sixties of underground queer coffee bars in Soho and Carnaby Street and the London School of Economics-based Gay Liberation Front of 1970. I confronted the power of an extraordinary transformative moment as I moved from being an outlawed, criminalized, sick, sinful little teenager to being an out proud gay man claiming my rights. In the same period, I got my first degree at Enfield College, started work on my PhD on homosexuality at the LSE, got a job as a sociology lecturer, and found my first serious boyfriend. How could this be? What might my life had been if I had been born in Biafra and not in Swinging London at this time?

I had been born into a white, London working-class background – with no books but lots of loving aspirations. Before 1966, I cried and suffered the pangs of outlawed gay youth. I had had enough of all this by the time I was 20. I started going to the furtive gay bars in Soho, counting around 100 at that time. I declared 'I am gay' to close friends, some of whom turned out to be gay themselves. And finally I told my parents, who took me straight to the doctor! All this was in the summer of 1966, a memorable period in the annals of my life. At that time, 'homosexuality' was 'against the law', and a 'mental illness'. I had a short flirtation with psychiatrists and mental hospitals, as that was the way of that time. It made me very suspicious of much psychiatry, psychology and even sociology. I learnt that the social sciences were definitely not as neutral as they pretended. And in the face of church nastiness, I

gave up my little boy Christian beliefs to become a life-long atheist
(until recently, when agnosticism has become my preferred route).
By 1967 I had sorted much of this 'sexual stigma' stuff out, and had
cheerfully started my 'new life' in this lively London scene. How
could this be? What might my life had been like if I had been born
in London 100 years earlier?

I also decided to do a thesis on homosexual life, and as the law
in England changed in 1967, this became my focus. In November
1970, I was among a very small group of people at the LSE for the
first meeting of the Gay Liberation Front – called by two young
students, Aubrey Walter and Bob Mellors. I recall meeting the
now renowned historian Jeffrey Weeks there, and we became life-
long friends. It was a critical turning point in my life, as I came to
appreciate that being sexual was also being intellectual, social and
political. How could this be? What might my life have been like if
I had never encountered the Gay Liberation Front in 1970?

My little tales of gay contingency could continue, but this will
do. Stories of my coming out in the 1960s soon became embel-
lished and changed. I have many versions of it. Indeed, I recall, 20
years on at a conference in Utrecht in 1988 (when I was speaking
to a cluster of very keen enthusiastic lesbian and gay European
students), announcing that I was even 'post-gay'. Oh dear: the
ways of academic pretension! Still, stories do not take a naturally
linear form and nor do they develop in naturally linear ways. They
bump you around and are contingent upon the events of everyday
life. They change from place to place and from time to time. They
offer you moments of choice and moments of utter fatalism. And
stories themselves are never free-floating and random. They have
historical roots, connect to wider patterns, cluster into structures
and habits, and indeed become our (often much-loved) habits –
part of what some sociologists now call our 'habitus'.

Textual tales

From the mid 1960s onwards, just as I was exploring my own
sexual feelings, I also started on my life-long journey of reading

the texts and stories of sexualities that others had written. I began reading the texts of plural sexualities – there are an awful lot of them. I guess it started when I had to inspect Kinsey's massive dull tome of statistics (1948) for a second-year undergraduate research methods course that I took in 1965. The methodological appendix was the key reading, but my eyes soon strayed elsewhere. I quickly picked up the statistics on homosexuality, premarital and extra-marital sex (as they were called then), masturbation, and other delights like sex with animals. I learnt that there was a lot of concealed, hidden taboo sex across a wide spectrum of activities going on behind closed doors. Little did I know then that a decade later I would spend a week at the Kinsey Institute with a bunch of professional self-styled 'sexperts' hearing about sex therapy, participating in masturbation workshops, gossiping with nuns about their sex lives, 'skinny-dipping' and participating in a male beauty contest. Or that three decades on, I would return, in the midst of a world conference on sexual methodology, with my mentor friend the pioneering John Gagnon, in pursuit of a stark and unloved Kinsey grave.

Gradually, I became a voracious reader of all the sexological classics: Richard Krafft-Ebing, Magnus Hirschfield, Sigmund Freud, Alfred Kinsey, Masters and Johnson, and the rest. I recall, for instance, picking up Richard von Krafft-Ebing's monumentally influential *Pyschopathia Sexualis* (originally published in 1886) from a pornographic bookstore. Although masked in scientific terminology, the founder sexologist psychiatrist introduced me to more than 200 vivid case studies of non-procreative sexual differences, ranging from coprophagia to handkerchief fetishists. It was he, probably more than any other, who helped provide the language of the modern perversions that some live with more easily today – sadism, masochism, exhibitionism, fetishism and, yes, homosexuality. Here was a simple opening taxonomy of differences: *paradoxia* (sexual desire at the wrong time of life), *anesthesia* (insufficient sexual desire), *hyperesthesia* (excessive sexual desire) and *paraesthesia* (misdirected sexual desire). The book had been through 12 expanding and increasingly popular editions by the time I came to pick up my much-popularized version in a grubby Soho 'dirty book' store (it was no longer in Latin). Originally concealed and specialist, nowadays the book can be downloaded in its entirety online. In one sense, the study of sexual differences over the past 100 years may be seen as little more than an attempt to classify and order an almost impossibly diverse array of desires.

My readings of Kinsey and Krafft-Ebing were soon joined by a scrutiny of Magnus Hirschfield, Havelock Ellis, Edward Carpenter, Wilhelm Reich and others. Magnus Hirschfield taught me of the dangers of sexual radicalism (he of the book burnings). I flirted with the imaginative Freud, and not least his constantly evolving *Three Essays on the Theory of Sexuality* (1905–25). This hugely influential work, shaped so much by Krafft-Ebing, formed most thinking on sexual aberrations, on infantile sexuality and 'the transformations of puberty' for the Western twentieth-century mind. And there were many others I read: Donald J. West's handy Penguin compendium tour of homosexuality (1955/1968) – a book I hurled at my beloved parents when I 'came out' as gay to them; Michael Schofield's (1965) early researches into homosexual life in England before the law changed (under his pseudonym of Gordon Westwood); Paul Robinson's (1976) elegant account of the democratization of sex. The list goes on and on. I learnt that human sexualities were deeply embroiled in different languages, and were given depth through metaphor.

Research tales

And all of this led me on from my limited gay research of the 1960s to a much wider concern with all the so-called 'sexual differences'. It was research that changed my life. In the mid-1970s I gained my first (and only) major research grant to investigate 'symbolic interactionism and sexual differentiation', which was a euphemism in order to resist the tabloid media inclination to sensationalize funding awarded to controversial projects. This was inspired by the work of John Gagnon (1977) and William Simon (1973/2005), who taught me that 'there are many ways to become, to be, to act, to feel sexual. There is no one human sexuality, but rather a wide variety of sexualities.' And the process of becoming human is also a process of acquiring the social meanings of sex. So in this project, Annabel Faraday and I interviewed and observed the life of a group of mid-twentieth-century 'perverts', people with stigmatized desires. Here was a research journey in which I encountered close up the multiple and fragmented human identities and social worlds of sadomasochism, transgender, fetishism, paedophilia, prostitution, pornography, rape and sexual violence, heterosexualities, homosexualities, bisexualities, sex dysfunctions and worlds possibly best identified as celibate and asexual. It was a major life experience, and I learnt that all these terms glossed the complex, multiple social experiences or life forms in which new labels, stories and identities were giving coherence to inchoate forms. Simultaneously, this has led to a lifetime of scholarly (and sometime not so scholarly) conflicts in the social worlds of sex research and sexual politics. Oddly, many of the stories they told were mundane; but sometimes they could be dramatically shocking, even threatening. By definition, all were outside the dominant sexual mores of the moment – then much more so than nowadays. All had their stories to tell and many things were learnt.

If there was one finding of substance to emerge, it was the strong sense of the distinct and diverging symbolic worlds that people inhabit when it comes to sex. Poets, dramatists and dreamers, of course, have always known this; but sexologists had to find it out the hard way: through research. Diverse sexual lives were lived mainly by ordinary people – your neighbours and the everyday people you meet on the street – who inhabited sexual worlds and got up to sexual things that their 'fronts' never revealed. They looked and acted as conventionally as anyone, seemed to subscribe to dominant values in most things, yet lived in a world of sexuality that went firmly against any dominant view of the time.

Here, for example, was the suburban housewife who turned hooker during the day while her husband was at work; the transvestite who was a highly successful local businessman; the paedophile who worked as a porter in a university; the doctor who relished sadomasochistic surgery; the gay student at teacher's training college who concealed his identity from other students; the genteel middle-class gentleman whom I interviewed with his wife and daughter about the sadomasochistic organization he had set up and run from his middle-class suburban home; the Eastern Orthodox priest who tried to rape me in my interviewing office at the LSE; the publisher who held regular heavy leather sex parties; the businessman who fashioned and collected sexual strait jackets; the foot fetishist, the pornographer, the eunuch, the child abuse victims – and so on. But enough!

Troubled tales

A great many difficulties ensued in the wake of this, some discussed in my book *Telling Sexual Stories* (1995). For example, one of the life story subjects for the funded project was a man we called Ed: a self-labelled paedophile who worked on my university campus and who offered to tell me his story. For some five years this led me – very naively – to consider the debates and issues around child adult sexualities. I wondered whether arguments made for homosexual reform and rights could also be made for 'the paedophile cause' which was being stated loudly at that time by the emerging paedophile movement (PIE, PAL and NAMBLA in particular). I soon discovered that this was a very dangerous area indeed to research; but a profoundly important one. I was hurtled into the problems not just of stigmatized desire, but also of childhood sexuality and their meanings, the nature of sexual exploitation, the issues of consent and power, the problems of frustrated adult desires, and the very deep fears and anxieties that this topic raises in wider publics: 'the moral panics' that my first tutor of sociology, Stan Cohen, had so brilliantly described. This research was on the cusp of the emerging 'paedophile panics' which have since dominated Western sexual debate for nearly 40 years. The 'paedophile' whom I was trying to understand soon started to become sexual public enemy number one, and all attempts to understand him (and sometimes her) have been more or less stopped by the presence of one single monolithic view of the predatory and necessarily abusive child molesting monster. So I was led to think more of the deep fears of sexualities, and the critical significance of sexual boundaries. I guess I had naively started my research thinking that all human sexual diversity was fine and should be celebrated; this little study brought me up with a shock. There were critical boundaries: we cannot live with all difference.

I left this field behind, more than a bit battered by it (and the battering continues to this day). But continuing with the problem of exploitation and violence, it led me to the heartlands of feminist theory. It led me to a little study of power, rape and sexual violence; and soon I was deeply immersed in what came to be known as the feminist sex wars. I made the connection between masculinity and many sexual problems, started to wonder how sexual variety is, perhaps unsurprisingly, deeply shaped by this gender order. I discovered (despite some recent changes) that men are much more likely than women to become sexual consumers: they will pay for sex in all its varieties – prostitution, pornography, striptease, sex tourism, massage, lap-dancing, telephone sex, fetish sales. Men are also much more likely to feel that they can assert themselves to 'take sex' when they want it: not just in obvious 'rape' situations, but more routinely from their wives (wife rape), girl friends (date rape), their children (son–daughter rape) and even other men (homosexual rape). They are much more likely than women to feel they have a specific turn-on – a little out of the ordinary – which must be met: where are all the women who 'must' steal underwear, who 'must' expose their genitals to men passing by in the street, who 'must' make obscene phone calls to unknown men? 'Perversion', said the late Robert Stoller – once a leading psychiatrist of sexual diversity – 'is far more common in men than in women; women practice almost none of the official diagnoses' (1979: 34). And men are much more likely than women to be driven to break the sex laws and become sex offenders: male sex offenders overwhelmingly outnumber female sex offenders in all areas except one – prostitution; and while women may commit crimes of passion, they are not the same as the so-called lust murders of men. Again: let's be clear that only a minority of men may be involved in all the above; but it does seem that many, many fewer women are.

So this awareness turned me towards feminism and soon I encountered their many divides. The much-debated 'feminist sex wars' suggest a long battle stretching back to at least the nineteenth century, and it is still very much alive today. It divides a feminist movement of multiple factions into, minimally, those who primarily highlight female sexuality as pleasure and those who focus on its violence, exploitation and dangers. The polar cases are 'pleasure feminists' desiring to use their bodies as they wish for all kinds of sexual desire; and 'danger feminists' claiming women are severely subordinated and abused by male sexualities, obviously with rape and sexual violence, but also in prostitution and pornography. These debates were not mild-mannered. They hurled me into worlds of anger and rage: lives and their dignity were being fought over.

At this stage, I started to live with a contradiction of opposing feminisms, finding truths in both. I may have started in the 1960s as a sexual liberationist – letting it all hang out, a believer in free love and all that; but by now I was becoming more cautious. And by the early 1980s, the pure liberationist position had become untenable. (I might note that the Gagnon and Simon models of sexuality had also made me suspicious of the repression and liberation model; Foucault's later ideas hence came as no surprise.) Feminism now brought me back sharply to a world where many forms of sexuality were not acceptable at all. Paedophilia and sexual violence then introduced me to the dark side of sexualities. Along the way I was being given lessons in human rage and anger, and the extraordinary vulnerability of the little human animal.

Mobile tales

And then. Just as I was starting to take all this in, suddenly, in the early 1980s, all my research projects and interests were disrupted by the unexpected and unwelcome arrival of the holocaustic AIDS. This change was not in vision a few years earlier: but now and for much of the 1980s, the spectre of AIDS and HIV came to dominate much of sexual life across the planet (it still does in certain parts). Here was more shame, rage and anger; but also a time of great grief and tragedy. It was also a time to sense the human energy pushing to develop a good response to AIDS. It was a time when social movements changed both sexualities and the world, bringing a whole new language and politics of sexuality into the public arena.

As millions died, new politics and global concerns were carved out. And I came to appreciate more and more that history was moving on, nothing remained the same; and sexuality, like life, does not step into the same river twice.

So the stories flow on and I must end. More than 30 years after the arrival of AIDS, I see flashing before my eyes: Madonna, who broke every public boundary of female sexuality and generated, though not single-handedly, the sexualization of Western culture; the arrival of Judith Butler and Michel Foucault as the overawing gurus of the late twentieth-century Western intellectual sexual life; a fellating United States President having sex with an office worker, and even as this became global knowledge, retaining his presidency; the arrival of postmodernism and globalization as academic clichés that permeated everything; 11 September 2001, the Twin Towers attack, which brought world religions, terrorism – and Muslim veils – back into world focus; and many undreamt of, absurd non-ideas of 50 years earlier – 'gay marriage', 'cybersex', 'global surrogacy', 'the sexualization of everything' – becoming the contemporary reality of many countries. And ultimately, even, the development of an industry of gender and sexual scholarship involving thousands of scholars doing advanced research in every conceivable nook and cranny of modern sexual life: research that could hardly have been imagined a half century ago. Every subfield of sexualities now has its army of specialists, its own journals, professional meetings and student training; and this holds for many countries around the world. The world and its stories really do keep moving on.

Notes

Introduction

1 The Nirbhaya Trust and Billion Women Rising.There is a fully referenced account of this at: http://en.wikipedia.org/wiki/2012_Delhi_gang_rape.

2 I started my intellectual life as a symbolic interactionist and I still see this as a valuable tradition (see Plummer, 2000a). But I have moved on a little, seeing myself now as a critical humanist, a position that incorporates pragmatism and interactionism but takes it further (Plummer, 2012b, 2013a). This book builds upon ideas from some of my key earlier works – Plummer, 1975, 1995, 2003a.

3 The term hegemony is used throughout this book and is drawn roughly from the works of Gramsci, 2000. It conveys the idea of dominance that is informal and invisible and works coercively in subtle ways.

4 See Clark, 2008: 170.

Chapter 1 Plural Sexualities: Making Valued Human Lives

1 Two key classic thinkers, William James and Hannah Arendt, are cited here because they directly shape the claims in this opening

paragraph, and they deeply infuse the whole book. James writes of the 'pluralistic universe'; Arendt sees plurality as distinctive to our humanity. For a guide to the ideas of James, see Richardson (2006); to Arendt, see Hayden (2014).

2 There are many contemporary social theorists who now take seriously the ideas of the plural, complexity and the agonistic. See, for example, the work of William E. Connolly, a leading North American political theorist, and his concern with difference, 'the ethos of pluralization', cosmopolitanism, the building of an 'agnostic politics' and the fragility of the world, all of which will feature in this book. From a long bibliography, see Connolly (1995, 2013).

3 Sumner continued: 'Each group nourishes its own pride and vanity, boasts itself superior, exalts its own divinities, and looks with contempt on outsiders. Each group thinks its own folkways the only right ones, and if it observes that other groups have other folkways, these excite its scorn. Opprobrious epithets are derived from these differences.' Sumner was a very influential early liberal sociologist though rarely considered these days. He was hostile to imperialism (Sumner, 1906). His work can be downloaded free from Project Gutenberg.

4 The title of William James's most celebrated book is *The Varieties of Religious Experience*. Emulating him, I have often aspired to write a book on the varieties of *sexual* experience. Sadly, this book is not it: in this book I do not take life documents and detail as my prime goal (which was the core concern of James); instead this is much more a book of social analysis, abstraction and theory.

5 The literature on sexual variety is now vast and there are many illustrative references to it throughout this book. We can find evidence in the early clinicians, especially Krafft-Ebing (1886/1931), Freud (1905/1962). The social research of the biologist Kinsey (1948, 1953) was a polemical landmark. The early anthropological work is reviewed in Ford and Beach (1952/1965); and Bullough was a pioneer historian who wrote more than 50 books and whose work is too neglected (see Bullough, 1976). More recently and controversially, Bornstein (1995) has suggested there may be a thousand genders! Let a thousand genders flourish, she proclaims! And Roughgarden (2004) writes of 'Evolution's Rainbow'.

6 See Dean (2009).

7 'Patriarchal sexualities' refers to sexualities organized by gender inequalities and power in which women are treated negatively. 'Hegemonic masculinities' is derived from the highly influential research and writings of Raewyn Connell (1995).

8 See also Said (2004). It should be clear that my humanism follows in the pragmatic tradition outlined originally by James, Cooley, Dewey and Mead; and more recently by Bernstein (2010), Unger (2009), Stuhr (2010).

9 A classic of modern humanism is Arendt (1958/1998). The work of Martha Nussbaum is also prominent (see especially 1999, 2011). Adam Smith's *The Theory of Moral Sentiments* (1759/2000) is the foundation for much modern thinking about the person. Advanced contemporary discussions of the human person can be found in Sayer (2011) and Smith (2010). My own position is outlined in Plummer (2013a).

10 Mazlish (2009) develops this argument more fully.

11 See Livingstone Smith (2011).

12 I discussed this first in Plummer (1975) and, most recently, in Plummer (2012a). The central inspiration for this view has come from Gagnon and Simon (1973/2005), Simon (1996), Gagnon (2004). Seidman (2003/2010) provides an introduction and the British feminist sociologist Stevi Jackson (1999) documents the development of such ideas in her work. A useful guide to the contemporary language of sexualities can be found in Weeks (2011); and for current work in this area, see the journal *Sexualities: Studies in Culture and Society*. Two widely read classics are Foucault (1976), Butler (1990).

13 For a valuable discussion, see Bellah and Joas (2012).

14 See Israel (2010, 2013) and his other works.

15 The writings on culture, biology and the complexity of human nature are vast. As I was writing this book, three more 'popular' books gained attention – see Everett (2012), Prinz (2012), Tallis (2011). These books all stressed the cultural nature of human nature. But it is one of those perpetually contested debates.

16 An important study on Smith is that by Forman-Barzilai (2010), who fills out ideas on sympathy and empathy in a 'circle of humanity'.

17 See Beck (2010), Bharat (2007).

18 Jordan (2006), Admirand (2012), Ellis (2010) all indicate the horrors of religion. Armstrong (2014) tries a defence.

19 Todorov (1999) is elegant on this. See also his defence of the Enlightenment more generally (Todorov, 2006).

20 For example, Braidotti (2013). However Nayar (2014) also equates this writing with a critical humanism.

21 For recent works, see, amongst others, Unger (2009), Smith (2010), Sayer (2011).

22 This may all well be linked to the fact that we are born immature, with undeveloped brains, unable to do anything, and dependent on others. For discussions of human vulnerability, see Mackenzie et al. (2014), as well as works by Arendt, Butler and Nussbaum. My own introduction to the theory of vulnerability started with a reading of Ernest Becker's *The Denial of Death* (1973), at the time of my father's death in 1978. A valuable collection of essays on Becker's work can be found in Liechty (2005).

23 Turner (2006: 127). Bryan S. Turner's work on rights has been a cornerstone of the sociology of rights.

24 See Schopenhauer (1915/2005: 51).

25 See Smith (2010), Sayer (2011).

26 See Dworkin (2000: 485, n1), and Appiah (2005: xiii). In broad brush strokes, ethicists can be seen to fall into three clusters: philosophers, psychologists and historical sociologists. They rarely speak to each other. Western philosophers trace back to Aristotle and Plato and broadly divide between those who centre on justice and rights and those who focus on virtue. Key contemporary examples include Ronald Dworkin, Martha Nussbaum, Amartya Sen and Michael Sandel. Few speak beyond the West. The modern psychologists have been largely shaped by the writings of Lawrence Kohlberg and Jean Piaget. The historical sociologists divide between those who focus on the 'genealogy of morals' shaped by Friedrich Nietzche and Michel Foucault, and those who work on the detailed work of specific groups and the formation of ethical ideas. Key examples of this include Hans Joas, Phillip Kitchner and, more recently, Kenan Malik. Much justice and inequality theory ignores or minimizes the deep structural inequalities of economy and gender and class which are the background to the workings of sociologists. During the late twentieth century, there were a number of alternative statements produced – often by feminist moral and political philosophers; here, the grounds for the arguments shifted towards matters of care (Carol

Gilligan, Nel Noddings), recognition (Iris Marion Young) and dia-logue (Seyla Benhabib). But curiously, the largely male writers on justice have more or less ignored these developments and continue with their own sophisticated, but limited, arguments. Likewise, there is a vast literature on theological ethics (e.g. Reinhold Niebuhr, José Porfirio Miranda) environmental ethics (e.g. Peter Singer) or even queer postgender ethics. It is a rich and complex world of thinking, but marked by its agonistic (or indifferent) differences.

27 Ricoeur (1992: 180; his italics).

28 Kitcher (2011: 411; my italics).

29 For an illuminating study of widespread prevalence of the Golden Rule, see Gensler (2013).

30 See, for example, Jordan (2006). Armstrong (2014) tries to tell a counterbalancing story.

31 See James (1967: 611), Berlin (1954/1969: 167–72).

32 For a clarification of this debate, see the guidance from Wenman (2013).

33 On global values and ethics, see Tremblay (2009), Van Hooft (2009), Widdows (2011). See also: Bloch (1938–47/1986), Sandel (2009), Sen (2009), Arnett et al. (2009), Benhabib (2011), Slote (2007), Lukes (2008).

34 The International Association for Religious Freedom: http://iarf. net/.

35 On the history and current status of interfaith, see Bharat and Bharat (2007). A short introduction is Pui-Lan (2012).

36 See Lauren (1998/2011), Glendon (2002), Morsink (2000).

37 See, for example, Widdows (2011) and the creation of an International Association of Global Ethics.

38 The sociologist Zygmunt Bauman had much to say about this process of ambivalence in his *Postmodern Ethics* (1993); he continues with these problems right up to his most recent book, *Moral Blindness* (2013).

39 But see Joas (2000, 2013), Kitcher (2011), as well as Ishay (2004), Hunt (2007) on the history of rights.

40 While I realize this is both presumptuous and contentious, I keep on struggling to find these values because I think they are much needed. If you believe in some sense in the significance of putting human beings first, and in the idea of us looking after each other, then my

hope is that you are likely to generally agree with much of this. It really does not need to be too complicated. At the same time, there is a bigger project searching for genealogies of key clusters of values. How have people throughout history practically developed ideas of the good life? Where did the goals of human flourishing and virtue come from? How did empathy, dialogue, sympathy and compassion develop out of earliest human life forms? How did care, kindness and love emerge in daily life? How did justice, freedom, equality and rights evolve not theoretically but in daily practices? And how did this dignity and rights become key features of modern life? These are troubling questions of value that haunt any humanist work; and, as we will see, they certainly haunt this one.

41 The writing on ethics fills the vast libraries of civilizations and much of it is written in the most opaque language, inaccessible to all but a small group of cognoscente that follows this issue. I will just point to a few useful popularizers who aim to write for a wider audience: Blackburn (2003), Dworkin (2000), Nussbaum (2006), Sandel (2009), Sen (2009).

42 Engster (2007: 1). Engster's book is a very important statement on how to blend 'care' with 'justice'. Other major writings on care that I draw from include Gilligan (1982), Noddings (1986), Sevenhuijsen (1998), Fine (2007), Robinson (2011).

43 The work on empathy and dialogue is substantial. I reference some of it later in the book (see Chapter 6).

44 The debate on human rights is vast, but I have found Woodiwiss (2005) and Turner (2006) useful.

45 This links with the Aristotelian view of virtue ethics. Key contemporary thinkers in this area would include Alasdair MacIntyre and Martha Nussbaum. Key psychologists – now completely out of fashion – would be Abraham Maslow (1943) and Eric Fromm (1993, 2013). Some would claim that these positions cannot be merged with the pragmatist one. I suggest that while they may deal with different things, they both have value. I cannot quite see why only one value can be taken into account.

46 Modern capability theory has its origins in the work of Sen (1980), who worked in the 1980s with Nussbaum to shape the Human Development Index. In 2004, the Human Development and Capability Association (HDCA) was formed; see Nussbaum (2011),

Deneulin and Shahin (2009), Deneulin (2014). Amongst the key capabilities are nutrition, security, emotions, reasoning, play, health, bodily health and, yes, even sexuality. Sen (2009) linked the theory to justice, Nussbaum (1999) to rights. The important idea is that of building social structures that enable human beings to flourish, and this surely entails both justice and rights.

47 For some key statements on the world's overpowering inequality and the problems this generates, see Bauman (2011), Dorling (2014), Therborn (2013). See also Jones (2014).

48 I use the word 'intersecting' here, aware of the full intellectual baggage this idea has been made to carry over the past 30 years. For an early example, see Collins (1990); for recent examples, see Yuval-Davis (2011) and the work in Taylor et al. (2011). There is now a veritable industry of intersectional studies that brings its own problems and many rival terms, such as 'assemblages'. Academic life remains as contested as ever.

49 Amongst the very many thinkers on justice are Sen (2009), Sandel (2009), Young (1990). For Sen, any theory of justice must begin with a recognition of the major contrast that exists between 'transcendental institutionalism' – e.g., Hobbes, Rousseau, Kant, Rawls and many more – and 'realized-focus comparison' – e.g., Adam Smith, Wollstonecraft, Bentham, Marx. The former is more abstract, while the latter contains real world events. From these contrasts, Sen builds his own theory, linking it, rather unfortunately in my view, to rational choice theory. Fraser (2009), in contrast, links justice to three conceptual fields: distribution (of resources), recognition (of the varying contributions of different groups) and representation (linguistic). I mention these only as examples of the many and very different conceptualizations of this whole field of analysis. There are, then, even plural theories of justice!

50 Many of these values are now open to some kind of social science measurement, and many are features of global UN measurement scales for countries across the world. We are now slowly starting to unfold how these human values are being implemented. We will look at the results a little later, riddled with problems as they are. See Box 6.2.

Chapter 2 *Transformational Sexualities:*
Making Twenty-First-Century Sexual Lives

1 I have reviewed a little of this truly vast literature in Macionis and Plummer (2012: 135–6). More than 20 books are mentioned there, suggesting interminable disagreement. Here, I take a position allied with multiple modernities, capitalism, reflexivity and individualization as core features. See also Peter Wagner (2012). My previous discussions of all this include Plummer (1995, 2000b, 2003a, 2012a).

2 From Bloch (1938–47/1986) to Bullogh (1976). See also Greenberg (1990), Rupp (1997, 2009).

3 On premodern shifts, see Phillips and Reay (2011), Bromley and Stockton (2013); on modernist shifts, Foucault (1976); on the history of gender, Laqueur (1990); on heterosexuality, Tin (2012); on homosexuality, Greenberg (1990), Rupp (2009); on orgasm, Jagose (2013); and on the arrival of a so-called sexual revolution, see Dabhoiwala (2012). A recent series of historical essays for students is Buffington et al. (2014). I have outlined the significance of these changes for notions of 'choice' in Plummer (2000b).

4 See Eisenstadt (2000).

5 Shibutani (1955: 566). See also the work of Anselm Strauss (1978), Adele Clarke (2005). A recent theoretical development suggests bridging the interactional social worlds to Bourdieu's ideas of field and habitat. I am not entirely convinced. But see Green (2013).

6 For a little sample of these worlds, see the edited collection by Seidman et al. (2008/2011). And for a sprinkling of exemplar case studies, see Agustin (2007), Bech (1997), El Feki (2013), Hennen (2008), Jeffreys (2009), Manalansan (2003), Rubin (2011), Rupp and Taylor (2003).

7 For various illustration and discussions of the new reproductive technologies and their social implications, see the work of Inhorn (e.g., 2007). See also Twine (2011), Nordqvist and Smart (2014). On lesbian motherhood, see Ryan-Flood (2009).

8 A very useful critical guide to all this can be found in Schaffner (2012).

9 See http://www.theguardian.com/books/badsexaward.

10 For useful discussions and histories of the modern media and sexuality

in the West see the very useful studies by McNair (2002), Williams (2004, 2009), Rutherford (2007). The classic on porn is Williams (1990), but the literature on this is vast. On gender and media, see Gill (2007). For samples of more global reach, see Berry et al. (2003), Biltereyst and Winkel (2013), Mankekar and Schein (2012).

11   On digital sex and porn, see Attwood (2009), McGlotten (2013), Mowlabocus (2010), Waskul (2004).

12   See Jacobs (2013) on Hong Kong and China and the 'cyber yellow danger'.

13   See Enemies of the Internet website (http://12mars.rsf.org/) as well as the World Press Freedom Index (http://rsf.org/index2014/en-index2014.php).

14   On 'personal life' see the important book of that name by Smart (2007).

15   D'Emilio and Freedman (1988/2012: xii; my italics).

16   See Buss and Herman (2003).

17   Therborn (2004: 73).

18   For examples, see Beck and Beck-Gernsheim (2013).

19   As of early 2015, the growing list includes: Argentina, Belgium, Brazil, Canada, Denmark, France, Iceland, Luxembourg, the Netherlands, New Zealand, Norway, Portugal, Spain, South Africa, Sweden, the United Kingdom and Uruguay, and 32 US states, and there are many countries where it is 'under review'.

20   For a discussion of this policy, see Hudson and Den Boer (2005).

21   See Stacey (2011). On polygamy, see Yamani (2008), Bailey and Kauffman (2010).

22   'Traditional female sexuality' has been radically changed. A long catalogue of authors in the western world have helped to redefine female sexuality – from Freud and Kinsey to Erica Jong, Shere Hite, Nancy Friday and countless others. See, for example, Kinsey (1953), Hite (1976).

23   'The world's most dangerous countries for women': http://in.reuters.com/article/2011/06/15/idINIndia-57704120110615.

24   The new masculinities literature is vast. I started to become interested in sexual violence and men in Plummer (1985), and took stock of it all 20 years later in Plummer (2004), which also suggested some of the changes in the making.

25   The trail-blazing classic history is Susan Brownmiller's hugely

influential book *Against Our Will* (1975). Much research has been done since this study. See, for example, Heinemann (2011).

26 Three books changed my personal understanding of this issue: Brownmiller (1975), which taught me about rape's long history; Dworkin (1981), which showed me how nasty, yet normalized, male violence was; and Kelly (1998), which gave me a sense of the sexual violence continuum as well as the urgent need for practice. The literature in this area is now vast: see, for example, Matthews (1994), Westmarland and Gangoli (2012).

27 There are many reports on all this. Parrot and Cummings (2006) have provided a valuable overview. The figures I give come from more recent reports; see WHO (2013), UNFPA (2012), UNICEF (2013). See also http://www.unwomen.org/en/what-we-do/ending-violence-against-women/facts-and-figures.

28 See Leatherman (2011: 2). In 2014, for example, a global summit to end sexual violence in conflict was held in London: see https://www.gov.uk/government/topical-events/sexual-violence-in-conflict.

29 Cited in Jafri (2008: 24).

30 For Schopenhauer (1891) honour falls into four types: knightly, civic, official and sexual. A good contemporary example that links it to 'young black people and trouble' is Anderson (1999). See also Anderson (2011).

31 See Bourdieu (1966: 191).

32 See Appiah (2006).

33 See Appiah (2010), Bowman (2006), Sessions (2010). On the crisis of masculinity, see Plummer (2004), Kimmel (2013), Aslam (2012), Anderson (2009).

34 See Jenkins (2013).

35 A straightforward and readable account of world religions can be found in Prothero (2011), and an account of sexuality and sex in Endsjo (2011). For empirical evidence of the changes around the secular and post-secular, see Inglehart and Norris (2003), Norris and Inglehart (2011). For wider debates, see Habermas (2010), Joas and Wiegandt (2009). 'Return of the Gods' is Ulrich Bech's phrase and his book (2010) provides a good introduction to the new need to civilize world religious conflict. The growth of new religious forms are discussed by Philip Jenkins in a trilogy of books (2013). Hefner (2013: 1)

claims that 'Pentecostalism is the fastest growing religious movement'.
36 Zelizer (2005) argues that intimate ties and connections are always bounded by economic activity. She develops an argument for connected lives – how lives bridge the public and the private, the personal and the economic.
37 A succinct critical review of capitalism can be found in Wright (2010), a readable critique is Chang (2010), and an extensive, influential one in Piketty (2014).
38 See Attwood (2009).
39 For example, see Constable (2003), Sender (2005).
40 See Illouz (2008).
41 See Burger (2012: 187).
42 See McNair (2002).
43 The title of a book by Chapkis (1997).
44 For field studies of sex work/prostitution around the world, see Agustín (2007), Aoyama (2009), Bernstein (2007), Brennan (2004), Chapkis (1997), Jeffreys (2009), Padilla (2007), Poulin (2011), Zheng (2009).
45 The International Labour Organisation estimated that there were 20.9 million people in global forced labour in 2012; Kara (2009: 17) estimates between 500,00 to 1.8 million in sex trafficking. For a critique of this whole field of inquiry, see Doezema (2010).
46 On 'baby markets' in general, see Goodwin (2010) and compare the arguments of Spar (2006), who favours baby markets, and Twine (2011), who shows the more damaging side and is more critical.
47 The quote is from Poulin (2003: 38); see also Poulin (2011). See also Jeffreys (2009), McNair (2002).
48 See Jeffreys (2009). See also Bernstein (2007), Poulin (2011).
49 See Aoyama (2009), Agustín (2007).
50 A useful guide to the research in this field is Hubbard (2012). My interest in this field of research was much stimulated by the early work of the Chicago sociologists and, more recently, by the path-breaking work of Henning Bech (1997).
51 See Mumford's classic account (1961); it is also cited in Hubbard (2012: 11).
52 See Bech (1997).
53 See Plummer (1988), Barnett and Whiteside (2006). The research on AIDS and HIV is a huge industry. For a telling account of it all, see Pisani (2008). For statistics, see http://www.who.int/gho/hiv/en.

54 See Lancaster (1994); also Scheper-Hughes (1993), Farmer (2003). A little while back I made an initial attempt at making sense of all this in Plummer (2005). For good reviews of inequality and poverty, see also Therborn (2013), Bauman (2011).

55 These are the 'wasted lives' as described by Bauman (2004), the 'bare lives' and the 'dispossessed' of Agamben (1998) Butler and Athanasiou (2013), and they show the brutalization of life that Arendt (1958/1998) feared. I originally named countries, but in truth there are too many of them and largely linked to refugee populations. In the face of all this brutalization, I personally worry sometimes that discussing 'liberating sexualities' in the West feels like an obscenity in itself.

56 Such figures as I use are always changing and problematic, and are readily available from a range of local and international reports on line. See, for example, the UN Human Development Report (2014), available at: http://hdr.undp.org/sites/default/files/hdr14-report-en-1.pdf. But there is a major research project to be carried out in this area. Studies of the world poor rarely mention sexualities, and sexualities studies all but ignore poverty.

57 The classic statement of this is C.B. Macpherson (1962). A neglected sociological update is Abercrombie et al. (1986).

58 Thus, as an undergraduate I was introduced to David Riesman's *The Lonely Crowd* (1950) and the classic Alexis De Tocqueville's *Democracy in America* (1835). My graduate days were the hippy days of Charles Reich's *The Greening of America* (1970) and Peter Berger's *The Homeless Mind* (1973). We had arrived at the time of Ralph Turner's 'impulsive self' (1976), Lois Zurcher's *The Mutable Self* (1977) and Tom Wolfe's '"Me" Decade' (1976). In the late 1970s, Richard Sennet's *The Fall of Public Man* (1977) and Christopher Lasch's *The Culture of Narcissism* (1979) became critical talking points. More recently, we have been introduced to Anthony Giddens's *Modernity and Self Identity* (1991), Ulrich Beck and Elizabeth Beck-Gersheim's *Individualization* (2002a), and Anthony Elliot and Charles Lemert's *New Individualism* (2006/2012). The titles of the books say a great deal. And so it continues.

59 These terms are derived from: Mazlish (2009), Friedman (2011), Joas (2013).

60 See Wouters (2004: 9). Wouters (2007) updates the ideas of Norbert Elias (1939/1978).

61 The works cited here are: on Mexico, Cantú, Jr (2009), Gonzalez-López (2005); on Filipino, Manalansan (2003); on Hong Kong, Kong (2010); on Peru, Vasquez Del Aquila (2013); on Cuba, Peña (2013). On the queer diaspora in general, see Patton and Sánchez-Eppler (2000) and the special issue of *GLQ* on Queer/Migration (2008, vol. 14, nos. 2–2). On migration patterns more generally, see UN (2013), UNCHR (2013).

62 The earliest statements of global sex can be found in Altman (2001), Binnie (2004), Padilla et al. (2007).

63 Writings on globalization is enormous. I have found Bauman (1998), Beck (2000b) and Nederveen Pieterse (2015/2004) especially useful.

64 See Inhorn (2007). Also see Browner and Sargent (2011), Knecht et al. (2012).

65 See Urry (2000, 2007).

66 These are very much the words of the global scholar Nederveen Pieterse (2015/2004).

Chapter 3 Cosmopolitan Sexualities: Living With Different Lives

1 See Clark (1997), Cheah (2006), Dallmayr (2002), Menocal (2002), Sen (2005).

2 Holton also excludes the popular meanings designated by Helen Gurley Brown, editor of the magazine *Cosmopolitanism*, or indeed the popular television series *Sex in the City*.

3 The quotes come from Appiah (2006: xv), Hannerz (1996: 103), Beck (2006: 7), Fine (2007: xii–xiii), Nussbaum (2006: 324). I have also found Delanty (2009, 2012) a valuable guide.

4 Tilly (2004) provides a short valuable history of social movements.

5 On these new global movements, see Moghadam (2012); and Stegger et al. (2012) for visions of the Global Justice Movement (GJM) and its organizations within the World Social Forum (WSF).

6 I use these three examples because they are clearly discussed in Parker et al. (2014). But there are many more. See, as further examples: for Africa, Currier (2012); for India, Dave (2012). For multiple cases, see also Lind (2010), Currier (2012), Tremblay et al. (2011).

7 On this history, see Antrobus (2004), Rupp (1997), Basu (2010). For specific country examples of the worldwide women's movement, see, for Iran, Barlow (2012); for Indonesia, Rinaldo (2013).

8 See Diez (2011).

9 See Marsiaj (2011).

10 For early histories of the gay movement, see Lauritsen and Thorstad (1995), Weeks (1997).

11 See Itaborahy and Zhu (2014). For these global developments, see Adam et al. (1999), Tremblay et al. (2012), Dave (2012), De La Dehesa (2010), Santos (2013).

12 See Petchesky (2003), Turshen (2007).

13 A point made by Kaldor (2003).

14 See Zenn (2012).

15 Mazower (2012) provides a very valuable history of world governance.

16 There is an important study by Sharratt (2011), which documents some of the decision-making at the ICTY concerning the rape and sexual violence war crimes.

17 This has long been central to the arguments of the leading sociologist Manuel Castells (2012). On contemporary activism and media, see Gerbaudo (2012). For critiques of the new social media, see Fuchs (2013), van Dijck (2013). These are heady times and there are both good stories and bad stories being told about the power of the new media in politics.

18 For a sample of cases studies, see Lind (2010).

19 The most valuable analyses include Aggleton and Parker (2010), Corrêa et al. (2008), Lee (2011), Petchesky (2003), Girard (2010), Parker et al. (2014).

20 I discuss the issue of rights more fully in Plummer (2010b).

21 As Witte and Green (2012) clearly show.

22 On the history of human rights, see Ishay (2004), Mazlish (2009). A more complex foundation is suggested by Joas (2013).

23 See this important and influential discussion in Arendt (1951/1979). For a discussion of this widely cited and critical idea of Arendt, see Birmingham (2006).

24 On the linkages between rights and citizenships, see Plummer (2003a: ch. 3). Classic statements on sexual citizenship include Evans (1993), Weeks (1998), Richardson (2000). Critical problems are raised in Bell and Binnie (2000), Roseneil (2013).

25 Petchesky (2000: 81).

26 On the European Court and gay rights in Europe, see Johnson (2012).

27 The full text of the Yogyakarta Principles, in all six UN languages, may be found at www.yogyakartaprinciples.org.

28 See UNHCHR (2012).

29 I prefer the odd little word 'nasty' over the more widely used word 'evil' – because that word really brings such a baggage with it. For an important discussion of the dangerous use of the word 'evil' in the modern world, see Bernstein (2005).

30 More general discussions of the 'trouble' with cosmopolitanism can be found in Braidotti et al. (2013) and Lettevall and Petrov (2014) even as they continue to champion it 'reluctantly' and call for a 'cosmopolitics'.

31 The idea of 'glocalization' appears to have been popularized by Roland Robertson (1992); it is now widely used to capture the way the local shapes the global.

32 In his study of the needed reforms, Goldin (2013) suggests that a lot of the perpetual reforming changes are little more than 'rearranging the deck chairs in the *Titanic*'. For a truly scathing critique of these organizations and the rights industry generally, see Hopgood (2013). See also Weiss, Thomas G. (2012).

33 The title of an important collection of essays by the leading legal feminist scholar Catharine MacKinnon (2006), in which she confronts many of the issues I raise head on with a strong universalist approach.

34 UNICEF (2013).

35 See Barlow (2012: 16).

36 Massad (2007: 49–50). Massad's work has been criticized for overstating the gay critique of the Muslim world, and underplaying the diversity of positions on the Western world and the gay movement.

37 On Mexico and Brazil, see De La Dehesa (2010); on Singapore, see Yue and Zubillaga-Pow (2012), which suggests how even in an illiberal authoritarian state, new forms of life emerge.

38 For the fullest instance of this argument, which has been hugely influential, see Puar (2007).

39 See Mohanty (2003). See also Barlow (2012) and, for the Indian case, Kapur (2005).

40 Lister (1997: 66). Lister draws, as I do, from Kymlicka (1995), in which a powerful claim is made for minority rights within citizenship frameworks.

41 See Appadurai (1990).

42 These ideas are themselves multiplying and are being developed in a number of directions. A good selection of these nomadic, moving, travelling ideas are discussed in the work of Braidotti (2012). On 'scattered hegemonies', see Grewal and Kaplan (1994); on mobilities, see Urry (2000, 2007).

43 See http://www.vatican.va/gpII/documents/homily-pro-eligendo-pontifice_20050418_en.html. The current Pope Francis continues to see this 'tyranny' as a major issue.

44 I have long been a fan of the work of Peter Berger, even though he has sometimes led me down strange religious and political paths that I do not agree with. See Berger and Zijderveld (2009).

45 There have been many references to this throughout this book. But classics include Krafft-Ebing (1886/1931), Kinsey et al. (1948), Ford and Beach (1952/1965), Roughgarden (2004).

46 Hundreds of basic universals have been detected across all societies. For a widely cited list of these, see Brown (1991).

47 See, for one example, the collection edited by Delanty and Strydom (2003).

48 As I see it, we need to build out of standpoint theory to realist theory.

49 See Berlin (1954/1969) for the original argument; and Lukes (2008) for a discussion.

50 See Berger and Zijderveld (2009: 158) for a prolegomena to a 'middle position between relativism and fundamentalism'.

51 Benhabib (2011: 2).

52 See the work of Ulrich Beck on this, available at: http://www.ulrichbeck.net-build.net/index.php?page=cosmopolitan.

53 See Kurasawa (2007) on human rights as practices in globalization movements.

54 Waltzer (1997: 80) asks: should we tolerate the intolerant? See also Abrahams and Williams (2008).

55 See Brown (2006: 202), Connell (2007).

56 See Walters (2014) for an analysis of the problems in the USA. Apparent tolerance does not bring true equality.

57 This classic debate has been most clearly outlined in Fraser (2009).

58 Kant's work *Perpetual Peace* was published in 1795 and speaks of 'world citizenship'. It has been very influential.

59 A wonderful essay on the fanatic can be found in Oz (2012).
60 See Braidotti et al. (2013).

Chapter 4 Cultural Sexualities: Cultivating Awareness of Complexity

1   The quote is from Benhabib (2002: ix). Chapter 1 of her book provides a very valuable discussion of the idea of culture.
2   A term taken from Elizabeth Gaskell's novel *Cranford* and adopted by theorists as diverse as Ernest Gellner, Homi Bhabha and Selya Benhabib to describe the commonplace of everyday life. See Benhabib (2002: 9).
3   On hybridity, see Burke (2009); for the postcolonial argument, see Canclini (1995).
4   Darwin (1871: ch. 8).
5   For a critical account of this biological approach and the way it dominates media reports, see Lancaster (2003). On the problem of human universals, see Brown (1991); and for recent discussions, see Everett (2012), Prinz (2012), Tallis (2011).
6   For an example of the controversial theories of the sociobiological basis of rape, see Thornhill and Palmer (2001).
7   Available at: http://oregonstate.edu/instruct/phl302/texts/mont aigne/montaigne-essays--2.html.
8   There is much written about the extraordinary Burton. For a rich biography, see Brodie (2003).
9   The literature on sexual variety is now vast. Illustrations of this are littered throughout this book; for example, from Krafft-Ebing (1886/1931) through Freud (1905/1962) and Kinsey et al. (1948, 1953) to Aggleton et al. (2013).
10 Debates over essentialism have a long and controversial history. The follies of superimposing Western 'essentialist' prejudices, often colonialist, on other cultures become more and more apparent.
11 For a history of these conferences up to 2013, see *Culture, Health and Sexuality* 15, suppl. 2, August 2013, pp. 128–136.
12 This is not the place to document this history, but I have done this elsewhere. See Plummer (2001b, 2008, 2012a).
13 Tamale (2011: 6).
14 See, for example, the discussions in Jackson et al. (2008), McLelland and Mackie (2014), Wieringa and Sivori (2013), Duangwises and

Jackson (2013). All in their own ways act as landmark books bringing together new authors from different parts of the world to demonstrate the complexity of world global sexual cultures.

15 As well as Huntington (1996), see Therborn (2010), Stearns (2010).

16 Jeff Hearn's (2009) idea of trans-patriarchy as a way of 'talking about patriarchies, intersectionality and transnationalization at the same time' is a provocative one.

17 There are now some excellent studies starting to appear – for example, an excellent review in the introductory essay in Tamale (2011); and the work of Mark Epprecht (2008, 2013) on gay issues is outstanding. A website has also been set up to counter all the general misinformation – see Africa Check at: http://africacheck.org/.

18 See McClintlock (1995), Young (1995).

19 On the change in Africa, see UNAIDS Update (2013). More generally, see the writings of Hunter (2003), Thornton (2008), Hunter (2010) and Squires (2013). Epstein (2008) describes her research into the sexual mores of Uganda, revealing the high frequency with which men and women engage in concurrent sexual relationships.

20 Epprecht (2008, 2013) has traced both the history of and current issues around same-sex practices in southern Africa, examining the emergence of gay and lesbian identities in the context of colonial rule, Christian education, apartheid and what he calls 'racial capitalism'.

21 On African politics and social movements, see Epprecht (2013), Nyeck and Epprecht (2013), Tamale (2011).

22 See Burger (2012: 6). There is growing writing on China: see especially Rofel (2007), Kong (2012), Zheng (2009).

23 Bouhdiba (1975/2004: 88, 19).

24 See Barlow (2012), El Feki (2013).

25 See Murray and Roscoe (1997), El-Rouayheb (2005), and, of course, Massad (2002, 2007).

26 Especially the Middle Eastern and Northern African (MENA) region; this is well documented by Whittaker (2011).

27 On Indonesia and gay life, see Bennett and Davies (2014), Blackwood (2010), Boellstorff (2005), Wieringa (2002).

28 This important idea is derived from Gramsci (2000) developed by Hall (1987) and applied to gender and masculinity by Connell (1995) with the now widely cited classic account of *hegemonic masculinity*.

29 I have written on this elsewhere – see Plummer (2009) – and was, long ago, much influenced by David Matza (1961). A major statement can be found in Maffesoli (1993). There is a now well-recognized strain of writing about the 'stranger' (Simmel, 1972; Schütz, 1944), the 'outsider' (Camus, 1942; Becker, 1963), the 'marginal' (Stonequist, 1937), and the 'invisible man' (Ellison, 1952) – as well as the Apollonian and the Dionysian (Nietzsche, 1886/2008); also, the misfits, the grotesque and the gothic; the 'tricksters', the 'liminal' and the 'sublime', much of which touches on the 'sexual outsider'. Here too are those who wear 'the mask' or the 'veil'; who travel, cross borders, who transgress liminal thresholds. The now widely used postcolonial idea of the 'subaltern' is also relevant here. See Spivak (1988).

30 See, for example, El Feki (2013), al-Haqq Kugle (2010), Tamale (2011).

31 This classification is loosely inspired by a famous typology developed by the sociologist Robert K. Merton in a widely cited article published in 1938. I also hint at how these 'anomic' subcultures may well be linked to 'social types' and here I think we could also valuably turn to Simmel (1972, esp. Part III) to start assembling a range of 'social sexual types'. I can only be sketchy here, but there is an interesting study to be conducted along these lines. Other responses could be developed: abusive sexualities seems to be another major tradition, but as I discuss this throughout the book, I have ignored it here.

32 See Phipps (2006).

33 Abbott (1999: 15–16).

34 See Carrigan (2011); also see the AVEN website at: http://www. asexuality.org/home/overview.html.

35 In using the word 'engulfment', I am thinking of Erving Goffman's classic article on role distance (1961), and how children on a merry-go-round move through incompetence, to engulfment and embracing and on to distance. Sexual rituals may well have similar phases.

36 On the history of masturbation, see Laqueur (2003). Betty Dodson was a key figure in developing masturbation workshops in the 1970s, and AIDS facilitated the emergence of 'buddy jerk off' groups in the 1980s.

37 For a lively ethnography of Faeries and Leathermen (and Bears), see Hennen (2008). Studies of BDSM include Beckman (2009) and Newmahr (2011).

38 Barbara Ehrenreich (2007) provides a marvellous history of 'collective joy', and ecstatic rituals.

39 A good start is made in Dollimore (1991).

40 Halperin (1995: 62).

41 While the ideas of Michel Foucault certainly loom large, the roots of contemporary queer theory (if not the term) are usually to be found in the works of Eve Kasofsky Sedgwick, David Halperin, Michael Warner and Judith Butler (and to a lesser extent Donna Haraway and Teressa de Lauretis). With Arlene Stein (1994), I long ago expressed some reservations about this stance, while also stressing the often dazzling originality of queer theory (Plummer, 2013b).

42 See, for example, Puar (2007).

43 See Muñoz (2009), Freeman (2010), Ahmed (2004), Halberstam (2011, 2012), Jagose (2013).

44 One useful volume of many that brings together queer theory writings is Hall and Jagose (2012). For some of the recent controversial statements, see, Edelman (2004), Halberstam (2011). See also Warner's (2012) sympathetic statement over the possible transforming demise of queer theory.

45 I am drawing here from my own knowledge of what was happening in this time. The history of safe sex has yet to be written.

46 See Dean (2009).

47 On some of these concepts and complexity, see Dowsett (1996), Kimmel (2007).

48 See Mead (1935), Herdt (1981), Humphreys (1970), Newton (1972), Connell (1995).

49 In order these studies were: Boellstorf (2005), Farrer (2002), Zheng (2009), Peña (2013), Manalansan (2003).

50 On the cultures of new gay movements, see Dave (2012) on India and Howe (2013) on Nicaragua; on women's Muslim movements, see Hélie and Hoodfar (2012) and Rinaldo (2013) on Indonesia.

51 See Boonmongkon and Jackson (2012).

52 The modern Western word for 'lesbian' (derived form the ancient Greek island Lesbos), takes many forms across the world; see Lelia Rupp's elegant history (2009: esp. 144).

53 See, for example, Chin and Finckenauer (2013).
54 See Gruenbaum (2000).
55 See Kulick (1998), Reddy (2005), Kong (2010, 2012). For the transgender case in China, see also Chiang (2012).
56 See Prince (1976), Benjamin (1966/1976). Both books were among the first I ever read on these areas; they are now, of course, seriously out of date.
57 See David Valentine (2007); also see The Transgender Road Map at: http://www.tsroadmap.com/start/tgterms.html.
58 See the website: http://www.tg-films.info/.

Chapter 5 Contested Sexualities: Inventing Enemies, Making Boundaries

1 There are those who argue for collective rights, and those who favour individual rights. And then there are similar tensions over citizenship and the contests over many versions of what is prime: economic, legal, welfare, intimate, cultural, feminist, global and the rest. For a good sample of rights debates, see Isin and Turner (2002).
2 It might also be added that conflict can indeed often be functional. For the classic statement of this, see Coser (1964), who suggests that conflict tends to be dysfunctional only for social structures in which there is insufficient toleration or institutionalization of conflict.
3 See the entire corpus of Jeffreys' work, but note, in particular, 2009 and 2012.
4 See, for example, Chauncey (1994), Doan (2001), Houlbrook (2005).
5 See Stein (1997), Robinson (2008), Hammick and Cohler (2009).
6 See Plummer (2003a: 34–40).
7 See the discussions in Corrêa et al. (2008).
8 On these global conflicts in general, see Huntington (1996).
9 On abortion in Poland, see Kramer (2005); on adultery in Turkey, see Pinar (2008). Valuable studies of community conflict include Stein (2003), Linneman (2003). See also Duggan and Hunter (2006) on sex wars and Hunter and Wolfe (2006) for the ongoing 'culture wars' debate in the USA.
10 Conflicts within a nation can soon spill over to the wider global world. In any event, there is now much global monitoring. See,

e.g., the very useful volume by Parker et al. (2010) and the Sexuality Policy Watch website: http://www.sxpolitics.org/?cat=1.

11 See the accounts on the Muslim women's movements: in Iran, Barlow (2012); in Indonesia, Rinaldo (2013); and, more generally, Hélie & Hoodfar (2012).

12 See, respectively: on transgender, Elliot (2010); on gay marriage, Bernstein and Taylor (2013); on Iran and women, Barlow (2012); and on sex work, Agustín (2007).

13 Claims of some recent strands of political theory suggest the need for an 'agonistic culture': see Mouffe (2013).

14 See Walby (2009).

15 Strikingly, though controversially, in the works of Anderson (2009), McCormack (2012), Dean (2014). This strand of argument suggests that in some Western cultures masculinity is changing alongside homophobia. How such arguments could be applied to the fears in some Muslim cultures remains to be seen.

16 On race and sexuality, see the important work by Nagel (2003). See also Eng (2010), Cohen (1999), Gopinath (2005).

17 Initially in the work of Mary Daly, now in the study by Sheila Jeffreys (2012).

18 This is illustrated in the 2011 Madeleva Lecture in Spirituality given by Kwok Pui-Lan; see Pui-Lan (2012).

19 Cited in Buss and Herman (2003: xiv).

20 See Alexander (2012). He speaks of cultural trauma, but I suspect his ideas could be readily developed into notions of 'cultural sexual trauma': the war rapes in Bosnia for example must have left many deep social wounds, and across generations. This is an interesting area for future investigation.

21 There have been many studies of these colonial tendencies. A classic example is McClintock (1995).

22 Bourdieu (1993: 95).

23 The earliest 'modern' sociological ideas on this derive from the sociologist Karl Mannheim (1893–1947), who suggested different kinds of generations – notably *nostalgic generations*, who are backward-looking, and *utopian generations*, who are forward-looking (they suggest 1968ers were and are utopians). Utopian generations are forward-looking – searching for new and better worlds; but within generations there will also be those who seek to return to past radical

sexual worlds. Old ways may be seen as achieving more than new ones. See Edmunds and Turner (2002), drawing from Mannheim. I have discussed all this in more detail elsewhere: see Plummer (2010a, 2015).

24 On the closed mind, see Rokeach (1960).

25 Studies of the regulation behind BDSM normativity include Newmahr (2011), Weiss, Margot Danielle (2012).

26 This imagery comes from Lévi-Strauss (1955/1973: 287–8).

27 See the crucial work of Durkheim (1895/1964: ch. 3). Of value also are Douglas (1966), Erikson (1966).

28 See Wolfe (1992: 323), Taylor (1989: 27), Beck (1997: 81). The anti-psychiatrist Thomas Szasz has said this even more pithily: 'In the animal kingdom, the rule is, eat or be eaten; in the human kingdom, define or be defined' (1973: 20).

29 It is in the work of John Urry (2000) that we find the idea of mobilities being fully developed as a key way of grasping the world. Social life is subject to flows, fluidities, transformations, amorphousness, networks, contingencies, movement and complexities.

30 The most influential writing on stigma is Goffman (1963).

31 See Rubin (2011: 137–93).

32 Rubin (2011: 151).

33 Douglas (1966: 48). I have used her work and discussed this idea in more detail elsewhere; see Plummer (2007).

34 There has been a very substantial writing on moral panics ever since the idea was first formulated in the works of Howard S. Becker (1963), Jock Young (1971) and Stanley Cohen (1971/2011). It does, however, raise significant theoretical, methodological, political and, increasingly, comparative problems. It is not at all clear, for example, that the ideas can be applied backwards in history or to a wider range of world cultures. I do make some gestures in this direction here, but I am not sure it can be done like this.

35 See Lancaster (2011: 11). This telling and timely book bridges a personal account of a school teacher accused of child sex abuse, together with the rise of the punitive state and fear of the 'sex monster' in the United States.

36 For recent accounts of moral panics and sexuality, see Herdt (2009), Lancaster (2011), Lee (2011). On 'punitive states', see Wacquant (2009).

37 I discuss this in Plummer (2003b). For further examples, see Jenkins (1998).

38 On Iran, see Najmabadi (2014: ch. 3); on the 2008 district of Jafferbad in Pakistan, see Khan (2012).

39 See Kaoma (2012).

40 See Abu-Lughod (1986/2000).

41 Richards (1991/2013: 1).

42 See Moore (2000); see also Robert I. Moore (1987).

43 Juergensmeyer (2008: 253).

44 There is a rich literature on all this. For a sample: in general, see Freud (1930/2005: 53–4); on death, see Becker (1973); on meaning, see Frankl (1946/1959) and Lifton (1979); on material desperation, see Agamben (1998); on status and 'rankism', see Fuller and Gerloff (2008); on cultural trauma, see Alexander (2012); on how 'ghosts' and ancestors shape our contemporary anxieties over generations, see Gordon (1997), Stein (2014). On modernity and ambivalence, see Bauman (1991). Most centrally, the brilliant work of Sen (2006) on identity and violence provided a stimulus to my thinking for this whole area.

45 There has long been talk about 'the new masculinity crisis' (Plummer, 2004) but see also the recent work of Kimmel (2013). Aslam (2012) links the debate to the current Islamic terrorist crisis and men.

46 A major start is to be found in the important study by Stan Cohen (2000).

47 See Bataille (2006: 11), Davis (1983: 12), Rubin (2011: 148).

48 I am not saying that sexuality itself is a powerful drive, a huge power 'in itself', that causes this vulnerability. What I am saying is that the human sexualities are contingent on the kinds of relations we encounter and how they bring to the fore our potentials for major vulnerabilities, fragilities, precariousness.

Chapter 6 Communicative Sexualities:
On the Hope and Empathy for a Common Global Humanity

1 *Communicative* sexualities must be clearly distinguished from *communicable* sexualities, which speaks to disease transmission and is widely used in the field of health and sexual disease. I am grateful to my friend Rob Stones for pointing out this distinction.

2 The term 'empathy' itself is a contested little mongrel word that does not seem to enter the English language until the early twentieth century (when it was translated from the German *Einfuehlung*). But the term 'sympathy', which is closely linked, has a longer life. We can find it being notably developed in the Scottish Enlightenment (*c.* 1750) and given pride of place by both David Hume in *A Treatise of Human Nature* (1739) and Adam Smith in *The Theory of Moral Sentiments* (1759) in their theories of the moral sentiments. A century or so later, this idea entered the languages of North American philosophy in the work of the early pragmatists, but especially the sociologist Charles Horton Cooley (1864–1929), who highlighted the ways in which we always 'dwell in the minds of others without knowing it' (see Cooley 1988). Cooley's compatriot in ideas, George Herbert Mead, is often seen as a key turning point in the history of this idea. He spoke of the necessity of the social self, of role-taking and the capacity for 'taking on the attitude of the other'. In *Mind, Self and Society*, he states: 'The individual experiences himself as such, not directly, but only indirectly, from the particular standpoints of other individual members of the same social group.' In addition, Mead was a dedicated internationalist and he saw that over the past few centuries, the modern world had been becoming more and more aware of an international other. Mead's cosmopolitanism is discussed in Aboulafia (2001: 18).

3 See Slote (2007), Baron-Cohen (2011), Kohut (1971: 306).

4 See Morrell (2010), Hoffman (2000), Haddon (2003), Decety and Ickes (2011), Rifkin (2009), Pinker (2011). See also Clohesy (2013) on the politics of empathy.

5 The links between diverse religions through notions of compassion has been well made by Armstrong (2011).

6 See Forman-Barzilai (2010: Part III).

7 On stranger compassion, see the summary statement by Ekman (2014) – and in conversation with the Dali Lama. More widely, on distant others, see Chouliaraki (2006).

8 See Arendt (1951, 1958, 1973). See also the work of Zimbardo (2007).

9 On prejudice, see Gadamer (1975/2013).

10 In order, these studies were Abu-Lughod (2000, 2013), Blackwood (2010), Inhorn (2012), Rahman (2014). A valuable collection of gay voices 'living out Islam' can be found in al-Haqq Kugle (2014).

11 See Stern (2003).
12 De Bary (2013) and Dallmayr (2002) have taken great strides towards this goal. Sen (2005) has helped us explore specific cultures – e.g., India and the 'Western imagination'. Critical problems of translation and 'sameness' are raised by Palumbo-Liu (2012).
13 On sympathy biography, see Clark (1997).
14 See Coles (2010).
15 Macintyre (1981/2011) has taught us the role of narrative in connecting to our past traditions, Arendt (1958/1998) about the ways narrative can repair our humanity and heal our wounds, Nussbaum (1997) about their role in cultivating humanity, and Frank (2010) about how stories are dialogic and can be 'good companions'. I raise many more issues around narrative elsewhere (Plummer, 2001a, 2013).
16 I have suggested elsewhere how much of this works (Plummer, 2005). See also Nelson (2001). For some telling counter-narratives on women's sexuality, see Pereira (2014).
17 See Ensler (2013) and the website for One Billion Rising at: http://www.democracynow.org/2013/2/14/one_billion_rising_playwright_eve_ensler.
18 See Mai (2007). There are many others. See films like *The Stoning of Soraya M* (2008). Abu-Lughod (2013) is critical of some of them, accusing them of becoming a kind of 'slave pornography'.
19 There is also a documentary film about him: see *Call Me Kuchu* (2012; dir Maliko Zouhali-Worrall). See http://www.guardian.co.uk/film/video/2012/nov/05/call-me-kuchu-david-kato-video.
20 For discussions of these 'celebrities', see Najmabadi (2014), Dworkin et al. (2013).
21 See Malala Yousafzai (2014).
22 See Bakhtin (1963/1984: 293). The works of many sociologists, theologians and philosophers – Kenneth Burke, David Bohm, Martin Buber, Hans Gadamer, Hannah Arendt, Ernest Becker, Mikhail Bakhtin, Seyla Benhabib, Eric Fromm, Arthur Frank, Paulo Freire, Jürgen Habermas, George Herbert Mead, and Paul Ricoeur and many others – can all help us to build a deeper understanding of dialogue. For illustrations of dialogue at work in religion, see Habermas (2010), Pui-Lan (2012).
23 Theories of recognition, e.g., Honneth (1996), are relevant here.

24 'The argument culture' is a nice phrase coined by the psychologist Deborah Tannen (1998) to suggest that our culture always seems to want to take sides on everything. Life is turned into a polarity, a binary, a dichotomy, a split, a struggle between good and evil. Might not life be more like a continuum of differences – more subtle and complex than brute divides?

25 See Rifkind and Picco (2014). Very frequently, interlocutors have personal histories with each other, sometimes involving personal hostility, and many dialogues flounder on these hidden hostilities – major wars may happen because of this. So even if a dialogue 'gets personal', these hostilities need to be clarified and made explicit.

26 There is of course a long history of trying to resolve world conflicts and seeking peace that we can learn from – most famously, Kant's search for perpetual peace. These days, we see key institutions, many treaties, as well as many centres for conflict resolution or peace centres. The challenge is to develop the skills of conflict transformation – moving the conflict into a better situation through power sharing, developing reconciliation, fostering trust, generating feasible options, making mutual benefit agreements and, ultimately, creating peaceful resolutions: peacekeeping, peacemaking and peacebuilding. Anyone new to this area would find Rambotham et al.'s *Contemporary Conflict Resolution* (2012) a useful read. They espouse a position they call 'cosmopolitan conflict resolution'. I also found Brewer (2010) and Daly and Sarkin (2007) very valuable. Important in showing the personal face is Rifkind and Picco (2014).

27 See Oz (2012).

28 I have discussed these ideas more fully elsewhere – see Plummer (2003a: ch. 6) – but they do need full book treatment.

29 These were dialogues set up by Sexuality Policy Watch, but it does not seem that the viewpoints expressed were very contentious. So there are dialogues with the like, and dialogues with the different. It is the latter that matter most.

30 An interesting study arising from all this would be one that examines both *empirically* the existence of these suggested global worlds of compassion and *theoretically* the wider historical structures of care, dignity, etc., from which they derive. I see some starts with Sznaider (2001), Joas (2013).

31 Cited in Coles (2010: 241).

32 The modern ethics of care has been largely fostered within feminism, centring on connectedness and a responsibility towards others across different situations that change over time. Grand abstract theories that dominate academic philosophy need to be grounded in local practices. The late twentieth century saw the full-scale intellectual recognition of the importance of this ethics of care (from Carol Gilligan's 1982 classic *In A Different Voice* onwards), one that could be found in the embodied care grounded in the human bond between mother/parent and the child, moving outwards through 'circles of sympathy' (Forman-Barzilai, 2010) to the human bond with community and, ultimately, both the wider politics of belonging (Yuval-Davis, 2011), security (Hudson et al., 2012) and the environmental family (Ehrlich and Ornstein, 2012).

33 As the feminist philosopher Alison Assiter (2009: 86) concisely says (drawing from Kierkegaard), 'each of us is an embodied, needy and dependent being'.

34 Tronto (1993: 101).

35 Tremblay (2009: 17).

36 For telling discussions of these bitter conflicts, see Petchesky (2003), Corrêa et al. (2008).

37 Ban Ki-moon's comments were given on Human Rights Day, 2010, and can be found at http://www.un.org/sg/statements/?nid=4992. He has made many similar critical comments since then. The full text of the *Yogyakarta Principles*, in all six of the UN languages, may be found at: www.yogyakartaprinciples.org. An *Activist's Guide to the Yogyakarta Principles* has also been developed and is available for download at: http://iglhrc.org/sites/default/files/Activists_Guide_Yogyakarta_Principles.pdf.

38 See Nussbaum (2011: x).

39 See Ahmed (2010).

40 Nussbaum (2005) discusses this point.

41 See Nussbaum (1999: 41-2; 2000: 78–80).

42 For contrasting versions of justice in general, see Fraser (2009), Sen (2009), Sandel (2009). For contrasting versions of sexual and gender justice, see Nussbaum (1999), Kapur (2005) (contrasting feminists); Kaplan (1997), Teunis and Herdt (2007) (mainly gay).

43 It has to be said that, overwhelmingly, the writings on cosmopolitanisms are by political scientists and they speak mainly of political

matters. See, for example, Held (2010). In this book I speak of wider matters.

44 For recent debates on cosmopolitan politics, see especially Ingram (2013).

45 Maybe the small Nordic countries are the most successful so far.

46 There is a seemingly infinite bibliography of writings on contemporary democracy that could include Archibugi (2008), Braidotti (2013), Connolly (2013), Fraser (2009), McNay (2014), Mouffe (2013), Unger (2009), Young (1990), among many others. Arguing for a more local and grounded approach, I found Goldfarb (2006) and Ingram (2013) to be refreshing.

47 See Kollman (2013).

48 See the critique by Cheah (2006) on 'inhuman conditions'; and Schwartz (2004) on choice and its limits. There has also been an internal backlash, seen in the work of, for instance, Puar (2007) and others on 'homonationalism'.

49 See Itaborahy and Zhu (2013: 12–20).

50 UN (2014: Table 5).

51 See the annual report of Reporters Without Borders, *Enemies of the Internet*. Available at: http://12mars.rsf.org/2014-en/enemies-of-the-internet-2014-entities-at-the-heart-of-censorship-and-surveillance/.

52 See Spijkerboer (2013).

53 On South Africa, see the work of Epprecht (2013), amongst others. On Spain, see the special issue of the journal *Sexualities* 14/5 (October 2011): pp 503–614. On Central and Eastern Europe, see Kulpa and Mizielińska (2011). On Southern Europe, see Santos (2013).

54 See Itaborahy and Zhu (2014: 84).

55 See Lennox and Waites (2013) for a detailed empirical overview of the issues in the Commonwealth.

56 See for examples Campbell (2013), Therborn (2013).

57 The conservative philosopher Roger Scruton has argued the case for pessimism. He has critiqued the modern world for its ameliorative reformist optimism and highlighted 'the uses of pessimism and the danger of false hope' (2010). I am more inclined to follow Popper and Gramsci. As Popper once remarked: 'What we can do is . . . make life a little less terrible and a little less unjust in every genera-

tion. A good deal can be achieved in this way' (1948: 115). And in another widely cited remark: 'I'm a pessimist because of intelligence, but an optimist because of will', Antonio Gramsci, 'Letter from Prison' (19 December 1929).

58 Unger (2009: 182*f*).
59 This is, though, a very controversial thesis. See the symposium and critical comments in *Sociology* 47/6 (2013): 1224–32.
60 On Scandinavian gay marriage, see Rydström (2011); on Latin American gay rights, see Corrales and Pecheny (2010), De La Dehesa (2010); on South Africa, see Epprecht (2013); on Europe, see Beger (2004), Downing and Gillett (2011). June 2013 saw the adoption of a Federal law banning 'homosexual propaganda' in Russia. See the reports in Itaborahy and Zhu (2014).
61 Bloch (1938–47/1986: vol. 1, p. 10). Bloch is critical of the idea of utopia, and I doubt if he would approve of my using Rodgers and Hammerstein on 'dreams' as an aphorism to start this part of the book. But I have found his ideas very valuable nevertheless. The late José Esteban Muñoz (2009), has used them very creatively.
62 Wells (1906: 367).
63 The Rorty quote comes from the obituary that Habermas published after Rorty's death in *Süddeutsche Zeitung* on 11 June 2007. Huxley is cited in Carlson (2002: 2).
64 See James (1920); also cited in Richardson (2006: 384).

References

Abbott, Elizabeth (1999) *A History of Celibacy*. Cambridge, MA: Di Capo Press.

Abercrombie, Nicolas, Stephen Hill and Bryan S. Turner (1986) *Sovereign Individuals of Capitalism*. London: Allen and Unwin.

Aboulafia, Mitchell (2001) *The Cosmopolitan Self: George Herbert Mead and Continental Philosophy*. Chicago: University of Illinois Press.

Abrahams, Kathryn and Mellisa S. Williams, eds (2008) *Toleration and Its Limits*. New York: New York University Press.

Abu-Lughod, Lila (1986/2000) *Veiled Sentiments: Honor and Poetry in a Bedouin Society*, 2nd edn. Berkeley: University of California Press.

Abu-Lughod, Lila (2013) *Do Muslim Women Need Saving?* Cambridge, MA: Harvard University Press.

Adam, Barry D., Jan W. Duyvendak and André Krouwel (1999) *The Global Emergence of Gay and Lesbian Politics: National Imprints of a Worldwide Movement*. Philadelphia: Temple University Press.

Admirand, Peter J. (2012) *Amidst Mass Atrocity and the Rubble of Theology*. London: Cascade Books.

Agamben, Giorgio (1998) *Homo Sacer: Sovereign Power and Bare Life*. Palo Alto, CA: Stanford University Press.

Aggleton, Peter and Richard Parker, eds (2010) *Routledge Handbook of Sexuality, Health and Rights*. London: Routledge.

Aggleton, Peter, Paul Boyce, Henrietta Moore and Richard Parker, eds (2013) *Understanding Global Sexualities*. London: Routledge.

Agustín, Laura (2007) *Sex at the Margins: Migration, Labour Markets and the Rescue Industry*. London: Zed Books.

Ahmed, Akbar S. (2003) *Islam Under Siege*. Cambridge: Polity.

Ahmed, Sara (2004) *The Cultural Politics of Emotion*. Edinburgh: University of Edinburgh Press.

Ahmed, Sara (2010) *The Promise of Happiness*. Durham, NC: Duke University Press.

Alexander, Jeffrey C. (2012) *Trauma: A Social Theory*. Cambridge: Polity.

al-Haqq Kugle, Scott Siraj (2010) *Homosexuality in Islam*. Oxford: One World.

al-Haqq Kugle, Scott Siraj (2014) *Living Out Islam: Voices of Gay, Lesbian and Transgender Muslims*. New York: New York University Press.

Altman, Dennis (2001) *Global Sex*. Chicago: University of Chicago Press.

Anderson, Elijah (1999) *Code of the Street: Decency, Violence and the Moral Life of the Inner City*. New York. W.W. Norton.

Anderson, Elijah (2011) *The Cosmopolitan Canopy: Race and Civility in Everyday Life*. New York: W.W. Norton.

Anderson, Eric (2009) *Inclusive Masculinity: The Changing Nature of Masculinities*. London: Routledge.

Antrobus, Peggy (2004) *The Global Women's Movement: Origins, Issues and Strategies*. London: Zed Books.

Aoyama, Kaoru (2009) *Thai Migrant Sexworkers: From Modernisation to Globalisation*. Basingstoke: Palgrave.

Appadurai, Arjun (1990) 'Disjuncture and difference in global cultural economy', *Theory, Culture and Society* 7: 295.

Appiah, Kwame Anthony (2005) *The Ethics of Identity*. Princeton: Princeton University Press.

Appiah, Kwame Anthony (2006) *Cosmopolitanism: Ethics in a World of Strangers*. London: Allen Lane.

Appiah, Kwame Anthony (2010) *The Honor Code: How Moral Revolutions Happen*. New York: Norton and Co.

Archibugi, Daniele (2008) *The Global Commonwealth of Citizens: Toward Cosmopolitan Democracy*. Princeton: Princeton University Press.

Arendt, Hannah (1951/1979) *The Origins of Totalitarianism*. New York: Harvest Books.

Arendt, Hannah (1958/1998) *The Human Condition*, 2nd edn. Chicago: University of Chicago Press.

Arendt, Hannah (1973) *Men in Dark Times*. Middlesex: Penguin.

Armstrong, Karen (2011) *Twelve Steps to a Compassionate Life*. London: Bodley Head.

Armstrong, Karen (2014) *Fields of Blood: Religion and the History of Violence*. London: Bodley Head.

Arnett, Ronald C., Janie Harden Fritz and Leeanne M. Bell (2009) *Communication, Ethics, Literacy: Dialogues and Differences*. London: Sage.

Aslam, Maleeha (2012) *Gender-Based Explosions: The Nexus Between Muslim Masculinities, Jihadist Islamism and Terrorism*. New York: United Nations University Press.

Assiter, Alison (2009) *Kierkegaard, Metaphysics and Political Theory*. London: Continuum.

Attwood, Feona, ed. (2009) *Mainstreaming Sex: The Sexualization of Western Culture*. London: I.B. Tauris.

Attwood, Feona, ed. (2010) *Porn.Com: Making Sense of Online Pornography*. London: Peter Lang.

Bailey, Martha and Amy J. Kaufman (2010) *Polygamy in the Monogamous World: Multicultural Challenges for Western Law and Policy*. Santa Barbara, CA: Praeger.

Bakhtin, Mikhail M., ed. (1963/1984) *Problems of Dostoyevsky's Poetics*. Minneapolis: University of Minnesota.

Barlow, Rebecca L. (2012) *Women's Human Rights and the Muslim Question: Iran's One Million Signatures Campaign*. Victoria: Melbourne University Press.

Barnett, Tony and Alan Whiteside (2006) *AIDS in the Twenty-First Century: Disease and Globalization*, 2nd edn. Basingstoke: Palgrave.

Baron-Cohen, Simon (2011) *Zero Degrees of Empathy*. London: Allen Lane.

Basu, Amrita, ed. (2010) *Women's Movements in the Global Era: The Power of Local Feminisms*. Westport: Greenwood.

Bataille, George (2006) *Eroticsm*. London: Marion Boyers.

Bauman, Zygmunt (1991) *Modernity and Ambivalence*. Cambridge: Polity.

Bauman, Zygmunt (1993) *Postmodern Ethics*. Oxford: Blackwell.

Bauman, Zygmunt (1998) *Globalization: The Human Consequences*. Cambridge: Polity.

Bauman, Zygmunt (2004) *Wasted Lives: Modernity and its Outcasts.* Cambridge: Polity.

Bauman, Zygmunt (2006) *Liquid Fear.* Cambridge: Polity.

Bauman, Zygmunt (2011) *Collateral Damage: Social Inequalities in a Global Age.* Cambridge: Polity.

Bauman, Zygmunt (2013) *Moral Blindness: The Loss of Sensitivity in Liquid Modernity.* Cambridge: Polity.

Bech, Henning (1997) *When Men Meet: Homosexuality and Modernity.* Cambridge: Polity.

Beck, Ulrich (1997) *The Reinvention of Politics: Rethinking Modernity in the Global Social Order.* Cambridge: Polity.

Beck, Ulrich (2000) *What is Globalization?* Cambridge: Polity.

Beck, Ulrich (2006) *Cosmopolitan Vision.* Cambridge: Polity.

Beck, Ulrich (2010) *A God of One's Own: Religion's Capacity for Peace and Violence.* Cambridge: Polity.

Beck, Ulrich and Elizabeth Beck-Gernsheim (1995) *The Normal Chaos of Love.* Cambridge: Polity.

Beck, Ulrich and Elizabeth Beck-Gernsheim (2002a) *Individualization.* London: Sage.

Beck, Ulrich and Elizabeth Beck-Gernsheim (2002b) *Reinventing the Family.* Cambridge: Polity.

Beck, Ulrich and Elizabeth Beck-Gernsheim (2013) *Distant Love: Personal Life in the Global Age.* Cambridge: Polity.

Becker, Ernest (1973) *The Denial of Death.* New York: Free Press.

Becker, Howard S. (1963) *Outsiders: Studies in the Sociology of Deviance.* Glencoe: Free Press.

Beckman, Andrea (2009) *The Social Construction of Sexuality and Perversion: Deconstructing Sadomasochism.* New York: Palgrave Macmillan.

Beger, Nico J. (2004) *Tensions in the Struggle for Sexual Minority Rights in Europe.* Manchester: Manchester University Press.

Bell, David and Jon Binnie (2000) *The Sexual Citizen: Queer Politics and Beyond.* Oxford: Polity.

Bellah, Robert N. and Hans Joas (2012) *The Axial Age and its Consequences.* Cambridge, MA: Belknap Press.

Benhabib, Seyla (2002) *The Claims of Culture: Equality and Diversity on the Global Era.* Princeton: Princeton University Press.

Benhabib, Seyla (2011) *Dignity in Adversity: Human Rights in Troubled Times.* Cambridge: Polity.

Benjamin, Harry (1966/1976) *The Transsexual Phenomenon*. New York: Dover Books.

Bennett, Linda Rae and Shartn Graham Davies, eds (2014) *Sex and Sexuality in Contemporary Thailand: Sexual Politics, Health, Diversity, and Representations*. London: Routledge.

Berger, Peter and Anton Zijderveld (2009) *In Praise of Doubt: How to Have Convictions Without Being a Fanatic*. New York: Harper One.

Berlin, Isaiah (1954/1969) *Four Essays on Liberty*. Oxford: Oxford University Press.

Bernstein, Elizabeth (2007) *Temporarily Yours: Intimacy, Authenticity and the Commerce of Sex*. Chicago: University of Chicago Press.

Bernstein, Mary and Verta Taylor (2013) *The Marrying Kind? Debating Same-Sex Marriage Within the Lesbian and Gay Movement*. Minneapolis: University of Minnesota Press.

Bernstein, Richard J. (2005) *The Abuse of Evil: The Corruption of Politics and Religion since 9/11*. Cambridge: Polity.

Bernstein, Richard J. (2010) *The Pragmatic Turn*. Cambridge: Polity.

Berry, Chris, Fran Martin and Audrey Yue, eds (2003) *Mobile Cultures: New Media in Asia*. Durham, NC: Duke University Press.

Bharat, Sandy and Joel Bharat (2007) *Interfaith: A Global Guide to Reflections from Around the World*. Abingdon: O Books.

Biltereyst, Daniel and Roel Vande Winkel, eds (2013) *Silencing Cinema: Film Censorship Around the World*. New York: Palgrave Macmillan.

Binnie, Jon (2004) *The Globalization of Sexuality*. London: Sage.

Birmingham, Peg (2006) *Hannah Arendt and Human Rights: The Predicament of Common Responsibility*. Bloomington: Indiana University Press.

Blackburn, Simon (2003) *Being Good: A Short Introduction to Ethics*, 2nd edn. Oxford: Oxford University Press.

Blackwood, Evelyn (2010). *Falling into the Lesbian World: Desire and Difference in Indonesia*. Hong Kong: Hong Kong University Press.

Bloch, Ernst (1938–47/1986) *The Principle of Hope*, 3 vols. Boston, MA: MIT Press.

Bob, Clifford (2012) *The Global Right Wing and the Clash of World Politics*. Cambridge: Cambridge University Press.

Boellstorf, Tom (2005) *The Gay Archipelago: Sexuality and Nation in Indonesia*. Princeton: Princeton University Press.

Boonmongkon, Pimpawun and Peter A. Jackson (2012) *Thai Sex Talk:*

The Language of Sex in Thailand. Chaing Mai: Mekong Press–Silkworm Books.

Borges, Jorge Luis (2000) *Labyrinths: Selected Stories and Other Writings*. London: Penguin Classics.

Bornstein, Kate (1995) *Gender Outlaw*. New York: Vintage.

Bouhdiba, Abdelwahab (1975/2004) *Sexuality in Islam*. London: Saqi.

Bourdieu, Pierre (1966) 'The sentiment of honour in Kabyle society', in J.G. Peristiany, ed., *Honour and Shame: The Value of Mediterranean Society*. Chicago: University of Chicago Press, pp. 191–241.

Bourdieu, Pierre (1993) 'Youth is just a word', in Bourdieu, *Sociology in Question*. London: Sage, pp. 94–102.

Bowman, James (2006) *Honor: A History*. New York: Encounter Books.

Braidotti, Rosi (2012) *Nomadic Theory*. New York: Columbia University Press.

Braidotti, Rosi (2013) *The Posthuman*. Cambridge: Polity.

Braidotti, Rosi, Patrick Hanafin and Bolette B. Blaagaard, eds (2013) *After Cosmopolitanism*. London: Routledge.

Brennan, Denise (2004) *What's Love Got to Do With It? Transnational Desires and Sex Tourism in the Dominican Republic*. Durham, NC: Duke University Press.

Brewer, John (2010) *Peace Processes: A Sociological Approach*. Cambridge: Polity.

Brodie, Fawn M. (2003) *The Devil Drives: A Life of Sir Richard Burton*. London: Eland Publishing.

Bromley, James W. and Will Stockton, eds (2013) *Sex Before Sex: Figuring the Act in Early Modern England*. Minneapolis: University of Minnesota Press.

Brown, Donald J. (1991) *Human Universals*. New York: McGraw Hill.

Brown, Wendy (2006) *Regulating Aversion: Tolerance in the Age of Identity and Empire*. Princeton: Princeton University Press.

Browner, Carole H. and Carolyn F. Sargent, eds (2011) *Reproduction, Globalization and the State*. Durham, NC: Duke University Press.

Brownmiller, Susan (1975) *Against Our Will: Men, Women and Rape*. New York: Simon and Shuster.

Buffington, Robert M., Eithne Luibhéid and Donna J. Guy, eds (2014) *A Global History of Sexuality: The Modern Era*. Chichester: Wiley.

Bullogh, Vern (1976) *Sexual Variance in Society and History*. New York: Wiley.

Burger, Richard (2012) *Behind the Red Door: Sex in China*. Hong Kong: Earnshaw Books.

Burke, Peter (2009) *Cultural Hybridity*. Cambridge: Polity.

Buss, Doris and Didi Herman (2003) *Globalizing Family Values: The Christian Right in International Politics*. Minneapolis: University of Minnesota Press.

Butler, Judith (1990) *Gender Trouble*. New York: Routledge.

Butler, Judith and Athena Athanasiou (2013) *Dispossession: The Performative in the Political*. Cambridge: Polity.

Campbell, Beatrix (2013) *End of Equality: The Only way is Women's Liberation*. London: Seagull.

Camus, Albert (1942) *The Outsider*. London: Penguin.

Canclini, Néstor García (1995) *Hybrid Cultures: Strategies for Entering and Leaving Modernity*. London: University of Minnesota Press.

Cantú, Lionel, Jr. (2009) *The Sexuality of Migration: Border Crossings and Mexican Immigrant Men*. New York: New York University Press.

Carlson, Richard (2002) *What About the Big Stuff? Finding Strength and Moving Forward When the Stakes Are High*. London: Hodder & Stoughton.

Carrigan, Mark (2011) 'There's more to life than just sex? Difference and commonality within the asexual community', *Sexualities* 14(4): 462–78.

Castells, Manuel (2012) *Networks of Outrage and Hope: Social Movements in the Internet Age*. Cambridge: Polity.

Change, Ha-Joon (2010) *23 Things They Don't Tell You About Capitalism*. London: Allen Lane.

Chapkis, Wendy (1997) *Live Sex Acts: Women Performing Erotic Labor*. New York: Routledge.

Chauncey, George (1994) *Gay New York: Gender, Urban Culture, and the Making of the Gay Male World, 1890–1940*. New York: Basic Books.

Cheah, Pheng (2006) *Inhuman Conditions: On Cosmopolitanism and Human Rights*. Cambridge, MA: Harvard University Press.

Chiang, Howard, ed. (2012) *Transgender China*. Basingstoke: Palgrave Macmillan.

Chin, Ko-lin and James O. Finckenauer (2013) *Selling Sex Overseas: Chinese Women and the Realities of Prostitution and Global Sex Trafficking*. New York: New York University Press.

Chouliaraki, Lillie (2006) *The Spectatorship of Suffering*. London: Sage.

Clark, Anna (2008) *Desire: A History of European Sexuality*. London: Routledge.

Clark, Candace (1997) *Misery and Company: Sympathy in Everyday Life*. Chicago: University of Chicago Press.

Clarke, Adele E. (2005) *Situational Analysis: Grounded Theory after the Postmodern Turn*. London: Sage.

Clarke, J.J. (1997) *Oriental Enlightenment: The Encounter between Asian and Western Thought*. London: Routledge.

Clohesy, Anthony M. (2013) *Politics of Empathy: Ethics, Solidarity, Recognition*. London: Routledge.

Cohen, Cathy J. (1999) *The Boundaries of Blackness: AIDS and the Breakdown of Black Politics*. Chicago: University of Chicago Press.

Cohen, Stanley (2000) *States of Denial: Knowing about Atrocities and Suffering*. Cambridge: Polity.

Cohen, Stanley (1971/2011) *Folk Devils and Moral Panics*. London: Routledge.

Coles, Robert (2010) *Handing One Another Along: Literature and Social Reflection*. New York: Random House.

Collins, Patricia Hill (1990) *Black Feminist Thought*. London: Routledge.

Connell, Raewyn, ed. (1995) *Masculinities*. Cambridge: Polity.

Connell, Raewyn (2007) *Southern Theory*. Cambridge: Polity.

Connolly, William E. (1995) *The Ethos of Pluralization*. Minneapolis: University of Minnesota Press.

Connolly, William E. (2013) *The Fragility of Things: Self-Organizing Processes, Neo-liberal Fantasies and Democratic Activism*. Durham, NC: Duke University Press.

Constable, Nicole (2003) *Romance on a Global Stage: Pen Pals, Virtual Ethnography and 'Mail Order Brides'*. Berkeley: University of California Press.

Cooley, Charles Horton (1988) *On Self and Social Organization*, ed. Hans-Joachim Schubert. Chicago: University of Chicago Press.

Corrales, Javier and Mario Pecheny (2010) *The Politics of Sexuality in Latin America*. Pittsburgh: University of Pittsburgh Press.

Corrêa, Sonia, Rosalind Petchesky and Richard Parker (2008) *Sexuality, Health and Human Rights*. London: Routledge.

Coser, Lewis (1964) *The Functions of Social Conflict*. London: Routledge.

Cuncun, Wu (2012) *Homoerotic Sensibilities in Late Imperial China*. London: Routledge.

Currier, Ashley (2012) *Out in Africa: LGBT Organizing in Namibia and South Africa* Minneapolis: Minnesota University Press.

Dabhoiwala, Faramerz (2012) *The Origins of Sex: A History of the First Sexual Revolution*. London: Allen Lane.

Dallmayr, Fred (2002) *Dialogue Among Civilizations: Some Exemplar Voices*. Basingstoke: Palgrave.

Daly, Erin and Jeremy Sarkin (2007) *Reconciliation in Divided Societies: Finding Common Ground*. Philadelphia: University of Pennsylvania Press.

Darwin, Charles (1871) *The Descent of Man, and Selection in Relation to Sex*. London: John Murray.

Dave, Naisargi N. (2012) *Queer Activism in India: A Story of Activism in India*. Durham, NC: Duke University Press.

Davis, Kevin, Angelina Fisher, Benedict Kingsbury and Sally Engle Merry, eds (2012) *Governance by Indicators: Global Power Through Classifications and Ranking*. Oxford: Oxford University Press.

Davis, Murray S. (1983) *Smut: Erotic Reality/Obscene Ideology*. Chicago: University of Chicago Press.

Dean, James Joseph (2014) *Straights: Heterosexuality in Post-Closeted Culture*. New York: New York University Press.

Dean, Tim (2009) *Unlimited Intimacy: Reflections on the Subculture of Barebacking*. Chicago: University of Chicago Press.

De Bary, Theodore W. M. (2013) *The Great Civilized Conversation: Education for a World Community*. New York: Columbia University Press.

de Beauvoir, Simone (1972) *All Said and Done*. Middlesex: Penguin Books.

Decety, Jean and William Ickes (2011) *The Social Neuroscience of Empathy*. Boston, MA: MIT Press.

De La Dehesa, Rafael (2010) *Queering the Public Sphere in Mexico and Brazil: Sexual Rights in Emerging Democracies*. Durham, NC: Duke University Press.

Delanty, Gerard (2009) *The Cosmopolitan Imagination: The Renewal of Critical Social Theory*. Cambridge: Cambridge University Press.

Delanty, Gerard, ed. (2012) *The Routledge Handbook of Cosmopolitanism*. London: Routledge.

Delanty, Gerard and Piet Strydom, eds (2003) *Philosophies of Social Science*. Maidenhead: Open University Press.

D'Emilio, John and Estelle Freedman (1988/2012) *Intimate Matters: A History of Sexuality in America*, 3rd edn. Chicago: University of Chicago Press.

Deneulin, Séverine (2014) *Wellbeing, Justice and Development Ethics.* London: Earthscan.

Deneulin Séverine and Lila Shahin (2009) *An Introduction to the Human Development and Capability Approach.* London: Earthscan.

Diez Jordi (2011) 'Argentina: A queer tango between the lesbian and gay movement and the state', in Mannon Tremblay, David Paternotte and Carol Johnson, eds, *The Lesbian and Gay Movement and the State: Comparative Insights into a Transformed Relationship.* Farnham: Ashgate, pp. 13–26.

Doan, Laura (2001) *Fashioning Sapphism.* New York: Columbia University Press.

Doezema, Jo (2010) *Sex Slaves and Discourse Masters: The Construction of Trafficking.* London: Zed Books.

Dollimore, Jonathan (1991) *Sexual Dissidence: Augustine to Wilde, Freud to Foucault.* Oxford: Clarendon Press.

Donnan, Hastings and Fiona Magowan (2010) *The Anthropology of Sex.* Oxford: Berg.

Dorling, Danny (2014) *Inequality and the 1%.* London: Verso.

Douglas, Mary (1966) *Purity and Danger: An Analysis of Ritual and Taboo.* Middlesex: Penguin.

Downing, Lisa and Robert Gillett, eds (2011) *Queer In Europe.* Farnham: Ashgate.

Dowsett, Gary W. (1996) *Practicing Desire: Homosexual Sex in the Era of AIDS.* Stanford: Stanford University Press.

Duangwises, Narupon and Peter Jackson, eds (2013) *Phet Lak Chet-Si: Phahuwattanatham Thang-Phet Nai Sangkhom Thai – Cultural Pluralism and Sex/Gender Diversity in Thailand.* Bangkok: Princess Sirindhorn Anthropology Centre.

Duggan, Lisa and Nan Hunter (2006) *Sex Wars: Sexual Dissent and Political Culture,* 2nd edn. London: Routledge.

Durkheim, Émile (1895/1964) *The Rules of Sociological Method.* New York: Free Press of Glencoe.

Dworkin, Andrea (1981) *Pornography: Men Possessing Women.* New York: Perigee.

Dworkin, Roland (2000) *Sovereign Virtue.* Cambridge, MA: Harvard University Press.

Dworkin, Shari L., Amanda Lock Swarr and Cheryl Cooky (2013) 'The (mis)treatment of South African track star Caster Semenya', in S.N.

Nyeck and Marc Epprecht, eds, *Sexual Diversity in Africa*. Montreal: McGill-Queens University Press, pp. 129–48.

Eco, Umberto (2009) *The Infinity of Lists*. London: MacLehose Press.

Eco, Umberto (2013) *Inventing the Enemy*. New York: Vintage.

Edelman, Lee (2004) *No Future: Queer Theory and the Death Drive*. Durham, NC: Duke University Press.

Edmunds, June and Bryan S. Turner (2002) *Generations, Culture and Society*. Milton Keynes: Open University.

Ehrlich, Paul R. and Robert E. Ornstein (2010) *Humanity on a Tight Rope*. Lanham, MD: Rowman & Littlefield.

Ehrenreich, Barbara (2007) *Dancing in the Streets: A History of Collective Joy*. London: Granta Books.

Eisenstadt, Shmuel N. (2000) 'Multiple modernities', *Daedalus* 129(1): 1–29.

Ekman, Paul (2014) *Moving Toward Global Compassion*. San Francisco: Paul Ekman Group.

El Feki, Shereen (2013) *Sex and the Citadel: Intimate Life in a Changing Arab World*. London: Chattus & Windus.

Elias, Norbert (Orig.1939; 1978) *The Civilizing Process*. New York: Pantheon.

Elliot, Anthony and Charles Lemert (2006/2012) *The New Individualism: The Emotional Costs of Globalization*. London: Routledge.

Elliot, Patricia (2010) *Debates in Transgender, Queer and Feminist Theory: Contested Sites*. London: Ashgate.

Ellis, Mark H. (2010) *Unholy Alliance: Religious Atrocity in Our Time*. London: SCM.

Ellison, Ralph (1952) *The Invisible Man*. New York: Random House.

El-Rouayheb, Khaled (2005) *Before Homosexuality in the Arab-Islamic World, 1500–1800*. Chicago: University of Chicago Press.

Endsjo, Dag Øistein (2011) *Sex and Religion: Teachings and Taboos in the History of World Faiths*. London: Reaktion Books.

Eng, David (2010) *The Feeling of Kinship: Queer Liberalism and the Racialization of Intimacy*. Durham, NC: Duke University Press.

Engster, Daniel (2007) *The Heart of Justice: Care Ethics and Political Theory*. Oxford: Oxford University Press.

Ensler, Eve (2013) *In the Body of the World: A Memoir*. New York: Metropolitan Books.

Epprecht, Marc (2008) *Heterosexual Africa? The History of an Idea from the*

Age of Exploration to the Age of AIDS. Athens: Ohio University Press/ University of Kwazulu-Natal Press.

Epprecht, Marc (2013) *Sexuality and Social Justice in Africa: Rethinking Homophobia and Forging Resistances*. London: Zed Books.

Epstein, Helen (2008) *The Invisible Cure: Why We Are Losing the Fight Against AIDS in Africa*. New York: Picador.

Erikson, Kai T. (1966) *Wayward Puritans: Studies on the Sociology of Deviance*. London: Wiley.

Evans, David (1993) *Sexual Citizenship*. London: Routledge.

Everett, Daniel (2012) *Language: The Cultural Tool*. London: Profile Books.

Farmer, Paul (2003) *Pathologies of Power: Health, Human Rights and the New War on Poor*. Berkeley: University of California Press.

Farrer, James (2002) *Opening Up: Youth Sex Culture and Market Reform in Shanghai*. Chicago: University of Chicago Press.

Fausto-Sterling, Anne (2000) *Sexing the Body: Gender Politics and the Construction of Sexuality*. New York: Perseus.

Fine, Michael D. (2007) *A Caring Society? Care and the Dilemmas of Human Service in the 21st Century*. Basingstoke: Palgrave.

Fine, Robert (2007) *Cosmopolitanism*. London: Routledge.

Ford, Clellan S. and Frank A. Beach (1952/1965) *Patterns of Sexual Behaviour*. Suffolk: Eyre & Spottiswood.

Forman–Barzilai, Fonna (2010) *Adam Smith and the Circles of Sympathy: Cosmopolitanism and Moral Theory*. Cambridge: Cambridge University Press.

Foucault, Michel (1976) *The History of Sexuality*. Vol. 1: *An Introduction*. London: Allen Lane.

Frank, Arthur W. (2010) *Letting Stories Breathe: A Socio-Narratology*. Chicago: University of Chicago Press.

Frankl, Victor (1946/1959) *Man's Search for Meaning*. Boston, MA: Beacon Press.

Fraser, Nancy (2009) *Scales of Justice: Reimagining Political Science in a Globalizing World*. New York: Columbia University Press.

Freeman, Elizabeth (2010) *Time Binds: Queer Temporalities, Queer Histories*. Durham, NC: Duke University Press.

Freire, Paulo (1972) *Pedagogy of the Oppressed*. New York: Herder and Herder.

French, Marilyn (2008) *From Eve to Dawn: A History of Women in the*

World, vol. 1. New York: The Feminist Press at the City University of New York.

Freud, Sigmund (1905/1962) *Three Essays on the Theory of Sexuality*. New York: Basic Books.

Freud, Sigmund (1930/2005). *Civilization and Its Discontents*. New York: W.W. Norton.

Friedman, Lawrence M. (2011) *The Human Rights Culture: A Study in History and Context*. New Orleans: Quid Pro Books.

Fromm, Eric (1993) *The Art of Being*. London: Constable.

Fromm, Eric (2013) *To Have or to Be?* London: Bloomsbury.

Fuchs, Christian (2013) *Social Media: A Critical Introduction*. London: Sage.

Fuller Robert W. and Pamela A. Gerloff (2008) *Dignity For All*. San Francisco: Berrett-Koehler.

Gadamer, Hans-Georg (1975/2013) *Truth and Method*. London: Bloomsbury.

Gagnon, John (1977) *Human Sexualities*. Glenview: Scott, Foresman and Company.

Gagnon, John (2004) *An Interpretation of Desire: Essays in the Study of Sexuality*. Chicago: University of Chicago Press.

Gagnon, John and William Simon (1973/2005) *Sexual Conduct: The Social Sources of Human Sexuality*, 2nd edn. New Brunswick, NJ: Aldine Transaction.

Garcia, J. Neil C. (1996) *Philippine Gay Culture: Binabae to Bakla, Silahis to MSM*. Quezon City: University of the Philippines Press.

Gensler, Harry J. (2013) *Ethics and the Golden Rule: Do Unto Others*. London: Routledge.

Gerbaudo, Paulo (2012) *Tweets and the Streets: Social Media and Contemporary Activism*. London: Pluto Press.

Giddens, Anthony (1992) *The Transformation of Intimacy: Sexuality, Love and Eroticism in Modern Societies*. Cambridge: Polity.

Gill, Rosalind (2007) *Gender and the Media*. Cambridge: Polity.

Gilligan, Carol (1982) *In a Different Voice*. Harvard: Harvard University Press.

Girard, François (2010) 'Negotiating sexual rights and sexual orientation at the UN', in Richard Parker, Rosalind Petchesky and Robert Sember, eds, *Sex Politics: Reports From the Front Lines*. Sexuality Policy Watch. Available at: http://www.sxpolitics.org/frontlines/book/pdf/sexpolitics.pdf.

Glendon, Mary Ann (2002) *A World Made New: Eleanor Roosevelt and the Universal Declaration of Human Rights*. New York: Random House.

Goffman, Erving (1961) *Encounters: Two Studies in Interaction*. Oxford: Bobbs-Merrill.

Goffman, Erving (1963) *Stigma: Notes on the Management of Spoiled Identity*. New York: Simon and Schuster.

Goldfarb, Jeffrey C. (2006) *The Politics of Small Things: The Power of the Powerless in Dark Times*. Chicago: University of Chicago Press.

Goldin, Ian (2013) *Divided Nations: Why Global Governance is Failing, and What We Can Do About It*. Oxford: Oxford University Press.

Gonzalez-López, Gloria (2005) *Erotic Journeys: Mexican Immigrants and Their Sex Lives*. Berkeley: University of California Press.

Goodwin, Michele Bratcher, ed. (2010) *Baby Markets: Money and the New Politics of Creating Families*. Cambridge: Cambridge University Press.

Gopinath, Gayatri (2005) *Impossible Desires*. Durham, NC: Duke University Press.

Gordon, Avery (1997) *Ghostly Matters: Haunting and the Sociological Imagination*. Minneapolis: University of Minnesota.

Gramsci, Antonio (2000) *The Gramsci Reader*. London: Lawrence and Wisehart.

Green, Adam Isaiah, ed. (2013) *Sexual Fields: Towards a Collective Theory of Sexual Life*. Chicago: University of Chicago.

Greenberg, David (1990) *The Construction of Homosexuality*. Chicago: University of Chicago Press.

Gruenbaum, Ellen (2000) *The Female Circumcision Controversy*. Philadelphia: University of Pennsylvania Press.

Habermas, Jürgen (2010) *An Awareness of What Is Missing: Faith and Reason in a Post-Secular Age*. Cambridge: Polity.

Haddon, Mark (2003) *The Curious Incident of the Dog in the Night-Time*. London: Random House.

Halberstam, Judith (2011) *The Queer Art of Failure*. Durham, NC: Duke University Press.

Halberstam, Judith (2012) *Gaga Feminism*. Boston, MA: Beacon Press.

Hall, Donald E. and Annamarie Jagose, eds (2012) *The Routledge Queer Studies Reader*. London: Routledge.

Hall, Stuart (1987) 'Gramsci and us', *Marxism Today* (June): 16–21.

Halperin, David (1995) *Saint Foucault: Towards a Gay Hagiography*. New York: Oxford University Press.

Hammick, Philip and Bernard Cohler (2009) *The Story of Sexual Identity: Narrative Perspectives on the Gay and Lesbian Life Course*. New York: Oxford.

Hannerz, Ulf (1996) *Transnational Connections: Culture, People, Places*. London: Routledge.

Hayden, Patrick, ed. (2014) *Hannah Arendt: Key Concepts*. London: Acumen Publishing.

Hearn, Jeff (2009) 'Patriarchies, transpatriarchies and intersectionalities', in Elżbieta H. Oleksy, ed., *Intimate Citizenships: Gender, Sexualities, Politics*. London: Routledge.

Hefner, Robert W., ed. (2013) *Global Pentecostalism in the 21st Century*. Bloomington: Indiana University Press.

Heineman, Elizabeth D., ed. (2011) *Sexual Violence in Conflict Zones: From the Ancient World to the World of Human Rights*. Philadelphia: University of Pennsylvania Press.

Held, David (2010) *Cosmopolitanism*. Cambridge: Polity.

Hélie, Anissa and Homa Hoodfar, eds (2012) *Sexuality in Muslim Contexts: Restrictions and Resistance*. London: Zed Books.

Hennen, Peter (2008) *Faeries, Bears and Leathermen: Men in Community Queering the Masculine*. Chicago: University of Chicago Press.

Herdt, Gilbert (1981) *Guardians of the Flutes: Idioms of Masculinity*. New York: McGraw Hill.

Herdt, Gilbert (1993) *Third Sex, Third Gender: Beyond Sexual Dimorphism in Culture and History*. New York: Zone Books.

Herdt, Gilbert, ed. (2009) *Moral Panics, Sex Panics: Fear and the Fight Over Sexual Rights*. New York: New York University Press.

Hite, Shere (1976) *The Hite Report: A Nationwide Study of Female Sexuality*. New York: Macmillan/Dell.

Hoffman, Martin (2000) *Empathy and Moral Development*. Cambridge: Cambridge University Press.

Holton, Robert (2009) *Cosmopolitanisms*. Basingstoke, Palgrave.

Honneth, Axel (1996) *The Struggle for Recognition: The Moral Grammar of Social Conflicts*. Cambridge: Polity.

Hopgood, Stephen (2013) *The Endtimes of Human Rights*. Ithaca, NY. Cornell University Press.

Horkheimer, Max and Theodor W. Adorno (1944/1997) *Dialectic of Enlightenment*. London: Verso.

Houlbrook, Matt (2005) *Queer London*. Chicago: University of Chicago Press.

Howe, Cymene (2013) *Intimate Activism: The Struggle for Sexual Rights in Postrevolutionary Nicaragua*. Durham, NC: Duke University Press.

Hubbard, Phil (2012) *Cities and Sexualities*; London: Routledge.

Hudson, Valerie M. and Andrea M. Den Boer (2005) *Bare Branches: The Security Implications of Asia's Male Population*. Boston, MA: MIT Press.

Hudson, Valerie M., Bonnie Ballif-Spanvill, Mary Caprioli and Chad F. Emmett (2012) *Sex and World Peace*. New York: Columbia University Press.

Hume, David (1739/1985) *A Treatise of Human Nature*. Middlesex: Penguin.

Humphreys, Laud (1970) *Tea Room Trade: A Study of Homosexual Encounters in Public Places*. New Brunswick, NJ: Aldine.

Hunt, Lynn (2007) *Inventing Human Rights: A History*. London: W.W. Norton.

Hunter, James Davison and Alan Wolfe (2006) *Is There a Culture War? A Dialogue On Values and American Public Life*. Washington, DC: The Brookings Institute.

Hunter, Mark (2010) *Love in the Time of Aids: Inequality, Gender and Rights in South Africa*. Bloomington: Indiana University Press.

Hunter, Susan (2003) *AIDS in Africa*. Basingstoke: Palgrave.

Huntington, Samuel P. (1996) *The Clash of Civilizations: Remaking the World Order*. New York: Touchstone.

Ilkkaracan, Pinar, ed. (2008) *Deconstructing Sexuality in the Middle East: Challenges and Discourses*. Farnham: Ashgate.

Illouz, Eva (2008) *Saving the Modern Soul: Therapy, Emotions and the Culture of Self Help*. Berkeley: University of California Press.

Inglehart, Ronald and Pippa Norris (2003) *Rising Tide: Gender Equality and Cultural Change Around the World*. Cambridge: Cambridge University Press.

Ingram, James (2013) *Radical Cosmopolitics: The Ethics and Politics of Democratic Universalism*. New York: Columbia University Press.

Inhorn, Marcia C. (2007). *Reproductive Disruptions: Gender, Technology, and Biopolitics in the New Millennium*. Providence, RI: Berghahn Books.

Inhorn, Marcia C. (2012) *The New Arab Man: Emergent Masculinities, Technologies and Islam in the Middle East*. Princeton: Princeton University Press.

Ishay, Micheine R. (2004) *The History of Human Rights: From Ancient Times to the Globalization Era*. Berkeley: University of California Press.

Isin, Engin F. and Bryan S. Turner, eds (2002) *Handbook of Citizenship Studies*. London: Sage.

Israel, Jonathan (2010) *A Revolution of the Mind: Radical Enlightenment and the Intellectual Origins of Modern Democracy*. Princeton: Princeton University Press.

Israel, Jonathan (2013) *Democratic Enlightenment: Philosophy, Revolution and Human Rights 1750–1790*. Oxford: Oxford University Press.

Itaborahy, Lucas Paoli and Jingshu Zhu (2013) *State-Sponsored Homophobia, 2013: A World Survey of Laws*. ILGA. Available at: http://Old.Ilga. Org/Statehomophobia/ILGA_State_Sponsored_Homophobia_2013. pdf.

Itaborahy, Lucas Paoli and Jingshu Zhu (2014) State Sponsored Homophobia, 2014: A World Survey of Laws. Available at: http:// old.ilga.org/Statehomophobia/ILGA_SSHR_2014_Eng.pdf.

Jackson, Peter, Fran Martin, Mark McLelland and Audrey Yue, eds (2008) *Asia Pacific Queer: Rethinking Genders and Sexualities*. Champaign: University of Illinois Press.

Jackson, Stevi (1999) *Heterosexuality in Question*. London: Sage.

Jacobs, Katrien (2013) *People's Pornography*. Chicago: University of Chicago Press.

Jafri, Amir H. (2008) *Honour Killing: Dilemma, Ritual, Understanding*. Oxford: Oxford University Press.

Jagose, Annamarie (2013) *Orgasmology*. Durham, NC: Duke University Press.

James, Henry (1920) *The Letters of William James*. Boston, MA: Atlantic Monthly Press.

James, William (1967) *The Writings of William James: A Comprehensive Edition*. Chicago: University of Chicago Press.

Jaspers, Karl (1951/2003) *Way to Wisdom: An Introduction to Philosophy*, 2nd edn. New Haven, CT: Yale University Press.

Jeffreys, Sheila (2005) *Beauty and Misogyny: Harmful Cultural Practices in the West*. London: Routledge.

Jeffreys, Sheila (2009) *The Industrial Vagina: The Political Economy of the Global Sex Trade*. London: Routledge.

Jeffreys, Sheila (2012) *Man's Dominion: The Rise of Religion and the Eclipse of Women's Rights*. London: Routledge.

Jenkins, Philip (1998) *Moral Panic: Changing Concepts of the Child Molester in Modern America*. New Haven: Yale University Press.

Jenkins, Philip (2013) *The Next Christendom: The Coming of Global Christianity*, 3rd edn. Oxford: Oxford University Press.

Joas, Hans (2000) *The Genesis of Value*. Cambridge: Polity.

Joas, Hans (2013) *The Sacredness of the Person: A New Genealogy of Human Rights*. Washington, DC: Georgetown University Press.

Joas, Hans and Klaus Wiegandt (2009) *Secularization and the World Religions*. Liverpool: Liverpool University Press.

Johnson, Paul (2012) *Homosexuality and the European Court of Human Rights*. London: Routledge.

Jones, Owen (2014) *The Establishment; And How They Get Away With It*. London: Allen Lane.

Jordan, Michael (2006) *In the Name of God: Violence and Destruction in the World's Religions*. Stroud: Sutton Publishing.

Juergensmeyer, Mark (2008) *Global Rebellion: Religious Challenges to the Secular State, From Christian Militias to Al Quaeda*. Berkeley: University of California Press.

Kaldor, Mary (2003) *Global Civil Society: An Answer to War*. Cambridge: Polity.

Kaoma, Kapya John (2012) *Colonizing African Values: How the Christian Right is Transforming Sexual Politics in Africa*. Somerville, MA: Political Research Associates.

Kaplan, Morris B. (1997) *Sexual Justice: Democratic Citizenship and Desire*. London: Routledge.

Kapur, Ratna (2005) *Erotic Justice: Law and the New Politics of Postcolonialism*. London: Glasshouse Press.

Kara, Siddharth (2009) *Sex Trafficking: Inside the Business of Modern Slavery*. New York: Columbia University Press.

Kelly, Liz (1998) *Surviving Sexual Violence*. Cambridge: Polity.

Khan, Hooria Hayat (2012) 'Moral panic: The criminalization of sexuality in Pakistan', in Anissa Hélie and Homa Hoodfar, eds, *Sexuality In Muslim Contexts: Restrictions and Resistance*. London: Zed Books, pp. 79–97.

Kimmel, Michael, ed. (2007) *The Sexual Self: The Construction of Sexual Scripts*. Nashville: Vanderbilt University Press.

Kimmel, Michael (2013) *Angry White Men*. New York: Nation Books.

Kinsey, Alfred C. et al. (1948) *Sexual Behaviour in the Human Male*. Philadelphia: W.B. Saunders.

Kinsey, Alfred C. et al. (1953) *Sexual Behaviour in the Human Female*. Philadelphia: W.B. Saunders.

Kitcher, Philip (2011) *The Ethical Project*. Cambridge, MA: Harvard University Press.

Knecht, Michi, Stefan Beck and Maren Klotz, eds (2012) *Reproductive Technologies as Global Form: Ethnographies of Knowledge, Practices and Transnational Encounters*. Frankfurt: Campus Verlag.

Kohut, Heinz (1971) *The Analysis of the Self*. New York: International Universities Press.

Kollman, Kelly (2013) *The Same Sex Unions Revolution in Western Democracies: International Norms and Domestic Policy Change*. Manchester: Manchester University Press.

Kong, Travis S.K. (2010) *Chinese Male Homosexualities: Memba, Tonghzi and Golden Boy*. London: Routledge.

Kong, Travis S.K. (2012) 'Chinese male bodies', in Bryan S. Turner, ed., *Routledge Handbook of the Body*. London: Routledge, pp. 289–306.

Krafft-Ebing, Richard von (1886/1931) *Psychopathia Sexualis*. London: W. Heinemann.

Kramer, Anne-Marie (2005) 'Gender, nation and the abortion debate in the Polish media', in Vera Tolz and Stephanie Booth, eds, *Nation and Gender in Contemporary Europe*. Manchester: Manchester University Press, pp. 130–48.

Kulick, Don (1998) *Travesti: Sex, Gender and Culture among Brazilian Transgendered Prostitutes*. Chicago: University of Chicago Press.

Kulpa, Robert and Joanna Mizielińska, eds (2011) *De-Centering Western Sexualities: Central and Eastern European Perspectives*. Surrey: Ashgate.

Küng, Hans and K.J. Kuschel (1993) *A Global Ethic: The Declaration of the Parliament's World Religions*. London: SCM Press.

Kurasawa, Fuyuki (2007) *The Work of Global Justice: Human Rights as Practices*. Cambridge: Cambridge University Press.

Kymlicka, Will (1995, 2000) *Multicultural Citizenship*. Oxford: Clarendon.

Lancaster, Roger N. (1994) *Life is Hard: Machismo, Danger and Intimacy in Nicaragua*. Berkeley: University of California Press.

Lancaster, Roger N. (2003) *The Trouble with Nature: Sex in Science and Popular Culture*. Berkeley: University of California Press.

Lancaster, Roger N. (2011) *Sex Panic and the Punitive State*. Berkeley: University of California Press.

Laqueur, Thomas W. (1990) *Making Sex: Body and Gender from the Greeks to Freud.* Cambridge, MA: Harvard University Press.

Laqueur, Thomas W. (2003) *Solitary Sex: A Cultural History of Masturbation.* New York: Zone Books.

Lauren, Paul Gordon (1998/2011) *The Evolution of International Human Rights: Visions*, 3rd edn. Philadelphia: University of Pennsylvania.

Lauritsen, John and David Thorstad (1995) *The Early Homosexual Rights Movement (1864–1935)*, rev. edn. New York: Times Change Press.

Leatherman, Janie L. (2011) *Sexual Violence and Armed Conflict.* Cambridge: Polity.

Lee, Harper (1960) *To Kill a Mockingbird.* New York: Harper Collins.

Lee, Julian C.H. (2011) *Policing Sexuality: Sex, Society and the State.* London: Zed Books.

Lennox, Corrine and Matthew Waites, eds (2013) *Human Rights, Sexual Orientation and Gender Identity in the Commonwealth.* London: Institute of Commonwealth Studies.

Lettevall, Rebecka and Kristian Petrov, eds (2014) *Critique of Cosmopolitan Reason.* Oxford: Peter Lang.

Lévi-Strauss, Claude (1955/1973) *Tristes Tropiques*, trans. John and Doreen Weightman. New York: Atheneum Press.

Levitas, Ruth (2013) *Utopia As Method: The Imaginary Reconstitution of Society.* Basingstoke: Palgrave.

Liechty, Daniel, ed. (2005) *The Ernest Becker Reader.* Seattle: University of Washington Press.

Lifton, Robert Jay (1979) *The Broken Connection.* New York: Simon and Schuster.

Lind, Amy, ed. (2010) *Development, Sexual Rights and Global Governance.* London: Routledge.

Linneman, Thomas J. (2003) *Weathering Change: Gays and Lesbians, Christian Conservatives and Everyday Hostilities.* New York: New York University Press.

Lister, Ruth (1997/2003) *Citizenship: Feminist Perspectives*, 2nd edn. Basingstoke: Palgrave.

Livingstone Smith, David (2011) *Less Than Human: Why We Demean, Enslave and Exterminate Others.* New York: St Martin's Press.

Lukes, Steven (2008) *Moral Relativism.* London: Profile Books.

Macintyre, Alasdair (1981/2011) *After Virtue.* London: Bloomsbury Academic Imprint.

Macionis, John J. and Ken Plummer (2012) *Sociology: A Global Introduction*, 5th edn. Harlow: Pearson Education.

Mackenzie, Catriona, Wendy Rogers and Susan Dodds, eds. (2014) *Vulnerability: New Essays in Ethics and Feminist Philosophy*. Oxford: Oxford University Press.

MacKinnon, Catharine A. (2006) *Are Women Human? And Other International Dialogues*. London: Belknap Press.

Macpherson, C.B. (1962) *The Political Theory of Possessive Individualism: From Hobbes to Locke*. Oxford: Oxford University Press.

Maffesoli, Michel (1993) *The Shadow of Dionysus: A Contribution to the Sociology of the Orgy*. Albany: State University of New York.

Mai, Mukhtar (2007*) In the Name of Honour: A Memoir*. London: Virago.

Malinowski, Bronislaw (1927) *Sex and Repression in Savage Society*. London: Routledge.

Manalansan, Martin F. (2003) *Global Divas: Filipino Gay Men in the Diaspora*. Durham, NC: Duke University Press.

Mankekar, Purniam and Louisa Schein, eds (2012) *Media, Erotics and Transnational Asia*. Durham, NC: Duke University Press.

Marsiaj, Juan P. (2011) 'Brazil: From AIDS to Human Rights', in Mannon Tremblay, David Paternotte and Carol Johnson, eds, *The Lesbian and Gay Movement and the State: Comparative Insights into a Transformed Relationship*. Farnham: Ashgate, pp. 57–72.

Massad, Joseph A. (2002) 'Re-orienting desire: The Gay International and the Arab world', *Public Culture* 14: 361–85.

Massad, Joseph A. (2007) *Desiring Arabs*. Chicago: University of Chicago Press.

Maslow, Abraham H. (1943). *Motivation and Personality*. New York: Harper.

Matthews, Nancy A. (1994) *Confronting Rape: The Feminist Anti-Rape Movement and the State*. London: Routledge.

Matza, David (1961) 'Subterranean traditions of youth', *Annals of the American Academy of Political and Social Science* 338(1): 102–18.

Mazlish, Bruce (2009) *The Idea of Humanity in a Global Era*. New York: Palgrave Macmillan.

Mazower, Mark (2012) *Governing the World: The History of an Idea*. London: Penguin.

McClintock, Anne (1995) *Imperial Leather: Race, Gender and Sexuality in the Colonial Contest*. New York: Routledge.

McCormack, Mark (2012) *The Declining Significance of Homophobia: How Teenage Boys are Redefining Masculinity and Heterosexuality*. Oxford: Oxford University Press.

McGlotten, Shaka (2013) *Virtual Intimacies: Media, Affect and Queer Sociality*. Albany: State University of New York Press.

McLelland, Mark and Vera Mackie, eds (2014) *Routledge Handbook of Sexuality Studies in East Asia*. London: Routledge.

McNair, Brian (2002) *Striptease Culture: Sex, Media and the Democratization of Desire*. London: Routledge.

McNay, Lois (2014) *The Misguided Search for the Political*. Cambridge: Polity.

Mead, Margaret (1935) *Sex and Temperament in Three Primitive Societies*. New York: William Morrow.

Menocal, Maria Rosa (2002) *The Ornament of the World: How Muslims, Jews and Christians Create a Culture of Tolerance in Medieval Spain*. New York: Little, Brown and Company.

Merton, Robert K. (1938) 'Social structure and anomie', *American Sociological Review* 3(5): 672–82.

Meston, Cindy M. and David M. Buss (2007) 'Why humans have sex', *Archives of Sexual Behaviour* 37(4): 477–507.

Moghadam, Valentine M. (2012) *Globalization and Social Movements: Islamism, Feminism and the Global Justice Movement*, 2nd edn. Rowman & Littlefield.

Mohanty, Chandra Talpade (2003) *Feminism Without Borders: Decolonizing Theory, Practicing Solidarity*. Durham, NC: Duke University Press.

Moore, Jr., Barrington (2000) *Moral Purity and Persecution in History*. Princeton: Princeton University Press.

Moore, Robert I. (1987) *The Formation of a Persecuting Society*. Oxford: Basil Blackwell.

Morrell, Michael (2010) *Empathy and Democracy*. Philadelphia: Penn State University Press.

Morsink, Johannes (2000) *The Universal Declaration of Human Rights: Origins, Drafting and Intent*. Philadelphia: University of Pennsylvania Press.

Mouffe, Chantal (2013) *Agonistics: Thinking the World Politically*. London: Verso.

Mowlabocus, Sharif (2010) *Gaydar Culture: Gay Men, Technology and Embodiment in the Digital Age*. Farnham: Ashgate.

Mumford, Lewis (1961) *The City in History*. San Diego: Harcourt, Brace & Co.

Muñoz, José Esteban (2009) *Cruising Utopia: The Then and There of Queer Futurity*. New York: New York University Press.

Murray, David A.B. (2003) 'Who is Takatāpui? Māori language, sexuality and identity in Aotearoa/New Zealand', *Anthropologica* 45(2): 233–41.

Murray, Stephen O. and Will Roscoe (1997) *Islamic Homosexualities: Culture, History and Literature*. New York: New York University Press.

Murray, Stephen O. and Will Roscoe, eds (2001) *Boy-Wives and Female Husbands: Studies of African Homosexualities*. New York: St Martins Press.

Nagel, Joane (2003) *Race, Ethnicity and Sexuality: Intimate Intersections, Forbidden Frontiuers*. New York: Oxford University Press.

Najmabadi, Afsaneh (2014) *Professing Selves: Transsexuality and Same-Sex Desire in Contemporary Iran*. Durham, NC: Duke University Press.

Nanda, Serena (1998) *Neither Man nor Woman: Hijras of India*. Belmont, CA: Wadsworth.

Nayar, Pramod K. (2014) *Posthumanism*. Cambridge: Polity.

Nederveen Pieterse, Jan (2015/2004) *Globalization and Culture: Global Mélange*. Lanham, MD: Rowman & Littlefield.

Nelson, Hilde Lindemann (2001) *Damaged Identities, Narrative Repair*. Ithaca, NY: Cornell University Press.

Newmahr, Staci (2011) *Playing on the Edge: Sadomasochism, Risk and Intimacy*. Indiana: Indiana University Press.

Newton, Esther (1972) *Mother Camp: Female Impersonators in America*. Englewood Cliffs, NJ: Prentice Hall.

Nietzsche, Friedrich (1886/2008) *The Birth of Tragedy*. Oxford: Oxford University Press.

Noddings, Nel (1986) *Caring: A Feminist Approach to Ethics and Moral Education*. Berkeley: University of California Press.

Nordqvist, Peter and Carol Smart (2014) *Relative Strangers: Family Life, Genes and Donor Conception*. Basingstoke: Palgrave Macmillan.

Norris, Pippa and Ronald Inglehart (2011) *Sacred and Secular: Religions and Politics Worldwide*, 2nd edn. Cambridge: Cambridge University Press.

Nussbaum, Martha (1997) *Cultivating Humanity: A Classical Defense of Reform in Liberal Education*. Cambridge, MA: Harvard University Press.

Nussbaum, Martha (1999) *Sex and Social Justice*. Oxford: Oxford University Press.

Nussbaum, Martha (2000) *Women and Human Development: The Capabilities Approach.* Cambridge: Cambridge University Press.

Nussbaum, Martha (2004) 'Patriotism and cosmopolitanism', *Boston Review* XIX(5) October: 3–16.

Nussbaum, Martha (2005) 'Women's bodies: Violence, security, capabilities', *Journal of Human Development* 6(2): 167–83.

Nussbaum, Martha (2006) *Frontiers of Justice: Disability, Nationality, Species Membership.* Cambridge, MA: Harvard University Press.

Nussbaum, Martha (2011) *Creating Capabilities: The Human Development Approach.* Cambridge, MA: Belknap/Harvard.

Nyeck, S.N., and Marc Epprecht, eds (2013) *Sexual Diversity in Africa: Politics, Theory, Citizenship.* Montreal: McGill-Queen's University Press.

Oz, Amos (2012) *How to Cure a Fanatic.* New York: Vintage.

Padilla, Mark (2007) *Caribbean Pleasure Industry: Tourism, Sexuality and AIDS in the Dominican Republic.* Chicago: University of Chicago Press.

Padilla, Mark, Jennifer S. Hirsch, Miguel Muñoz-Laboy, Robert E. Sember and Richard Parker, eds (2007) *Love and Globalization: Transformations of Intimacy in the Contemporary World.* Nashville, TN: Vanderbilt University Press.

Palumbo-Liu, David (2012) *The Deliverance of Others: Reading Literature in a Global Age.* Durham, NC: Duke University Press.

Parker, Richard, Rosalind Petchesky and Robert Sember (2010) *Sex Politics: Reports From the Front Lines.* Sexuality Policy Watch. Available at: http://www.sxpolitics.org/frontlines/book/pdf/sexpolitics.pdf.

Parker, Richard, Jonathan Garcia and Robert M. Buffington (2014) 'Sexuality and the contemporary world: Globalization and sexual rights', in Robert M. Buffington, Eithne Luibhéid and Donna J. Guy, eds, *A Global History of Sexuality: The Modern Era.* Chichester: Wiley, pp. 221-60.

Parrot, Andrea and Nina Cummings (2006) *Forsaken Females: The Global Brutalization of Women.* New Jersey: Rowman & Littlefield.

Patton, Cindy and Benigno Sánchez-Eppler (2000) *Queer Diasporas.* Durham, NC: Duke University Press.

Peletz, Michael G. (2009) *Gender Pluralism: Southeast Asia Since Modern Times.* London: Routledge.

Peña, Susana (2013) ¡*Oye Loca! From the Mariel Boatlift to Gay Cuban Miami.* Minneapolis: University of Minnesota Press.

Pereira, Charmaine (2014) *Changing Narratives of Sexuality: Contestations, Compliance and Women's Empowerment*. London: Zed Books.

Petchesky, Rosalind P. (2000) 'Sexual rights: Inventing a concept: Mapping an international practice', in Richard Parker, Regina Maria Barbosa and Peter Aggleton, eds, *Framing the Sexual Subject: The Politics of Gender, Sexuality and Power*. Berkeley: University of California Press, pp. 81–103.

Petchesky, Rosalind (2003) *Global Prescriptions: Gendering Health and Human Rights*. London: Zed Books.

Phillips, Kim M. and Barry Reay (2011) *Sex Before Sexuality: A Premodern History*. Cambridge: Polity.

Phipps, William E. (2006) *Clerical Celibacies*. London: Continuum.

Piketty, Thomas (2014) *Capital in the Twenty-First Century*. London: Belknap Press.

Pinker, Steven (2011) *The Better Angels of Our Nature: The Decline of Violence and Its Causes*. London: Allen Lane.

Pisani, Elizabeth (2008) *The Wisdom of Whores: Bureaucrats, Brothels and the Business of AIDS*. London: Granta.

Plummer, Ken (1975) *Sexual Stigma: An Interactionist Account*. London: Routledge & Kegan Paul.

Plummer, Ken (1985) 'The social uses of sexuality: Symbolic interaction, power and rape', in J. Hopkins, ed., *Victims of Sexual Assault*. London: Wiley, pp. 37–56.

Plummer, Ken (1988) 'Organising AIDS', in Peter Aggleton and Hilary Homans, eds, *Social Aspects of AIDS*. Basingstoke: Falmer Press, pp. 20–51.

Plummer, Ken (1995) *Telling Sexual Stories: Power, Change and Social Worlds*. London: Routledge.

Plummer, Ken (2000a) 'Symbolic interactionism in the twentieth century', in Bryan Turner, ed., *A Companion to Social Theory*, rev. edn. Oxford: Blackwell, pp. 193–222.

Plummer, Ken (2000b) 'Intimate choices', in Gary Browning, Abigail Halcli and Frank Webster, eds, *Understanding Contemporary Society: Theories of the Present*. London: Sage, pp. 432–44.

Plummer, Ken (2001a) *Documents of Life. 2: An Invitation to a Critical Humanism*. London: Sage.

Plummer, Ken, ed. (2001b) *Sexualities: Critical Concepts in Sociology*. Four Volumes. London: Routledge.

Plummer, Ken (2003a) *Intimate Citizenship: Personal Decisions and Public Dialogues*. Seattle: University of Washington Press.

Plummer, Ken (2003b) 'The sexual spectacle: Making a public culture of sexual problems', in George Ritzer, ed., *Handbook of Social Problems: A Comparative International Perspective*. London: Sage, pp. 521–41.

Plummer, Ken (2004) 'Male sexualities', in Robert Connell, Jeff Hearn and Michael Kimmel, eds, *Handbook of Studies on Men and Masculinities*. London: Sage, pp. 178–95.

Plummer, Ken (2005) 'Intimate citizenship in an unjust world', in Mary Romero and Judith Howard, eds, *The Blackwell Companion to Social Inequalities*. Oxford: Blackwell, pp. 75–9.

Plummer, Ken (2007) 'The flow of boundaries: Gays, queers and intimate citizenship', in David Downes, Paul Rock, Christine Chinkin and Conor Gearty, eds, *Crime, Social Control and Human Rights: From Moral Panics to States of Denial. Essays in Honour of Stanley Cohen*. Devon: Willan Publishing, pp. 379–93.

Plummer, Ken (2008) 'Studying sexualities for a better world? Ten years of sexualities', *Sexualities* 11(1/2): 7–21.

Plummer, Ken (2009) 'Outsiders, deviants and countercultures: Subterranean tribes and queer imaginations', in Gurminder Bhambra and Ipek Demi, eds, *1968 in Retrospect: History, Theory, Alterity*. Basingstoke: Palgrave, pp. 43–56.

Plummer, Ken (2010a) 'Generational sexualities, subterranean traditions, and the hauntings of the sexual world: Some preliminary remarks', *Symbolic Interaction* 33(2): 163–91.

Plummer, Ken (2010b) 'The social reality of sexual rights', in Peter Aggleton and Richard Parker, eds, *Routledge Handbook of Sexuality, Health and Rights*. London: Routledge, pp. 45–55.

Plummer, Ken (2012a) 'Critical sexualities studies', in George Ritzer, ed., *Wiley-Blackwell Handbook of Sociology*. Oxford: Blackwell, pp. 243–68.

Plummer, Ken (2012b) 'Towards a cosmopolitan symbolic interactionism', in Andrea Salvini, Joseph A. Kotarba and Bryce Merill, eds, *The Present and Future of Symbolic Interactionism*. Milan: FrancoAngeli.

Plummer, Ken (2013a) 'A manifesto for a critical humanism in sociology: On questioning the social world', in Daniel Nehring, ed., *Sociology*. Harlow: Pearson.

Plummer, Ken (2013b) 'Editorial changeover: Farewell from Ken Plummer'. *Sexualities* 16(7): 755–63.

Plummer, Ken (2015) 'Liberating generations: Continuities and change in the radical queer Western era', in David Paternotte and Manon Tremblay, eds, *Companion to Lesbian and Gay Activism*. Farnham: Ashgate.

Popper, Karl (1948) 'Utopia and violence', *Hibbert Journal* 46: 109–16.

Poulin, Richard (2003) 'Globalization and the sex trade: Trafficking and the commodification of women and children', *Canadian Women Studies / Les cahiers de la femme* 22(3–4): 38–43.

Poulin, Richard (2011). *La Mondialisation des industries du sexe*. Paris: Imago.

Prieur, Annick (1998) *Mema's House, Mexico City: On Transvestites, Queens, and Machos*. Chicago: University of Chicago Press.

Prince, Virginia Charles (1976) *Understanding Cross Dressing*. Los Angeles: Chevalier.

Prinz, Jesse (2012) *Beyond Human Nature: How Culture and Experience Shape Our Lives*. London: Allen Lane.

Prothero, Stephen (2011) *God Is Not One*. New York: Harper One.

Puar, Jasbir K (2007) *Terrorist Assemblages: Homonationalism in Queer Times*. Durham, NC: Duke University Press.

Pui-Lan, Kwok (2012) *Globalization, Gender and Peacebuilding: The Future of Interfaith Dialogue*. New York: Paulist Press.

Rahman, Momin (2014) *Homosexualities, Muslim Cultures and Modernity*. Hampshire: Palgrave.

Ramsbotham, Oliver, Tom Woodhouse and Hugh Miall (2012) *Contemporary Conflict Resolution*. Cambridge: Polity.

Reddy, Gayatri (2005) *With Respect to Sex: Negotiating Hijra Identity in South India*. Chicago: University of Chicago Press.

Richards, Jeffrey (1991/2013) *Sex, Dissidence and Damnation*, rev. edn. London: Routledge.

Richards, Jesse (2010) *The Secret Peace: Exposing the Positive Trend of World Events*. New York: Book and Ladder Press.

Richardson, Diane (2000) *Rethinking Sexuality*. London: Sage.

Richardson, Robert D. (2006) *William James: In the Maelstrom of American Modernism*. New York: Houghton Mifflin.

Ricoeur, Paul (1992) *Oneself As Another*. Chicago: University of Chicago Press.

Rifkin, Jeremy (2009) *The Empathic Civilization: The Race to Global Consciousness in a World of Crisis*. Cambridge: Polity.

Rifkind, Gabrielle and Giandomenico Picco (2014) *Fog of Peace: The Human Face of Conflict Resolution.* London: I.B. Tauris.

Rinaldo, Rachel (2013) *Mobilizing Piety: Islam and Feminism in Indonesia.* Oxford: Oxford University Press.

Robertson, Roland (1992) *Globalization: Social Theory and Global Culture.* London: Sage.

Robinson, Fiona (2011) *The Ethics of Care: A Feminist Approach to Human Security.* Philadelphia: Temple University Press.

Robinson, Paul (1976) *The Modernization of Sex.* London: Paul Elek.

Robinson, Peter (2008) *The Changing Gay World of Gay Men in Australia.* Basingstoke: Palgrave.

Rofel, Lisa (2007) *Desiring China: Experiments in Neo Liberalism, Sexuality and Public Culture.* Durham, NC: Duke University Press.

Rokeach, Milton (1960) *The Open and Closed Mind.* New York: Basic Books.

Roscoe, Will (2000) *Changing Ones: Third and Fourth Genders in Native America.* New York: St Martin's Press.

Roseneil, Sasha, ed. (2013) *Beyond Citizenship: Feminism and the Transformation of Belonging.* Basingstoke: Palgrave.

Roughgarden, Joan (2004) *Evolution's Rainbow: Diversity, Gender and Sexuality in Nature and People.* Berkeley: University of California Press.

Rubin, Gayle S. (2011) *Deviations: A Gayle Rubin Reader.* Durham, NC: Duke University Press.

Rupp, Leila (1997) *Worlds of Women: The Making of an International Women's Movement.* Princeton: Princeton University Press.

Rupp, Leila (2011) *Sapphistries: A Global History of Love Between Women.* New York: New York University Press.

Rupp, Leila and Verta Taylor (2003) *Drag Queens at the 801 Cabaret,* 2nd edn. Chicago: University of Chicago Press.

Rutherford, Paul (2007) *A World Made Sexy: Freud to Madonna.* Toronto: University of Toronto Press.

Ryan-Flood, Roísín (2009) *Lesbian Motherhood: Gender, Families and Sexual Citizenship.* Basingstoke: Palgrave.

Rydström, Jens (2011) *Odd Couples: A History of Gay Marriage in Scandinavia.* Amsterdam: Amsterdam University Press.

Said, Edward W. (1978) *Orientalism.* New York: Pantheon Books.

Said, Edward W. (2004) *Humanism and Democratic Criticism.* Basingstoke: Palgrave MacMillan.

Sanday, Peggy Reeves (2007) *Fraternity Gang Rape: Sex, Brotherhood and Privilege on Campus*, 2nd edn. New York: New York University Press.

Sandel, Michael (2009) *Justice: What's the Right Thing To Do?* London: Allen Lane.

Santos, Ana Christina (2013) *Social Movements and Sexual Citizenship in Southern Europe*. Basingstoke: Palgrave.

Sayer, Andrew (2011) *Why Things Matter to People: Social Science, Values and Ethical Life*. Cambridge: Cambridge University Press.

Schaffner, Anna Katharina (2012) *Modernism and Perversion: Sexual Deviance In Sexology and Literature, 1850–1930*. Basingstoke: Palgrave.

Scheper-Hughes, Nancy (1993) *Death Without Weeping: The Violence of Everyday Life in Brazil*. Berkeley: University of California Press.

Schofield, Michael (1965) *Sociological Aspects of Homosexuality*. London: Longman.

Schopenhauer, Arthur (1891) *The Wisdom of Life*. Cosmo Classics.

Schütz, Alfred (1944) 'The stranger: An essay in social psychology', *American Journal of Sociology* 49(6): 499–507.

Schwartz, Barry (2004) *The Paradox of Choice: Why More Is Less*. New York: Harper Collins.

Scruton, Roger (2010) *The Uses of Pessimism: And the Danger of False Hope*. Oxford: Oxford University Press.

Sedgwick, Eve Kasofsky (1990) *The Epistemology of the Closet*. Berkeley: University of California Press.

Seidman, Steven (2003/2010) *The Social Construction of Sexuality*, 2nd edn. New York: W.W. Norton.

Seidman, Steven, Nancy Fischer and Chet Meeks, eds (2008/2011) *Introducing The New Sexuality Studies*, 2nd edn. London: Routledge.

Sen, Amartya (1980) 'Equality of what?' in Sterling McMurrin, ed., *The Tanner Lectures on Human Values*. Cambridge: Cambridge University Press.

Sen, Amartya (2005) *The Argumentative Indian: Writings on Indian Culture, History and Identity*. London: Penguin.

Sen, Amartya (2006) *Identity and Violence: The Illusion of Destiny*. London: Allen Lane.

Sen, Amartya (2009) *The Idea of Justice*. London: Allen Lane.

Sender, Katherine (2005) *Business Not Politics: The Making of the Gay Market*. New York: Columbia University Press.

Sessions, William Lad (2010) *Honor For Us: A Philosophical Analysis, Interpretation and Defense*. London: Bloomsbury.

Sevenhuijsen, Sekma (1998) *Citizenship and the Ethics of Care: Feminist Considerations of Justice, Morality and Politics*. London: Routledge.

Sharratt, Sara (2011) *Gender, Shame and Sexual Violence: The Voices of Witnesses and Court Members at War Crimes Tribunals*. Farnham: Ashgate.

Shibutani, Tamotsu (1955) 'Reference groups as perspectives', *American Journal of Sociology* 60: 562–9.

Simmel, Georg (1972) *Georg Simmel on Individuality and Social Forms*, ed. Donald N. Levine. Chicago: University of Chicago Press.

Simon, William (1996) *Postmodern Sexualities*. London: Routledge.

Slote, Michael (2007) *The Ethics of Care and Empathy*. London: Routledge.

Smart, Carol (2007) *Personal Life*. Cambridge: Polity.

Smith, Adam (1759/2000) *The Theory of Moral Sentiments*. New York: Prometheus Books.

Smith, Christian (2010) *What Is a Person?* Chicago: University of Chicago Press.

Solnit, Rebecca (2009) *A Paradise Built in Hell: The Extraordinary Communities that Arise in Disaster*. London: Penguin.

Spar, Deborah (2006) *Baby Business: How Money, Science and Politics Drives the Commerce of Conception*. Boston, MA: Harvard Business School Press.

Spijkerboer, Thomas (2013) *Fleeing Homophobia: Sexual Orientation, Gender Identity and Asylum*. New York: Routledge.

Spivak, Gayatri Chakravorty (1988) 'Can the subaltern speak?' in Cary Nelson and Lawrence Grossberg, eds, *Marxism and the Interpretation of Culture*. Urbana: University of Illinois Press, pp. 271–313.

Squires, Corinne (2013) *Living with HIV and ARV's: Three Letter Lives*. Basingstoke: Palgrave.

Stacey, Judith (2011) *Unhitched: Love, Marriage, and Family Values from West Hollywood to Western China*. New York: New York University Press.

Stearns, Peter N. (2010) *World History: The Basics*. London: Routledge.

Stegger, Manfred B., James Goodman and Erin K. Wilson (2012) *Justice Globalism: Ideology, Crises, Policy*. London: Sage.

Stein, Arlene (1997) *Sex and Sensibility: Stories of a Lesbian Generation in the USA*. Berkeley: University of California Press.

Stein, Arlene (2003) *The Stranger Next Door: The Story of a Small*

Community's Battle Over Sex, Faith and Civil Rights. Boston, MA: Beacon Press.

Stein, Arlene, with Ken Plummer (1994) 'I can't even think straight: Queer theory and the missing revolution in sociology', *Sociological Theory* 12(2): 178–87.

Stern, Jessica (2003) *Terror in the Name of God: Why Religious Militants Kill.* New York: Harpercollins.

Stoller, Robert (1979) Sexual Excitement: Dynamics of Erotic Life. New York: Pantheon.

Stonequist, Everett V. (1937) *The Marginal Man: A Study in Personality and Culture Conflict.* New York: Charles Scribner's.

Strauss, Anselm (1978) 'A social world perspective', *Studies in Symbolic Interactionism* 1(1): 119–28.

Stuhr, John J., ed. (2010) *100 Years of Pragmatism: William James and the Revolutionary Philosophy.* Bloomington: Indiana University Press.

Sumner, William Graham (1906) *Folkways.* Boston, MA: Atheneum Press.

Szasz, Thomas (1973) *The Second Sin.* London: Routledge.

Sznaider, Natan (2001) *The Compassionate Temperament: Care and Cruelty in Modern Society.* Oxford: Rowman & Littlefield.

Tallis, Raymond (2011) *Aping Mankind: Neuromania, Darwinitis and the Misrepresentation of Humanity.* London: Acumen.

Tamale, Sylvia, ed. (2011) *African Sexualities.* Cape Town: Pambazuka Press.

Tannen, Deborah (1998) *The Argument Culture.* New York: Random House.

Taylor, Charles (1989) *Sources of the Self.* Cambridge,MA: Harvard University Press.

Taylor, Yvette, Sally Hines and Mark E. Casey, eds (2011) *Theorizing Intersectionality and Sexuality.* Basingstoke: Palgrave.

Teunis, Nils and Gil Herdt, eds (2007) *Sexual Inequalities and Social Justice.* Berkeley: University of California Press.

Therborn, Göran (2004) *Between Sex and Power: Family in the World, 1900–2000.* London: Routledge.

Therborn, Göran (2010) *The World: A Beginner's Guide.* Cambridge: Polity.

Therborn, Göran (2013) *The Killing Fields of Inequality.* Cambridge: Polity.

Thornhill, Randy and Craig Palmer (2001) *A Natural History of Rape: Biological Bases of Sexual Coercion*. Boston, MA: MIT Press.

Thornton, Robert (2008), *Unimagined Community: Sex, Networks, and AIDS in Uganda and South Africa*. Berkeley: University of California Press.

Tilly, Charles (2004) *Social Movements 1768–2004*. London: Paradigm.

Tin, Louis–Georges (2012) *The Invention of Heterosexual Culture*. Boston, MA: MIT Press.

Todorov, Tzvetan (1999) *Facing the Extreme: Moral Life in the Concentration Camps*. London: Phoenix.

Todorov, Tzvetan (2006) *In Defense of the Enlightenment*. London: Atlantic Books.

Tremblay, Mannon, David Paternotte and Carol Johnson (2011) *The Lesbian and Gay Movement and the State: Comparative Insights into a Transformed Relationship*. Farnham: Ashgate.

Tremblay, Rodrigue (2009) *The Code for Global Ethics: Toward a Humanist Civilization*. Victoria, BC: Trafford Publishing.

Tronto, Joan (1993) *Moral Boundaries: A Political Argument for an Ethic of Care*. London: Routledge.

Turner, Bryan S. (2006) *Vulnerability and Human Rights: Essays in Rights*. Philadelphia: Penn State University Press.

Turner, Ralph (1976) 'The real self: From institution to impulse', *American Journal of Sociology* 81(5): 989–1016.

Turshen, Meredeth (2007) *Women's Health Movements: A Force for Change*. Basingstoke: Palgrave.

Tutu, Desmond (1999) *No Future Without Forgiveness*. New York: Doubleday.

Twine, France Winddance (2011) *Outsourcing the Womb: Race, Class and Gestational Surrogacy in a Global Market*. London: Routledge.

UN (2013) *International Migration Report*. Available at: http://www.un.org/en/development/desa/population/publications/migration/migration-report-2013.shtml.

UN (2014) *Human Development Report: Sustaining Human Progress*. Available at: http://hdr.undp.org/sites/default/files/hdr14-report-en-1.pdf.

UNAIDS Update (2013) *How Africa Turned AIDS Around*. Available at: http://www.unaids.org/en/media/unaids/contentassets/documents/unaidspublication/2013/20130521_Update_Africa.pdf.

UNCHR (2013) *War's Human Cost: Global Trends 2013*. Available at: http://www.unhcr.org/5399a14f9.html.

UNFPA (2012) *Marrying Too Young: End Child Marriage*. New York: United Nations. Available at: http://www.unfpa.org/public/home/publications/pid/12166.

Unger, Roberto M. (2009) *The Self Awakened: Pragmatism Unbound*. Cambridge, MA: Harvard University Press.

UNHCHR (2012) *Discriminatory Laws and Practices and Acts of Violence Against Individuals Based on Their Sexual Orientation and Gender Identity*. New York: United Nations. Available at: http://www2.Ohchr.Org/English/Bodies/Hrcouncil/Docs/19session/A.HRC.19.41_English.Pdf.

UNICEF (2013) *Female Genital Mutilation/Cutting: A Statistical Overview and Exploration of the Dynamics of Change*. Available at: http://www.unicef.org/publications/index_69875.html.

Urry, John (2000) *Sociology Beyond Societies: Mobilities for the Twenty-First Century*. London: Routledge.

Urry, John (2007) *Mobilities*. Cambridge: Polity.

Valentine, David (2007) *Imagining Transgender: An Ethnography of a Category*. Durham, NC: Duke University Press.

Vance, Carole S., ed. (1984) *Pleasure and Danger: Exploring Female Sexuality*. London: Routledge.

van Dijck, José (2013) *The Culture of Connectivity*. Oxford: Oxford University Press.

Van Hooft, Stan (2009) *Cosmopolitanism: A Philosophy for Global Ethics*. Stocksfield: Acumen.

Vasquez Del Aguila, Ernesto (2013) *Being a Man in a Transnational World: The Masculinity and Sexuality of Migration*. London: Routledge.

Wacquant, Loïc (2009) *Punishing the Poor: The Neoliberal Government of Social Insecurity*. Durham, NC: Duke University Press.

Wagner, Peter (2012) *Modernity: Understanding the Present*. Cambridge: Polity.

Walby, Sylvia (2009) *Globalization and Inequalities: Complexity and Contested Modernities*. London: Sage.

Walters, Suzanna Danuta (2014) *The Tolerance Trap: How God, Gay Genes and Good Intentions are Sabotaging Gay Equality*. New York: New York University Press.

Waltzer, Michael (1997) *On Toleration*. New Haven, CT: Yale University Press.

Warner, Michael (1999) *The Trouble with Normal: Sex, Politics and the Ethics of Queer Life*. Cambridge, MA: Harvard University Press.

Warner, Michael (2012) 'Queer and then: The end of queer theory?' *Chronicle Review*, 1 January.

Waskul, Dennis (2004) *Net. SeXXX: Readings on Sex, Pornography and the Internet*. London: Peter Lang.

Weeks, Jeffrey (1997/1990) *Coming Out: Homosexual Politics from the Nineteenth Century to the Present*, 2nd edn. London: Quartet.

Weeks, Jeffrey (1998) 'The sexual citizen', *Theory, Culture and Society* 15(3/4): 35–52.

Weeks, Jeffrey (2007) *The World We Have Won*. London: Routledge.

Weeks, Jeffrey (2011) *The Languages of Sexuality*. London: Routledge.

Weiss, Margot Danielle (2012) *Techniques of Pleasure: BDSM and the Circuits of Sexuality*. Durham, NC: Duke University Press.

Weiss, Thomas G. (2012) *What's Wrong with the United Nations and How to Fix It*, 2nd edn. Cambridge: Polity.

Wells, H.G. (1906) 'The so-called science of sociology', *Sociological Papers* 3: 367.

Wenman, Mark (2013) *Agonistic Democracy: Constituent Power in the Era of Globalization*. Cambridge: Cambridge University Press.

West, Donald (1955/1968) *Homosexuality*. Harmondsworth: Penguin.

Westermarck, Edward (1891) *The History of Human Marriage*. London: MacMillan.

Westmarland, Nicole and Geetanjali Gangoli, eds (2012) *International Approaches to Rape*. Bristol: Policy Press.

Whittaker, Brian (2011) *Unspeakable Love: Gay and Lesbian Life in the Middle East*, 2nd edn. London: Saqi.

WHO (2013) *Global and Regional Estimates of Violence Against Women: Prevalence and Health Effects of Intimate Partner Violence and Non-Partner Sexual Violence*. Geneva: World Health Organization.

Widdows, Heather (2011) *Global Ethics: An Introduction*. Durham: Acumen.

Wieringa, Saskia (2002) *Sexual Politics in Indonesia*. Basingstoke: Palgrave.

Wieringa, Saskia and Horacio Sivori, eds (2013) *The Sexual History of the Global South: Sexual Politics in Africa, Asia and Latin America*. London: Zed Books.

Wikan, Unni (1977) 'Man becomes woman: Transsexualism in Oman as a key to gender roles', *Man* 12/2: 304–19.

Williams, Linda (1990) *Hard Core*. London: Rivers Oram Press.

Williams, Linda, ed. (2004) *Porn Studies*. Durham, NC: Duke University Press.

Williams, Linda (2009) *Screening Sex*. Durham, NC: Duke University Press.

Williams, Raymond (1989) *Resources of Hope*. London: Verso.

Witte, John Jr and M. Christian Green, eds (2012) *Religion and Human Rights: An Introduction*. Oxford: Oxford University Press.

Wolfe, Alan (1992) 'Democracy versus sociology: Boundaries and their consequences', in Michele Lamont and Marcel Fourier, eds, *Cultivating Differences*. Chicago: University of Chicago Press.

Woodiwiss, Anthony (2005) *Human Rights*. London: Routledge.

Wouters, Cas (2004) *Sex and Manners: Female Emancipation in the West, 1890-2000*. London: Sage.

Wouters, Cas (2007) *Informalization: Manners and Emotions Since 1890*. London: Sage.

Wright, Erik Olin (2010) *Envisioning Real Utopias*. London: Verso.

Yamani, Maha A.Z. (2008) *Polygamy and Law in Contemporary Saudi Arabia*. Reading, UK: Ithaca Press.

Young, Iris Marion (1990) *Justice and the Politics of Difference*. Princeton: Princeton University Press.

Young, Jock (1971) *The Drugtakers: The Social Meaning of Drug Use*. London: Judson, McGibbon & Kee.

Young, Robert J.C. (1995) *Colonial Desire: Hybridity in Theory, Culture and Race*. London: Routledge.

Yousafzai, Malala (2014) *I am Malala: The Girl Who Stood Up for Education and Was Shot by the Taliban*. London: Phoenix.

Yue, Audrey and Jun Zubillaga-Pow (2012) *Queer Singapore: Illiberal Citizenship and Mediated Cultures*. Hong Kong: Hong Kong University Press.

Yuval-Davis, Nira (2011) *The Politics of Belonging: Intersectional Contestations*. London: Sage.

Zelizer, Viviana A. (2005) *The Purchase of Intimacy*. Princeton: Princeton University Press.

Zenn, Jacob (2012) *Boko Haram in West Africa*. Washington, DC: Jamestown Foundation.

Zheng, Tiantian (2009) *Red Lights: The Lives of Sex Workers in Postsocialist China*. Minneapolis: University of Minnesota Press.

Zimbardo, Philip (2007) *The Lucifer Effect: How Good People Turn Evil*. London: Rider.

Index:
100 Samples of Multiple Sexualities

Cosmopolitan Sexualities discusses many different kinds of sexual varieties and aims to clarify an emerging new vocabulary that might help us better understand diverse sexualities in the twenty first century. This specialised index is intended to help the reader find where discussions and their contexts are introduced in the book. (A more general Index follows it).

Index: General